Sweet and Sour Milk

By the same author

From a Crooked Rib
A Naked Needle

Nuruddin Farah

Sweet and Sour Milk

Allison & Busby

First published 1979 by
Allison and Busby Limited
6a Noel Street, London W1V 3RB
Copyright © Nuruddin Farah 1979
All rights reserved

ISBN 0 85031 294 9

Set in 11 pt Lectura
and printed in Great Britain by
Villiers Publications Limited
Ingestre Road, London NW5

The quotations on pages 125-6 are from John Wain's
poem "The Murderer" in Weep Before God, published
by Macmillan, 1961.

For
my mother, my sisters
and
Koschin my son
again

My thanks and love go unreservedly to Martine whose help and love have been consistent; to Edo and Daniela; to Scott and Katie; to Renato for an unrepayable loan; to Sandro; to Francesco; to Laura Diaz and Nadia Spano; to Susie; and to Kryscia, my enormous thanks.

Make my house your inn
Inns are not residences.

MARIANNE MOORE

They hoist sails, the dying, they weigh anchor, they go out on
a little breath, they do not care.

MARY WEBSTER

Prologue

Like a baby with a meatless bone in his mouth, a bone given him by his mother to suck while she is in the kitchen minding the pot which has now begun to sing. . . .

There was something very disturbing about his features today, there was something which suggested an untidiness of a sort — rather like a cotton dress washed in salty water and worn until it reeks of human sweat. There was something very vulnerable about his looks, something quite restless. He breathed billows his lungs' size. His tongue, swollen and red, rolled in the discharge of pain. Soyaan held his mother's hand, held it lovingly and tightly, and he pressed it.

"Drink this," she said. "It will do you a lot of good."

A beetle entered, and cut the heat-waves of the room. The beetle headed upwards, it dog-fought with another there, returned and, for a while, circled just a few inches away from Soyaan's eyes. He closed and opened them. This pained his eyes. And the beetle was gone.

"Please drink it up."

But he wouldn't drink the medicinal concoction his mother held in front of his unseeing eyes. Nor would he give a plausible explanation of why he had come home with a stomach disorder. What had he eaten? With whom had he been? What poisonous food had he been given? He had feared that his mother's persistent queries would make a rent in his defensive armour, he had feared that his sister's appeal would make a small tear or two in his cloak of privacy. No fear of that now. For he had become inarticulate with the groans of pain. He need not offer answers to their questions. "Soyaan, my son," his mother had said.

Soyaan: healthy as the antimony of her kohled vision. Never had she known him fall ill. Never had she known him unwell for long. Unlike Loyaan, his twin brother, unlike his sister Ladan, unlike them both, Soyaan had been a catapult of order; all three were quite unlike their father Keynaan, who was the epitome of hypochondria. But what had Soyaan eaten? What unearthly potions had he taken? What had he come into contact with, whom? Why had he vomited a colourful mixture of vegetables, meat and spaghetti? His skin, for one thing, had turned unpleasantly pale, almost anaemic. His head had become unduly heavy for the rest of his body: to lift it from the pillow, he needed to be helped.

"With your mother's blessing . . . ," she said.

He shook his head. No. He wouldn't take it.

"Please."

She held a straw fan in her hand. With it, she chased away the flies. With it she also dispersed the heat. As she fanned, some of the flies fled, some stirred but remained where they had been, while those which she had struck landed on the floor. They made a pattern there, a pattern ugly and unhealthy.

He wondered if the room could be sprayed. All these flies, mosquitoes. Where there were flies, there were health hazards, inconveniences.

He motioned to her to help him lift his head off the pillow. She put one of her arms under his head and with her other supported the weight of his body — frail and yet heavy-boned. She suffered the painful effort of watching him place a pillow conveniently under his back. She stood back and eased her features into a relaxed smile when she saw him accomplish, with maintained grace, the difficult task of remaining in a propped-up position. Then she nodded an acknowledgement when he mumbled a word of gratitude.

She sighed as she took her seat again. She felt a pain in her back, a pain which reminded her of childbearing and other complications. But she took refuge in the menopausal safety of her age. Thank the Lord: three childbirths and a near-fatal fourth; and a terror for a husband. She remembered that Soyaan had vomited all she had forced down his throat. A friend of his, a Dr Ahmed-Wellie, had come and provided another long list of prescriptive remedies. Qumman picked up the straw fan again. She worked herself into a mood of fury, she fanned and she fanned. Abruptly she stopped to inquire if Soyaan would take at least a few spoonfuls of the yogurt he had originally requested.

"No, thank you."

"What is wrong with it?" She looked strangely at the bowl in her hand. She brought it nearer her nose and smelt it. Maybe to sense if

8

he, too, had scented the dash of herbs the traditionalist savant had administered to the yogurt.

Her tone of voice became desperate: "You haven't had anything since yesterday."

That wasn't quite true and she knew it. He had taken a little salted yogurt. When he couldn't stand the taste, he had asked for it to be sugared. But then he still didn't want any of it.

"Loyaan will be here any time now," she told him.

This alerted his tired senses, though his reaction to the news about his twin brother's arrival wasn't instantaneous. First he smiled his pleasure. A little later the lines of his face were cast in a mould of cheer. They hadn't met for several months.

"He should be here any time now."

As Soyaan breathed, his nostrils issued a whistle. His mother helped herself to the yogurt. The family's economy couldn't afford the slightest waste. The house in which they were had only just been paid for. *My precious son*, she said to herself, *we cannot afford to lose you.*

"Before I go, is there anything you specially want me to get for you?" she asked as she touched him, feeling his temperature.

"No."

Her hand pressed his stomach which in reaction made a noise something like a belch. He knitted his brow as though from a fresh start of pain. She smoothed his wrinkles with her open palm.

"All these when you are only twenty-nine!" she commented.

"Please." He pointed at a table by the door. His voice was feeble, his stare pale and unfocused.

On the table to which he pointed there lay, as though on display, an assortment of bottles of various groupings and dimensions. But his mother shook her head determinedly. No, she wouldn't get them for him. No. She wouldn't pass the bottles to him. Not before he promised her something. What? He knew that she had little faith in the miracles of modern medicines. He knew that she would exhaust what little faith she had in them long before the curded taste of malaria tablets melted flat out on the tongue which had drenched them. Qumman made no secret of this. She would argue with sustained passion that she favoured traditional medicines; in the event that they didn't work, then Allah's providential cures. Her sons and daughters found it

9

inexplicably curious that she nevertheless tolerated injections when it really came to making the ultimate choice.

"You don't need any of these," she said.

She went to the table and stood there for a while. She took two of the bottles, one in each hand, and studied them. She held them in front of her and stared at them. Knowing she couldn't read the instructions on the bottles, Soyaan wondered what it was that made her look at them in that strange, bewitched manner.

"If only you heard yourself. Of course, you weren't lucid, and your gaze was fixed on the unclear mist of the mad. Your temperature was exceptionally high. The inconsistencies you speak in your sleep — the obscenities your disturbed sleep utters. Is it that woman who gave you whatever has upset you so terribly?"

"What woman?"

Qumman's mouth opened but closed after only having softly pronounced the first letter of that woman's name. Her tongue had stumbled on the vowel-formation of the name, but she rose, with dignity, before she tripped over the wire trap of unuttered thoughts.

"Decency, Mother — and I should like to quote your own words," said Soyaan, "doesn't hide only in the skirt-folds of a young lady of perfumed modesty, whose movements are inconspicuous, unpretentious, a young lady who is discreet. If you pull the string, once you undo the hem — the nude is too obscene and too commonplace whatever the sex. Decency."

She moved away a little, quiet as dust. Her mind settled with and wouldn't do away with the choice she had made. She would not waver like agitated air between this and that pocket of the wind's pressure. She would stay firm.

"You always lose hold of your own reality," she said. "You are very sick. So I suggest you put your trust in us and we will, in no time, loosen *her* grip on your soul."

"Come to the point, Mother."

"You're bewitched, my son."

"No, no. I meant, what was it I said in my disturbed, bewitched sleep?"

"Inconsistencies."

"Be specific, Mother."

"Ask Ladan. Ask your sister." She held the bottles in front of her as before.

10

"Please," he appealed, looking at the bottled tablets.

"These haven't done you any good, anyhow."

"Just pass them to me." He looked at his watch. Time he took the hourly prescription Ahmed-Wellie had approved of. He should tell her that medicine takes a long time for its effect to work; but he dared not. "Please."

She set the bottles down on the table again. She walked back towards her chair. The floor stirred under her feet. There was a small breeze in the room now that the wind had pushed the window open.

"How about this," his mother challenged: "if I pass them to you and I let you take them, will you do something for me in return?"

"Let's hear it."

"When the sheikh arrives, will you promise not to make a mock of his efforts or deride mine? The Koran is all we know that cures without complications. We'll forget about the yogurt, as a compromise," she bargained.

No word from Soyaan. There was a light scatter of dust falling on the aluminium roof. Qumman looked up at the ceiling while she waited for his response. He looked up from his Neruda. Against the bottles, he noticed now, there stood the family copy of the Koran.

"Promise," he said.

She went out of the room to tell the sheikh to prepare.

Whereupon Soyaan searched for further clues to life's mysteries as he focused his stare on a gecko which moved, with consummate grace, up and down the uneven crevices of the wall in front of him. The silence helped lift the weight off his thoughts. He slowed down. He let his mind sail away. He spread his sailcloth at a very convenient spot. He lay there — feeling light as a sail, fleeing from all but *her*, feeling wanted. *Do enter if you will. I am spread like water. Come into me but slowly, lovingly. . . .*

The water was knee-high. They were in the shallow edge of the sea. Soyaan's friend was fully clothed, as the law of the land required of women. Her dress, recently tailored to order, was low-cut in the front. Her large breasts showed every now and again. The water lapped against her shapely thighs. And the waves, tamed by the shallowness of the water, made her dress detour slightly, made her skirt climb up

11

at the back and stay glued to her gorgeous body. The contours of her beautiful figure mapped their sexual geography.

He had known her for one and a half years, or nearly. He would admit he had enjoyed every moment of it. But there were difficulties to this relationship. Yes, although neither spoke the name, there was another. A man important enough to be recognised in public at every gathering in Mogadiscio. So whenever Soyaan met her, they did so in private.

Now she held him by the ankles. Soyaan's strokes were well-timed. He swam like a professional. He let his long arms descend upon the water from as far and as high as he could stretch them. He dived and remained under the water for as long as his lungs could hold out. The solidity of his body in the water's transparency flowed into ripples of fantasy. She pulled him upwards, catching him by the hair. They embraced. She gently kissed him. When she let him go, he swam away, his strokes superbly executed. She went over to where he now was.

"I've enjoyed reading it," she said.

"I was wondering how you found it." But he didn't wait to say any more.

He made a dive, improvised and clumsy. She followed him in. She couldn't stay under for as long as he did. The sea spat her out. Up and out, and she panted. She waited for him to re-emerge.

When he did, she asked: "Has anybody else seen it?"

"Why?"

"Dangerous stuff."

"Do you think so?"

"It certainly is a strong political statement."

He made no comment. He swam away doing the butterfly. He returned. He joined her where the water had been breast-high. They swam together. He stopped. He splashed water up at the heavens. He swallowed a mouthful.

"Can you hold on to it for me?"

"Of course."

They came out. They still believed they had the beach to themselves.

She wrote his name on the sand. The sea washed away her writing. They silently watched the water recede. He wished he could read her

12

message in the water receding. She wished she could make him see reason about the political statement he had made. Would he?

"You haven't shown it to anybody else, have you?"

He didn't reply. He tugged at the string of his swimming-suit tied tightly round his waist. He was a hairy man. Tall. Slim. And handsome. She was a few inches shorter than he. When they both stretched their arms out, side by side with their shoulders nearly touching, it appeared that they were the same height. He dug his big toe into the sand. And he was ready to change the topic.

"How is the little angel?" he asked.

"Growing wings of youth, independence and teeth."

A spatter of water fell on to Soyan's forehead. He looked up. No, to describe accurately: he started. He stared up in surprise. There was a small child dripping sandy water, a child barely two who stood above him. The child's smile lit a fire of delight in Soyaan's eyes whose lids had opened to reveal sparkles of his memory's dotage. The little angel had grown wings of youth, independence and teeth. But the newly arrived child wouldn't go, nor would he speak and explain how he came to be there. Soyaan gazed up at the child. His sight was now misted with unexplained mysteries and the child's sudden appearance from nowhere. The child did not return Soyaan's solicitous greetings. Nor did he respond to the woman's queries, but milled around without speaking. The name of a man came to Soyaan's and her mind, a name which both found convenient to immediately consign to the outskirts of their busy brain-centres. The child went away as quietly and as mysteriously as he came without saying anything. Soyaan wondered if the beach was really as private as he had thought. He wondered if there were other persons, adults, in the area. Neither spoke for a long while. Only much, much later when they had made love behind the bushes:

"The emaciated poor upon whom feed the hungry lice. Well-put that," she commented.

"But you've forgotten."

"What?"

"Once in a while the police gather these beggars as though they were a season's pick."

They lay side by side. The shadow of the clouds spread a short-lived umbrella all along the shore. Way down on the horizon, a couple of swallows chased each other playfully.

13

"When they finally come, having broken the pride of dawn, they will find me prepared. No, I don't belong to the class of the humiliated. I shall have readied myself like a woman who awaits her lover."

A defiant look from him. Her gaze avoided his: she appeared offended. And for an instant, she thought she saw a vulture perched on the precipice at the far end of the shore. She called back to her mind the apparition of the child who'd come and who'd gone. Her cheeks poured wet with a cataract of tears. She was up and on her feet. She ran away from him. She went to wash her hot tears in the salted water of the sea.

The sheikh had consulted his concise concordance. He had chosen which passages to read, which Suras of the Koran would suit the occasion, and he chanted them. Soyaan, as promised, made no comment nor mocked their efforts. The incense pot which she placed in the doorway burned an odorous mixture of frankincense and myrrh. Soyaan's sensitive nose detected something bizarre in the smell. Should he ask his mother to name what she had in that pot? What ungodly odour was that? Hair burning? Did she really think he had been bewitched by that woman?

His father was announced. The sheikh withdrew as Keynaan entered.

Of late, the two had been on very bad terms. Soyaan had cut the small allowance which used to be earmarked for the maintenance of Keynaan and his other wife, Beydan. He told his mother and sister that he had done this in order to pay for the house of which, it turned out, Mother would eventually take full possession. There was, however, another untold reason. Soyaan had learned that the old man had been courting a young girl Ladan's age and he had spent on her what money he had received for Beydan, despite the fact that Beydan was heavy with nine months' pregnancy. Of course, Soyaan didn't inform Beydan about this; nor his mother, sister or twin brother. Keynaan would feel the pinch, had said Soyaan to himself. He would speak. He would explain. He would say what had happened. And he did. "My son has abandoned me to the wolves of shame and disgrace," he said. "He has listened to the counsel of women. A man who seeks and follows women's advice is a man ruined."

14

"I've applied for a job," Keynaan told Soyaan now.

Silence. He couldn't take it, Soyaan couldn't. His itching nerve, Soyaan's inner impatience hazarded a move: he switched the radio on. He turned the volume unnecessarily loud. Keynaan, to be heard, spoke at the top of his voice. When his throat pained, Keynaan turned the volume down. The two listened to Dulman, the country's most famous actress, sing the psalms of the General's praise-names. Soyaan rubbed his eyes harder. The smoke of burning incense had stung them. Anyway, was it worthwhile asking what job Keynaan had applied for? A former police inspector, a man forced to retire because of scandalous inconveniences he had created for the régime, what job might he qualify for? An informer, a daily gatherer of spoken indiscretions, an "ear-servant" of the National Security Service since he was semi-literate?

"I am sorry I wasn't there when you came to Afgoi. Beydan told me of your visit," Keynaan said.

"How is she?"

"Nine months. Heavy as guilt with the weight of her pregnancy."

Beydan, on one of their last encounters, spoke to Soyaan of a dream she had seen, a dream in which she, the centre figure, wasn't there. "Like a ghost," she said, "whose shadow isn't reflected in mirrors, I do not see myself in the dreams I dream." Poor woman. "Neither are you there, my Soyaan. No. Loyaan stands high among the pall-bearers, tall, sad, unsmiling." Poor woman! Keynaan, fidgety in his chair, looked visibly uneasy. Was he, too, now thinking the same thoughts? Dulman's praise-songs of the country's Grand Patriarch provided him with a pretext for changing the subject of their conversation, supplied him with a cue.

"Listen to these ludicrous eulogies of the General," Soyaan said. "The father of the nation. The carrier of wisdom. The provider of comforts. A demi-god. I see him as a Grand Warden of a Gulag."

"I won't ask you to unsay that. But I suggest you be careful. It seems you take too many things for granted. If I were you, I wouldn't do that. I would be more careful if I were you. Gulag or no, you are doing well. I don't see why it is you who puts a neck out. Why you? Where are the others? Why must you carry the standard? Why must you be its bearer?"

"I am no bearer of anybody's banner. But I feel humiliated, I feel abused, daily, minutely. A friend of mine is in for anti-Soviet

15

activities. But where are we? What era is this? Is this Africa or is this Stalin's Russia? I am disgusted. As soon as I feel better, I promise you. . . ." He hiccupped.

"I warn you."

"As soon as I feel better, I *hic* will *hic*. . . ."

"Have a glass of cold water."

Hiccup. "No."

Soyaan switched off the radio. He thus strangled the singer in the middle of a syllable, made Dulman choke on the consonants of sycophancy. But just before either had time to think of things to say, there came the voice of a beggar chanting alms-songs.

Keynaan went out. Soyaan returned to Neruda's *Macchu Picchu*.

"Read it to me, please."

"Which sonnet?"

"Number X."

Gestures of love and tenderness: Ladan. Yes, of such gentle gestures were loving sisters made, thought Soyaan as he listened to the cadences of her beautiful voice, as she lifted her head and looked at him, as she rolled her eyes in tears of tenderness. She had just returned home from school where for the past four or so months she had taught, this being part of her two-year National Service. Before her, there had come and gone several other persons, her mother told her. There was Dr Ahmed-Wellie who had stayed by him for a very long time. There was "Siciliano". There was Keynaan. Plus some others. There were women from the neighbourhood who suggested that the family brand the body of the ailing with the cauterants of studied medical traditions. Once when Ladan had stolen in on them like a shadow, she thought she overheard a conversation in which the name of Koschin occurred more than twice. Wasn't the man "Il Siciliano", the one who was extremely courteous and who bowed as he took leave, as he bid them farewell? She finished reading the sonnet and sat silently, her feet heavy — like the cold wetness of a sweaty dream. Come what might, she told herself, she would contain the secret, she wouldn't repeat to him what he had spoken in his sleep. Yes, she would keep under control her alchemy of emotions.

She turned a page. The wick of her memory had lit, with a fresh flash, a page of her past. She read to herself the lyrics of love. A chapter of gratitude dedicated to Soyaan; another of sympathetic

16

understanding to her mother; a third of assurances to Loyaan; a sonnet of love to Koschin, which especially rhymed with that name. There was no mention of Keynaan, no reference to him. To Ladan, Soyaan was the braille of her otherwise unguided vision; to her, Loyaan was the brother who enabled her to sow her moons and bright days with nightly stars.

Soyaan turned towards her and said: "Mother says that I speak in my sleep."

"Does she?"

He took Neruda's book from her and put it aside. "She says I utter inconsistencies."

"You know what Mother is like."

"No, Ladan dearest. Tell me. Do I?"

She now had his hand in hers. She kissed it. "One has tumultuous moments and intervals of lucidity when one is ill, with a temperature as high as yours. So what does it matter what you've said and what you haven't?"

"What did I say?"

"Nothing of importance."

"What did I say?"

A tender smile framed her worried look. But she remained silent as curtainfall for a very long time. She looked away. She let his hand go. The air in the room was heavy as the gas a stove emits. Then:

"You spoke of pale ghostly beings which jabbed you with needles."

He regarded her with renewed interest.

"Yes, you said that," she assured him.

Pale ghostly beings jabbing him with needles? He changed the position in which he had lain: these injections, thought he to himself, how they pained! He remembered a scene in a hospital room, white as death and dull as a knife gone rusty. Or was he dreaming? They had tied him to a chair, there were three men, and they gave him an injection.

"What else?"

"You uttered obscenities about the General. But these were moments of tumultuous confusion and high fever. I was there. So was Mother. 'The Koran, the Holy Koran,' she once shouted. 'Read a passage, let us take refuge in the word of God.' "

"Anything else?"

17

"That was sufficient evidence, she argued, that you were bewitched. She interpreted it this way: the pale ghostly beings you saw were none but the masters of the *mingis*-bewitching ceremonies, the men who, for the performance of the rite, smear their black faces with the powder of lime-ash."

Another pause. Whispered asides. Inaudible murmurs: Soyaan's. Then there was a noise, which, although feeble, made Soyaan turn and open his eyes. The noise came from behind Ladan. She turned round. The robed angels of her dreams: heaven's God. *What do I see?* It was Loyaan. Loyaan in person. For a good five minutes, no one would recall who did what, who said what, who hugged or kissed whom.

Ladan left the twins together to talk things over.

A beggar's chant: the singing voice of a youth which alternated with that of an old man. Even beggars had classes, Soyaan was thinking, as he allowed his brother to take his temperature and ask questions for which he would get no answers. There were those in white, in clean robes, who were learned and who professionally chanted only religious incantations; these were usually considered as pupils of a principal sheikh, an imam at a mosque and were thus treated well. There were the others who wore tatters, whose manners were uncouth and harsh as their voices. They were treated as were street cats and masterless dogs.

"Feed the hungry tongues of the needy with the fats of the
  Almighty.
Wet the dry mouths of famine with the waters of the Wonder-
  maker.
Give and God will offer you more in return and also in abund-
  ance."

Ladan and Qumman went to fill the beggars' stomachs and empty containers with mouthfuls of residuals. *Pray for the sick among us, pray for the souls of the dead relative and Muslim anywhere they may be found.*

Meanwhile: Loyaan had felt Soyaan's pulse and taken his temperature. At first he got nowhere with his persistent questions about where his brother had been, with whom and what he had eaten. It transpired after an hour's talk, however, that Soyaan had been to Beydan's and had eaten something there. It also became clear that he had seen a doctor at the Military Hospital. The doctor's sug-

18

gestions were on the table, Loyaan could read the instructions himself. But who was the doctor? Soyaan, however, dragged the conversation on to topics of the day's politics. On the spree of improvised vitality, surprising Loyaan and himself too, he embarked on a long-winded monologue about how the General was serving a cocktail of poisonous contradictions to the masses. He said, with sufficient conviction, that if a small group, with a small following, were to organise, say, a picket or a sit-in of a sort, if this small group informed the masses of what really was happening, information being essential in a country where everything was censored . . . hiccup. . . .

"Come, come, now. Hold your breath. Inhale."

"A knock on a door at *hic* dawn. The Security take the man away *hic* and leave behind them a wife *hic* who suffers from the insomnia of restless nights *hic*."

"Come, come, now. Hold your breath. Inhale."

But he wouldn't hold his breath. There was no cold water either. Should Loyaan resort to the traditional method? Should he shock him, tell him the most horrid of news? "Your love is dead." Who? Who was Soyaan's love? Did he have one? What was her name? Or should he resign himself to one simple fact: that he knew hardly anything of Soyaan's private life, who his closest friends were. Hiccup.

"How is Beydan?"

The saliva in the floor of Soyaan's mouth soured into anger at the mention of her name, anger at himself more than at anybody else. He should do something for that woman. Would Loyaan please help give her some money? Would he please see to it that she got it in person? No. He chose not to tell even Loyaan about the young woman whom Keynaan intended to marry. That would only make things worse. Soyaan: a man of intrigue, rhetoric, polemic and politics. Loyaan: a man of melodramatic scenes, mundanities and lost tempers. Loyaan would insist, for instance, on removing all inverted commas from phrases like "revolution in Africa", "socialism in Africa", "radical governments", whereas Soyaan was fond of dressing them with these and other punctuational accessories; he was fond of opening a parenthesis he had no intention of closing. Years ago as a matter of fact it was Soyaan who had suggested that Loyaan should avoid politics as should a patient unprescribed drugs: "You stay where you are, in that region of Baidoa, you do your job well and you are the most revolutionary of revolutionaries" — inverted

19

commas removed! Hiccup. Soyaan lay quiet under the sheet like a
tucked-in child. Hiccup.

"And how is Father?"

"He was *hic* here a while ago."

"How is he?"

"A powerless *hic* patriarch, the grandest of them *hic* all. We are
on the worst *hic* of terms."

"On account of Beydan?"

"Not only that."

"What?"

"The politics of confron-*hic*-tation."

"I don't understand."

"The demystifica-*hic*-tion of in-*hic*-formation. Tell the *hic* mas-
ses in the simplest *hic* of terms what is happening. Demystify *hic*
politics. Empty those heads filled with tons of rhetoric. Uncover
whether hiding *hic* behind pregnant letters such as KGB, CIA, or other
hic wicked alphabet of mysteries *hic*. Do you *hic* understand now
hic?"

Soyaan's eyes were trained on Loyaan. "I am not sure if I do."

A smile. A hiccup. Then:

"You will in *hic* time."

Soyaan's silence elicited a further comment from Loyaan. The
aluminium sheet rattled as a MiG-21 flew past overhead.

"Koschin, by the way, *hic*, is in terrible *hic* need of help."

"Where are they keeping him?"

"In the underground prison *hic* the East Germans *hic* have con-
structed. A super-prison *hic* as aid from one Soviet *hic* satellite to *hic*
a fake socialist but really *hic* fascist Somalia."

"How can I be of any help?"

"Ask Ahmed-Wellie. He will know."

Loyaan's chair sat in the perforation of the sun's needle of rays.
Soyaan's knees stood out as they strained against the sheets which
covered him. He changed position and was ready to change topic of
conversation as well. But Loyaan was somewhere else. He had gone
back to and was walking the passageways of a past he had for-
gotten. . . . The twins were at play; there was a sandy beach; Merca;
sandy castles under construction. Yes, out of the hidden depths
emerged a ball with illustrations drawn on it, a globe, a world map,
complete with the physical as well as the political colouring of

20

colonies, mountains and lakes. This came and for a long while stayed hung in front of him brightly like a lantern. Keynaan was there as well, Keynaan the grand patriarch, Keynaan with a knife in hand, feet in boots, Keynaan heartless, gutless, and the knife tore into the ball. "A world round as a ball. Whoever heard of that?" Hiccup.

Soyaan lay silent and spreadeagled. Under one of his arms, there was a copy of Machiavelli's *The Prince*. Loyaan picked up the book. He read out a passage Soyaan had underlined:

" *'There is nothing more difficult to take in hand, more perilous to conduct, or more uncertain in its success then to take the lead in the introduction of a new order of things. Because the innovator has for enemies all those who have done well under the old conditions, and lukewarm defenders in those who may do well under the new.'* "

When Loyaan stopped reading, he saw that Soyaan had fallen asleep.

An hour later. Soyaan awoke and found him still seated there. They discussed serious as well as banal topics which concerned the family's life, politics of the General, et cetera. Then suddenly Soyaan's eyes, like the sun's light in the room, dimmed. Soyaan hiccupped a series of involuntary spasms of breathlessness. He looked all the more disturbed as he stretched his hand out to Loyaan who took it and held it in his. He repeated and repeated and repeated Loyaan's name in between these spasms of breathlessness.

First, the warmth went out of Soyaan's hand. Then the brightness out of his eyes. Everything assumed an artificial quietness, for an unbroken fraction of a second.

And Soyaan hiccupped his last.

Part I

Chapter One

Like two tyres of a bicycle that never touch, never come together, to tell each other of a wish to retire from serving an ungrateful master — each remains isolated within its own limits of space, a system, a code of behaviour that perpetuates and makes possible the serving; each is, for a purpose, locked, tied, screwed to a bar which runs between, which makes possible the moving, gives the article an existence, offers the metallic composition a name — and a label at that.

The sun re-emerged draped in the brown dust of noon; it re-appeared looking tanned. The sun had turned on its time-telling pivot and gathered round itself a robe blue as the heavens. For its crown, a wreath of clouds, white as the skull of death. Now the sun canoed through a fern of vapour and heat mist, swam to a clearing and was swallowed up by a swamp of tropical haze.

Soyaan, Loyaan's twin brother, hiccupped his last.

"Remember, remember the pledge you made, remember the wish of the dead, remember the family," Loyaan said to himself now. The room was very quiet, the air in the room of the dead had the chilling touch of brass at dawn. Loyaan, still and thoughtful, sat by the bed upon which his brother's corpse had lain shrouded in white. And he discovered there were huge and unfillable gaps which stared at his inability to repeat with sufficient accuracy all that had been said, who had said what, and what had happened. How could he narrow the gap, with what might he fill the hole to make it smaller? He remembered two remarks, one his mother had made, the other his father's. "The soul is God's, the body is the earth's," his mother had said, responding viscerally to Loyaan's suggestion that Soyaan's corpse be subjected to a post-mortem examination. "No, no, bless the soul of the dead — and may the generous earth which receives him be pacified, thus. We needn't discuss this any further, my son. We needn't discuss whether or not we shall allow a mad surgeon, with foul thoughts, to render Soyaan's body impure by touching it with the knife of science. No. There will be no autopsy. There will be none of that governmental bureaucracy." A second after she had spoken that cutting statement, indeed before the guillotine of the second had fallen sharply on the ticking head of the minute . . . an accusation, yes, Qumman had made a grave accusatory statement against "a certain woman whose name I shan't mention, a certain woman who poisoned my son's food." Would Keynaan come forward and make any comment? He would limit himself to saying that, on matters regarding life or death, no man should be allowed to question the authority of the Almighty. He preferred to see to it that Soyaan "re-encounters his Creator as undissected as the day He lent him the breath which had opened his lungs of cry". And the twins' sister, what of the twins' sister Ladan? Ladan had behaved strangely. She had sobbed and sobbed and sobbed, and for a long time wouldn't say a thing. Then she spoke in rhetoric: "Does it matter how you dispose of dead bodies? Does it matter whether or not you find out what has caused the death?" Then came shrieks of hysteria, her throat went hoarse, her cheeks were primed with a coat of dried tears. Loyaan resolved to leave her alone.

"Would a post-mortem examination have told us something you wouldn't want us told?" said he to the corpse. "What if we had you cut up and restitched, what if we had science do its bit, would that reveal an untoward secret?"

He stared at a poster on the wall in front of him: the tightly closed fist of a black man's protest against oppression, a fist raised as high as the Roman eagle of power. Then, through the haze of time he could see two children building palaces of sand, and behind them the battered body of an abandoned truck. The haze cleared, time past merged with time present, and Loyaan was back in the room of the dead, sitting still and quiet. The women's wailing, their mourning the dead had reached him in that room; women cleaning, clearing the mess of the living, women washing, women shouting to one another as they cried, women speaking Soyaan's praises as they stood mats against the walls. A torrent of noises which flowed, but with pauses, and theatrical silences. Loyaan exploited one such pause and addressed the bed of the dead:

"You had an appointment with somebody. Let us see your diary, a notepad hardly used. Against today's date, your neat hand has penned something which I cannot read. And the mystery: 'M to

26

the power of 2.' What does this mean? Beside it you have written: 'very important'."

More noise again, sounds that approached and faded; there was a wave of irritable sound that invaded the room. In vain would he pursue peace of mind in that room, he realised. He was certainly tempted to come out and tell these women to respect silence while on the patio, or else leave. But what could he say to Ladan whose solo led the chorus of cries? And yet again a brief pause.

" 'M to the power of 2. I/M comrade-in-project.' Who is I/M? You and your mysteries! Who are these people? What role have they played in your life? Where do I start? With whom do I speak? Ladan, your closest, can hardly articulate a thought; in any case I doubt if she was in on your mysterious moves, I doubt if she knows what underground political movements you may have belonged to or what political views you subscribed to. Very vaguely, yes. But not beyond naked generalities, not beyond generalisations."

Overwhelmed with fear and suspicion ("Could *they* have . . . oh, no, not that," he instantly dismissed the thought which had crossed his head), Loyaan's unbeguiled gaze fell and dwelled on a wormeaten wooden beam. Somebody, meanwhile, had knocked on the door then withdrawn. Loyaan couldn't bring himself to worry about who that was. He knew his mother and his sister were still on the patio. He could hear Ladan's solo. He could hear his mother's instructions about what to do with this or that. Now he was about to light a cigarette. He remembered he hadn't had one since the previous night. Out of respect for the dead, he surely shouldn't, he thought. His mind travelled elsewhere. When it returned, he said:

"A trivial thing, say, a journey up or down a hundred miles in any direction: even this leaves its imprint on one's life. An insect-bite, an itch — don't these trivia unbalance things for one? The sightless retina of a future vision, do you recall saying that to me when you talked of the General's lack of political perspective, the General's lack of a sense of humour?"

They were surely rich the dividends Loyaan's travelled mind had reaped and returned with! However, he staggered with the weight of guilt, he moved unsteadily with a heavy burden on his brain. He couldn't bear it any longer. He said:

"Father hit Mother last night, did you know? Just before you hiccupped your last, the two had conflicting views on a certain mystery,

27

the details of which, I am sure, you wouldn't be in the least interested in. Does this shock you? Does anything shock the dead? Eh? What did I do? Nothing to stop their fight. Your warm hand froze on mine — that's all."

And Loyaan rose to his feet. He stood behind the window, and watched the sun ride across his concentrated gaze. He turned and moved about for a while. He stopped. He said to the corpse:

"Mother had invoked maledictions, Mother had cursed, Mother had accused the name of Beydan. Father overheard; they argued. Father lost his temper. He moved in on her and hit her. Then I intervened, yes, I did, that's right."

Another stroll up and down the small space. "The place is in bad need of being done up, the walls must be repainted and the ceiling, which has begun to fall apart from lack of maintenance, must be tended with caring hands. Spiders come out of the crevices," wrote Soyaan in a letter to Loyaan barely a week previously, "and remain ensconced in the safety of the night's pockets and the creases in the leathered purses of dusk. The blisters on the walls show: they speak of the unnursed wound which poverty's scars haven't healed. When we've had the place whitewashed. . . ." But Loyaan had already sat down. He reached for the shroud in which the corpse was wrapped after the first and unceremonial washing. Loyaan pulled at it, to check if any part of the body had become uncovered. For, according to tradition, the wicked eyes of the living mustn't sin on any naked part of a corpse. He remained motionless, half-bending forward, with the corpse lying quiet under him — and unresponding, too.

Then there was another knock at the door, this time a gentle and unassuming tapping: it felt as though it was a soft knock on the entrance to Loyaan's attention. The knocking was immediately followed by a breeze which entered, a breeze slight although profane. The breath of the tropics, for a moment, managed to interfere with the quietness in the room. The white sheet, which until that instant had screened off the eyes of the sinful living from the body of the dead, stirred. Loyaan clumsily hurried to still it with his hand. And he *touched*.

He looked over his left shoulder.

Qumman, his mother, had already walked in. He stood up to meet her full height and furious look. Coincidentally, the inner courtyard that was open to the sky came to life: there was a commotion

28

of communal wailing, there came Ladan's hoarse crying. He requested his mother to close the door. This she did, although her eyes rested on his hands which had *touched*. He said nothing to defend himself. He allowed her to take her time; he, without saying anything, gave her time to advance further into the room.

"Bless his soul," she said.

"Amen."

"Bless the soul of the relations and all the Muslims whose souls have departed to the Other World. My precious, our own Soyaan. He harmed nobody. He never had, I can tell you that."

She wiped away a pool of moisture from below her eyes. She looked more aged. Her face, convulsed, appeared lined with the wells of ice-cold reserve. She had something of a charge in all her gestures. She wouldn't match nor meet anybody's description of a beautiful woman. It was as if different parts of her body had been dismantled at puberty and reassembled, in a rush, at old age. Also, today, she had bruises. Her forehead had bled and dried. There was a scar a night old on her arm as well.

"Thanks be to God, He that gives and He that takes what He has given. Thanks be to God, He that sees our inside. We pray for his forgiveness and his understanding. And, my son," she addressed Loyaan.

"Yes, Mother?"

A cry of irreverence: Ladan's cry pierced the air. In silence the two looked at each other. Qumman picked the theme of discussion over and turned it in her head. A pause, at first. Then:

"I've told her. Nobody can say I haven't. I've told Ladan that every tear she drops earns him that died (may God's mercy be on him) an extra stroke of heat-lashes from the hell which burns with the bodies of sinners. Every tear anyone drops. I've told her that."

"Should I go and talk to her?"

Qumman raised her palm: no. "When her body tires, her head will reason," she added.

She was now wearing a shield which she had devised over the years, she had put on her mask of non-expressiveness. She squinted, her face became a trifle troubled, and her lips moved. Was she saying a string of rosary secrets to Allah? Indeed. She told her beads quietly, she whispered her prayer of needs. After a minute, she dispensed with the mask, discarded it. Before God, before her Creator, she could

29

show herself as she was. "God, O God, forgive us all our sins. Amen."
Suddenly:

"What is that?" she cried angrily.

She pointed at the poster on the wall, the poster of the raised
fist. She looked at it intently, fixedly. In profile, she seemed a woman
much younger — but more fragile.

"Remove it, please."

Representational art, figurative art — and miscellanea! A fist
raised upwards at the heavens, defiant as the devil himself. (A dark
figure hidden in the darker shades of a stadium-light?) Loyaan wasn't
prepared to start on that. He did not talk back. He went and took
down the poster. He folded it and put it under his armpit.

"Do you know when we shall bury him?"

She invoked a pantheon of saintly reflections. She thanked God
again, sought His mercy, asked for His pardon not only for Soyaan
but for all Muslims who had died. She continued:

"It isn't very hot. We presume that around about three in the
afternoon will be fine. If the weather maintains, that is."

"And where is my father?"

Her arms opened, her arms rose as though on their own — like
the wings of a wounded bird, slow, pained. She addressed herself to
the universe in a philanthropic manner:

"Be sincere with yourself, my son. That is the first and most
important thing of all. Hold no grudge against your own father. He
is your father, don't you forget that." Her voice was now vibrant
with accusation.

"I only asked: where is he?"

His mother was silent. Loyaan decided to chance upon the
courage to say the unfinished but charged phrase:

"Wicked thoughts. . . ."

An avalanche of a hundred unpronounceable ideas tumbled
down upon them all at once. Keynaan. Beydan. Ladan. Soyaan. The
mystery of his death. Power. Last night's fight. Money. What was to
become of the family. However, their terms of reference were dif-
ferent. The sources upon which they drew were not the same. But she
was his mother; he, the son.

"Let us not talk about him here in the room of the dead," she
suggested. "Let us talk about him another time. Let us not pollute
the air in this room by pronouncing *her* name, either."

30

He conceded her that. But: "Will he take part in the burial rites as he is the father?"

She nodded. She changed the subject. "I wonder, will it rain?"

"If it doesn't, we might have to bury him earlier than three o'clock." He changed the position of the poster.

As she sat down, she said: "Let me be with him for a while. Alone."

The sun, the colour of charred flames gone dead but still hot, paraded across the sky.

"If you wish to win people's praise, die young," Loyaan quoted a Somali proverb to himself. There was sense in that. It would be said there was no person like you. A harvest of stories with new life as planted by the tellers. Some people had already begun telling such stories about Soyaan, stories which were, to a great extent, made up. But who were his friends? Who were his real friends? Who were the closest to him among his colleagues at the Presidency? Soyaan: the most discreet of men when it came to personalising details of one's public life; quiet; reserved; well-read; and a very conscientious man. He had been for many years the Economic Adviser to the Presidency, responsible directly to and answerable only to the General. There was nobody like him. He had been the most clear-headed among his peers. A special man, very special. Every man or woman who was there and who pronounced his name today praised it. But what if he hadn't died? If he hadn't died, would all these people still hold his name in such veneration and admiration? Was he not the man whom some of these very people had nicknamed "Soyaan the planner of deceits"? Had not some of them disapproved of him because of his political views? Had not some of the women here found it unbearable that he would not bend over backwards for anybody because he or she was tribally related? Principled persons make more enemies than friends in societies such as ours, he used to say. Loyaan, for one, didn't share his views on this. At any rate. . . .

He was standing in the heart of the patio which gave easy access to the four rooms which comprised the house. Four rooms of different sizes despite there being a striking similarity in structure and conception. Under normal conditions, none of these rooms, save that in which Soyaan had lain covered in white, could comfortably hold more than five persons at once. In each room, depending on size and

31

purpose, beds and other related oddities had been squeezed in. Wherever there was extra space, Mother's paraphernalia of odds and ends had rained in. One of the rooms had been Soyaan's. In it were his books, his tape-recorder, his record-player and his assortment of sea-things — shells, star-fish — and photographs of the sea. He had moved into the house with his mother and sister only a month and a half before his death. The largest of the rooms was Ladan's. There was also the one which was used as a store-room for the time being. Mother's room had two beds which had developed dales in the middle of their springs. A huge wooden crate, in which lay a thousand and one items bought over the years, occupied over one-eighth of the room's space. "Mother," said Soyaan, "knows not how to throw anything away. Mother is herself a souvenir from another age."

Hush. A sob. Quiet again, like a bundle in a corner: that was Ladan. He went to her. He helped her stand. He held her in his embrace as she shook, as she trembled, as she choked on her phlegm of tears. He took out a handkerchief. He wiped her face clean and dry.

"Come on."

Her eyes were blood-shot. She cleared her throat which was sore from the grating wailing of her keening. The place now was reverent-quiet. The few women who had come to help the family went about their business without saying anything to one another.

"Come on."

She hugged him to herself.

"It won't help," he said.

"I know."

She was nearly as tall as he. The children had taken after their father and not Qumman. Ladan had the handsome and receptive face of Keynaan. She was six years younger than the twins. But they were to her more than brothers. Soyaan meant more now that he had died. Soyaan's death had caused a profound disturbance in her. It made her look different. She was no longer a light-hearted girl, she was no longer full of youthful vitality, bursting with energy and creativeness. He wondered: would she have the key to those initialled mysteries — M to the power of 2, or I/M? He wondered: how much did she know of Soyaan's life?

"No more crying, no more wailing. Please."

"I won't," she half-sobbed.

32

"Promise?"

"Promise."

She would find herself something to do. She would put one of the rooms into some order. She would furnish it with chairs. She would have one of the women give her a hand in sweeping it. When the men came, there would be a room for them to retire to.

"I won't cry any more."

He kissed her on the forehead. "Good."

She picked up a broom and walked in the direction of the room she had in mind to prepare for the male guests and the sheikhs. There was a fever of anxiety in the atmosphere. Enveloped in numerous shadows of past and present polemic, Loyaan's mind jerked as though it were a compass pointing to a direction, indicating the point in a detail. He turned Mecca-wards — the Kaaba of darkened stones.

"God gives; He takes that which He only can give," said an old woman who had come to mourn with the family. "We shall all go there, if not today then tomorrow."

Loyaan let her press his arm.

"I knew Loyaan," she added. "I was there when the two of you were born. I recall how you wet my dress one day when I dropped in on my way to a wedding. Loyaan was quieter than you, Soyaan. Your mother could tell it was you crying, that it was you who had broken the clay water-pot, that it was you who had disobeyed an order. Such a reverent man, your twin Loyaan."

She had very beautiful skin, smooth as oil and shining. He couldn't remember her name if even he wanted to. Perhaps she was related to the family tribally. But this didn't and wouldn't affect Loyaan's attitude towards her in the least.

"Loyaan had enormous respect for the old and the young alike. How often did I come to him, and he but almost penniless: he shared the little he had with me. He said one day when he earned more he would contribute towards my trip to Mecca. He said he would first send Qumman, his mother. I am sorry he died before he was able to make that possible."

There came a long silence. Loyaan decided to exploit the pause.

"My name is Loyaan."

Was she hard of hearing? Need he shout?

"I am Loyaan."

33

The sun's light radiated out to the horizon. The old woman pulled at the sleeves of his shirt and beamed in the rays of his warmth.

"How I loved him. Like my own child."

Loyaan nodded and grinned his appreciation. She looked to this and that side, checking if there was anyone in the vicinity who might overhear their conversation.

"The pillar of the family household. He was the most solid of foundations any family could have structured itself on. Of course, you were not here; of course, you lived elsewhere, in another town. But he was ever so caring, ever so nice to his parents and the aged, too. The most solid of family foundations."

"Yes, yes."

She pulled him closer, she smiled her conspiracy, whispered her gossip. She wanted to know: "Don't misunderstand me, please don't. But has there been a small family discord, some disagreement as to what to do about Soyaan's money? I've heard a most disturbing story. Your father has been mean, I've heard. Is that true? He hit your mother, I've heard. Did he?"

A long pause. She let his sleeve go. She waited for his answer patiently. He took his time. He surveyed the scene. He saw women who entered, he saw others leave; there came and went a stream of persons moving about the patio doing something or other. Suddenly, a hush. The sheikhs had arrived. And with them the male guests. Loyaan said to the old woman as he took leave of her:

"Let me welcome the sheikhs and the men. Pardon me."

The women quietly withdrew.

It was now men who stirred and moved about the inner courtyard. The sheikhs were given mats on which to sit, in the room which Ladan had prepared for them. Some of the other women began to make tea, while others took refuge in another room and squatted in circles, keeping silent or quietly uttering the keen. Ladan, as she had promised, cried no more.

"We will all go there eventually. One after the other," said a man.

Loyaan turned. The face of the speaker sent him reeling backwards in time. The man was of the same clan as Keynaan's family. Other tribesmen, supportive, nodded their heads in unison. They in turn shook or held Loyaan's hand. They paid him tribal condolences. His gaze darted in all other directions in search of someone to save

34

him from the whirlpool of present-day controversies in which he was caught. "I am of nobody's tribe, neither was Soyaan," he said to himself. He picked his way through the people and shouted a greeting to a friend of his and Soyaan's. After they had embraced, Dr Ahmed-Wellie drew back and said:

"What is all this? What has happened? What did he die of?"

At first Loyaan appeared surprised. A moment later, he found that he was at a loss for an explanation. Hadn't it occurred to him that anyone would ask that question? What had Soyaan died of? Wasn't that why he had wanted a post-mortem examination? He resolved not to tell Ahmed-Wellie of his failure to convince his parents to have this performed on the body. But what had Soyaan died of? *Address yourself to the question. Come on.* A voice spoke to Loyaan from inside him. A voice? *Address yourself to the challenge.* And he improvised a response, safe, vague:

"He died of complications."

Ahmed-Wellie wasn't satisfied. "What complications? I met him only this morning. What is all this? Complications? What complications? As a doctor and a friend of his, I never knew him come to me with any complaint graver than venereal itches. So what are these complications?"

The roaring noise had died down a little. Loyaan felt taunted by the undaunted look with which Ahmed-Wellie challenged him. Should he admit that he, too, was searching for an acceptable answer, a scientific one? Did he dare ask Ahmed-Wellie if he knew anything of Soyaan's whereabouts in the last few days? *Address yourself to the question.*

"There is my father. He has just returned. Excuse me."

And yet again, Loyaan was able to go away without answering a question.

Enraged, furious, Keynaan greeted his son with a query: "Who is in the room with Soyaan?"

"Mother is."

"Her presence defiles the room, that evil woman. Have her brought out of there. Or else I shall go in and drag her out myself. And I am serious, Loyaan. I will do that if you don't."

"No, you won't."

The two were of equal height. The perilous difficulty of standing firm against his father's challenge made Loyaan stiffen. His expression wouldn't soften even when he acknowledged greeting-condolences from a few passers-by. In the thickening dejection all around him, Loyaan looked dazed, a man broken. His thoughts zigzagged through small, toe-dug squares of childhood games way back in his infancy. He was a child again; the moon was mild, and he and Soyaan had quarrelled over a ball. Keynaan's crooked smile; his towering height. The fist of power; the power of the patriarch; eyes hard as knuckles. Keynaan had picked up the ball and, without much ado, without any uprush of rage or anger, punctured it and tore it in two. "I will kill him one day," Soyaan had said. "I really will. When I am strong as he. When I can handle a knife, when I can carry a gun."

"Go and substitute her, then," ordered Keynaan now.

"Please. Peace."

Keynaan was speechless with rage. In the shade of a tree outside he could see there stood waiting for him friends of his, yes, former colleagues from the Security Service. This calmed him down. Whereupon Loyaan noticed there came in front of him a fellow tribesman who unfolded a wrapper and produced, for Loyaan's approval, the coffin-cloth Keynaan had ordered.

"And I've paid the gravediggers as well," added the young man who was Loyaan's age. "We should be ready in half an hour. But we should send somebody over to the Local Government to have the vans ready as well. Will you do that? You can borrow my car if Soyaan's isn't here."

"No. You arrange that. Get the water vans there earlier if possible."

The three went their different ways.

The sky was overcast. A grey ceiling of dampness and sweat. More people had called. The neighbours had come. Colleagues of Soyaan's, friends of the twins, men and women whose faces were familiar to Loyaan, men and women whose faces and names weren't familiar to him. Ladan was in a state again and had to be locked up in a room. Qumman, veiled in a gloom of silence, re-emerged from the room of the dead, as the sheikhs replaced her. Keynaan followed them.

"Death is mysterious," Ahmed-Wellie said to Loyaan. "And this more so than many deaths I've put my signature to. He died of complications, you said? What complications did he die of?"

36

Loyaan cast his glance elsewhere. "You tell me!"

Ahmed-Wellie didn't quite understand. "What of a post-mortem? Have you had one done?"

"Complications."

"That seems to be the password. What's wrong with you?"

"Family."

"Oh, my God."

Helpers shuffled by. Everything had gone a shade browner. Keynaan's colleagues stood to one side, Loyaan noted to himself. Close by, leaning against another tree, there was a one-armed man. Loyaan sensed that his rage had developed into a feeling of self-deprecation. Would Ahmed-Wellie assist, if asked, to decipher the meaning of those mysteries? "M to the power of 2." Would he know what they meant? Would he be able to tell Loyaan who were Soyaan's closest collaborators in the projects he had worked on?

"I can't believe he's dead," said Ahmed-Wellie.

"Neither could I when it happened."

Loyaan frowned in silence. The sun advanced up the rungs of the afternoon's heat. The rush of impotence in his hot blood set him at a remove from everybody and everything. Loyaan silently walked away from Ahmed-Wellie.

Chapter Two

Like a dry weed in the wind, blowing along with the breeze, light and skinny; a dry weed nodding in approval to the forceful wind blowing about; a dry weed bowing. A few yards away, there is a lone tree in the heart of barren terrain. Surrounding the base of the tree are a number of twigs which have been tamed by time and climate, twigs which fence the stalk, twigs which tease the root-stock. Something climactic runs havoc; the weed, in a headlong rush, somersaults hurriedly towards the growth at the bottom of the lone tree and breaks in two.

"Clowns. Cowards. And (tribal) upstarts: these are who I work with. The top civil service in this country is composed of them. Men and women with no sense of dignity, nor integrity; men and women whose pride has been broken by the General's Security; men and women who have succumbed and accepted to be humiliated. Are you married? Do you have children? How many? Five? A wife and a mistress? Plus the tribal hangers-on who have just arrived and whom you support? Listen to the knock on your neighbour's door at dawn. Hearken: the army-boots have crunched grains of sand on the road leading away from your house. Listen to them hasten. When will your turn come? Yesterday was your colleague's turn. You saw his wife wrapped in tears, you saw how she averted her eyes. Does she know where they have taken her husband? She goes from one police station to another. The police know who she is, and what she is seeking, but no one will tell her anything. She won't return home, in fact she cannot bear to: she has four small children to face and somehow feed. What has he done? What has her little clerk of a husband done? But what have all the others done, what have the thousands who languish in prisons done? The methods of the General and of the KGB are not dissimilar, I can tell you that. Instructions: Know who do not know you. Plant seeds of suspicion in every thinking brain and hence render it 'unthinking'. I remember what a friend of mine once said to

38

another: 'Raise your children, but not your voice nor your head. To survive you must clown. You must hide in the convenience of a crowd and clap. Don't put your neck out; why do that? There must be millions like you who are suffering the same ill-treatment. When in the company of the newly groomed upstarts (the men whom the General's sense of tribal priorities have supplied with the unquestioned authority to do what they please, when and where they please), make sure your profile is kept low. Take my counsel seriously, don't detect the note of cynicism in what I've just said. Clowns. Cowards. And upstarts.' Well, well. They trot the unprincipled line of the General's régime. I say: let's together humour the General. Let us sing his astral titles. The withered hope of a dream leafy as autumn. Our throats have pained, the latest encomium is too long to give an encore to. Listen to the knock on your neighbour's door at dawn. Hearken: the army boots have crunched grains of sand on the pavement by your window. Listen to them hasten. Listen to the revving of the engine. They've taken another. When will your turn come? The wife doesn't switch the electric lights off. The brightness of dawn overpowers them in the end. The sun will have sent her on her fearsome errand. She gives the morning terror to the brother of the detainee. The brother has himself once been imprisoned for nine months without trial. He has been through water – and other primitive methods of torture. The triumph of fear over anger engages his pensée, whereas the flames of rage indulge the understanding sympathy of the sister-in-law. Will he do something to avenge his brother's unfair detention? 'Go home and don't worry,' is all he says. 'I will supply your needs, will pay for the children's school fees.' Listen to his heart reject the reasoning of his head. See the expression on his face harden. Hearken: the cry of naked hunger is in the wind."

The piece was not signed. Qumman had found it in the folds of the pillowcase Soyaan had used, and, since she was unable to read it, had given it to Loyaan. A page and a half of neat double-spaced script. He stared at it now. He re-read the first two sentences and decided that the deletions had been made by another hand, not Soyaan's, although in all probability Soyaan had written the illegible comment in the margin. Unthinkingly, he passed the paper to Ahmed-Wellie, in whose car he was seated, Ahmed-Wellie who had started the engine despite being told that the procession might not start until half an hour later.

It was past two in the afternoon. The sun hammered dusty rays to the ground. The women's noise had faded to polite whispers of pass-the-shovel, pass-the-pail. The principal sheikh and a student of his of advanced age were talking to Keynaan about the funeral van and wished they knew what had caused the delay. Past doubt, thought Loyaan, this was the height of this régime's inefficiency. Previously, there had been fewer papers of bureaucracy to fill in before hiring a van. One would go and book the van just like that. One wouldn't be required to file the request earlier than it took the Local Government clerk to register it in the main ledger. Besides, many people didn't use such vans at any rate. But whatever could have caused the delay? Half an hour late. The inefficiency of this oligarchy.

"My condolences, *jaalle* Loyaan."

There was a man standing in the same shade as the car. Loyaan could not recall where he had scraped acquaintance with the man who now addressed him as "comrade". From the corner of his eye, he saw that Ahmed-Wellie had folded up the paper to hand it back before switching the engine off.

"Thanks," said Loyaan.

Loyaan suspected there was something the man was dying to say. He did not rush him. Instead, he encouraged him by looking up at him and by being silent. Finally:

"The van will be here in a moment."

A heavy pause.

"Thank you."

Loyaan and Ahmed-Wellie exchanged surreptitious eye-encounters.

"But who are you?" asked Loyaan.

"I am a colleague of your brother's. I work in the Presidency."

A conspiratory wink from Ahmed-Wellie, meaning: "Don't indulge him."

"There," the man said. "There is the Green Van just come."

As the man walked away, Ahmed-Wellie commented:

"A tribal upstart. An oligarch. A man of the ruling clan. I know him. One of Soyaan's bosses. And the only thing the man has ever done was to finish his primary."

40

Silence. The sun battered everything under it with its unrelenting heat. A chorus of *Allaahu-akbar* and *Alxamdulillaah,* and a recitation of mini-prayers were shouted across distances as the wooden casket was carried through the outer door, a casket clad in a colourful silk piece. Sticks, more pails and shovels. Loyaan and Ahmed-Wellie joined the pall-bearers lifting the coffin into the green van. They, too, whispered a word of gratitude to the All-hearer, the Omnipresent. They, too, had their hands clasped behind their backs as they prayed for the soul of Soyaan. God bless the dead. Amen.

And when all and sundry moved in single file in the direction of the cemetery, Loyaan went with and got into Ahmed-Wellie's car. The funeral procession of cars moved so slowly they could see, with precise detail, where the lamp-post had been dented by a military jeep.

"They came one dawn a week ago," Ahmed-Wellie said to Loyaan. "There were three of them. They had masks on. They knocked on my door and threatened to break in if I refused to open it immediately and quietly. They blindfolded me, pushed me into a military jeep and drove off. We hadn't gone half a mile when they turned left, then right, then left, then right. They thought that would confound my sense of direction. They drove in circles, over small humps, fast, cutting ferocious gusts of sand and wind. Distance driven: I would say fifty kilometres. The jeep stopped. We were in a 'village'. I was told to get down and helped to do so. I was led by the hand into the habitat of smelly humans. They removed the cloth with which they had blinded me. I was made to sit in front of a man whose identity was concealed to me: his whole upper part was covered in what felt, when I touched, like a length of hemp. They turned on a brighter light. The man's lower part was naked and he had a bellyband tied round his waist. The only things I can now describe with any sense of accuracy are the size, colour, and texture of the skin of his genitals. But I won't go into that."

Ahmed-Wellie changed gear, he slowed down. The spear-slits of the sun had increasingly become sharper. An ungainly young man in a Green Guards uniform led away a donkey which had been blocking the progress of the procession. The swamp of machinery began to flow as the Green Guard whistled.

"I was confronted with a moral dilemma," Ahmed-Wellie went

41

on. "The man was clearly someone important politically, who would serve the interests of the General's régime alive and in detention. I couldn't tell who he was. I thought he might be the former Prime Minister or one of the former Vice-Presidents of the first cabinet. I had evidence shown me that the man's kidney filters had ceased functioning; that his blood-pressure had risen in the past five hours; that the albumen found in his urine denoted a curious combination of high fever and constant vomiting. Another doctor was there. 'Chronic nephritis,' said the other doctor (his face was covered) whom they had probably used on other occasions, I deduced. 'Haemorrhage in the brain,' came my cue. 'Heart failure,' came his. 'Uraemia,' my turn. 'Comma, signs of epilepsy.' The Security bully wrongly thought we were speaking in code. 'Stop talking,' ordered the officer who still had his identity hidden from me. It had been my intention to uncover the other doctor's identity and I was sure he, too, was trying the same. 'Get on with your work.' 'It may be nephrosis,' I challenged. 'I would therefore like to see whether there are signs of oedema in the face of the patient.' 'Now that you mention it,' he said, 'I see that his ankles are swollen.' And meanwhile I reminded myself that my moral dilemma lay in whether or not I should perform my civic duty which was that of a doctor, but not whether I should prove to myself and to those bullies from the Security that I had principle, that I was a man of dignity, et cetera. I resolved that I had played enough games with this doctor whom they had brought before me. Thus I pronounced the medical verdict: the man suffered from pyelitis, I said. And I asked for the right instruments. I requested the necessary drugs."

By the roadside, huge as history, were displayed numbers of revolutionary billboards cashing in on the General's fabrications of the nation's realities. Loyaan was overawed at the prospect of refusing categorically to pay the price for the same plate as everybody else. And what a price to pay. *One follows the pattern all the way through,* thought he. *The price-tags stick, payment is made with life.* And one was humiliated on top of that. Like the political prisoner of Dr Ahmed-Wellie's story. Why would that prisoner wear a bellyband? Was it primarily to disorient Ahmed-Wellie and the other doctor, send them off the track? Why would an adult tie a bellybound round his waist, especially when he was from the northern region of the country?

42

"They returned two nights ago. Another case, this time a woman. They had tortured her. We were in an attic. I could see the sloping ceiling. But it was the same house as the one to which they had taken me previously. It smelt the same. The walls felt greasy. The woman was young, barely past her mid-twenties. They had given her shock treatment. She had a temperature. In fact, any well-trained nurse could have dealt with that. But she was to appear at the National Security Court as witness the following morning. They wanted everything done in a hurry. They requested that I perform a miracle, dye her bruises the same colour as the rest of her skin, or something. What stupid bullies they are."

The car slowed down. The procession came to a complete halt. The General's motorcade zoomed past. The noise the sirens made was beastly. Loyaan and Ahmed-Wellie exchanged drowsy glances. More people had joined the procession. Hundreds of men had climbed up into the trucks. They believed that by escorting a dead body to its resting place, a Muslim was in a posiiton to earn for himself a favour of the angels. It was also believed that the soul of the dead was given a less strenuous interrogation by the angels the more participants there were. They moved. When they had settled into a constant speed of gear-shifts, Loyaan, lighting a cigarette offered him by Ahmed-Wellie, said:

"You know anything about Koschin?"

"Koschin?"

"Do you know what prison he is being held in?"

"No. Why?"

"He is not feeling well."

"How do you know?"

"Soyaan told me. He wondered if we could do something for him."

"How did he know?"

"Perhaps the report came from the doctor who attended to him. Perhaps the news reached Soyaan through one of those doctors whom they drove out of bed at dawn to treat him for something or other."

"Oh, my God!"

They were at the impasse just before the main gate of the cemetery.

Mounds. Burial mounds. Some numbered, some carrying the date the person was buried, and some undated. The wealthy built a square stone-marker, the wealthy and the powerful spent on a single tomb what could buy for the very poor a zinc shack on the periphery of the city. Mounds. Burial mounds. When a person met violent death at the hands of the Security Service it was common knowledge that his family could not ask even to be shown the body of their beloved. Loyaan told himself as he walked away slightly from Ahmed-Wellie who had started conversing with another man. But why was he thinking about all this? Why had Ahmed-Wellie told him those bizarre stories which would break anyone's heart as would a pick a plot of cultivable earth? Was Ahmed-Wellie trying to plant a seed of suspicion in the fertile soil of unfounded doubts? Would he know of a clue to "M to the power of 2"? What about the I/M and the projects? Would he know more about Soyaan's movements and dealings than Ladan, say? Could he trust him with these secrets? "M to the power of 2"! And those statements about clowns, cowards and (tribal) upstarts. Were they made by Soyaan? Under what stressful conditions had they been written? And who was it that gave the news about Koschin? Perhaps Ladan would know, Ladan who loved Soyaan more dearly than she had loved anyone else in her life. Ahmed-Wellie had come in level with him.

"The water-van hasn't come. I wonder why." He consulted his watch. "It is very late. It should've been here a long while ago."

Those who had accompanied the corpse to the cemetery dispersed in all imaginable directions. The sheikhs were standing to one side, offering softly voiced prayers to God on behalf of the dead. They were indeed preparing to say the ultimate prayer, the "Janaaza". Whereas the other mortals who had dispersed in other directions would call at the tomb of their dead relatives or that of a friend.

"This, for example, is unnumbered. This tomb," commented Ahmed-Wellie.

"Yes. What about it?"

"Persons executed by a firing squad for their political beliefs are buried in unnumbered tombs. No member of their immediate family is allowed to see their dead bodies. I wonder if these are the tombs we are walking past."

He checked the time again. Of course, it shouldn't have upset him nor should it have affected him that the water-van was delayed. However, inexplicably, he felt very nervous. Was it the horror stories

44

that Ahmed-Wellie had narrated to him which had set him on an agitated course?

"See these."

"Where?"

"I've counted these. They've been patterned into a circle. There are eleven tombs. And they are not numbered. I wonder if these are the tombs of the ten sheikhs and the woman the General had executed."

Loyaan looked in the direction of the sheikhs who, together, had bowed and had risen as they performed the Janaaza prayer. Ahmed-Wellie walked ahead, he didn't wait for him. The sun's brightness levelled the sandy dust. What difference did it make whether a tomb was or wasn't unnumbered? Loyaan put this question to Ahmed-Wellie.

"He would feel exposed, the General, if he allowed these tombs to be numbered, for one thing. People would react differently to these burial mounds. People would garland them with flowery secrets. They would call on these tombs as you would on a martyr's."

"Do you think this would happen?"

He stole a quick glance at his wristwatch. More than three-quarters of an hour late. Should he go and seek somebody to telephone the depot concerned? Had that tribal fellow forgotten to give the time, the exact time? Maybe he should have driven the car himself, thought he. If he had this ludicrous delay wouldn't have occurred.

"Absurd, this is absurd!" Loyaan shouted now, incapable of withholding his emotions any longer. "No respect for the dead. None whatsoever."

"Patience. Patience. And look."

"Look what? Look where?"

"Not at your watch. Nor the impotence of the sun either. Just look and you will see that after all this delay, the van is here. And look who we have for a visitor."

A thousand thoughts crossed the heads of those present as they saw a member of the Supreme Revolutionary Council come out of one of the cars. He was the Minister to the Presidency. His presence stirred a quiet commotion; there were lips which moved, there were whispers and low voices which parted with so far unrevealed thoughts. To remark that they all looked frightened or worried and stop at that would be to grossly oversimplify a reaction. Had their fresh memory of the executions made them more nervous?

Whereupon, Loyaan assuming the role of the responsible, parted company with Ahmed-Wellie and also with those whose sense of defiance to naked authority had been dislodged by a moment of suspense. Keynaan followed him. Meanwhile, the others speculated. Somebody said: "What do they think *they* can do to a dead man?" The Minister to the Presidency stood apart from his entourage. The driver of the water-van got into the vehicle again and drove closer to the tomb.

"Yes?" Loyaan was hot with rage.

"I am the Minister to the Presidency. I've come on behalf of the General. I believe you are Loyaan. I believe this *jaalle* is the father. My condolences."

The sheikhs continued the burial rites with more fervour: "O God, help us, help the dead, help the family of the dead, bless us, bless the family of the dead, bless and protect the weak against the powerful."

Loyaan stared fixedly at the Minister who, a year or so ago, was a captain in the navy or something. Keynaan then took leave of the Minister and Loyaan. And a single gesture of the Minister's sent asunder the ten-strong entourage; some joined their voices to those chanting small prayers, and some waited on the fringe of those whose bent backs protruded as they shovelled earth on to the grave. *"The wave of the hand of the powerful, a single, simple burning look — everything is done,"* Loyaan reminded himself. This was from a letter Soyaan had sent him, with reference to whether or not the General's wave-of-hand would "open-sesame" Koschin's prison-gates.

"What did he die of?" asked the Minister.

"What?"

"Soyaan, what did he die of?"

Just this very minute, since it was the second time anyone had seriously put this query to him, Loyaan admitted to himself that Soyaan's death actually struck him as an activity peculiarly perverse. But he wouldn't openly admit a failure on his part to deal squarely with that question. He remembered the answer he had given to Ahmed-Wellie.

"Complications."

"Complications?"

46

"Yes. He died of blood complications."

"Blood complications?"

"Yes. Complications."

The Minister remained silent for a time. He would not immediately delve into the details surrounding Soyaan's death. Blood complications? Why had he said that? Blood complications, what kind? The Minister had another thing to ask:

"What were his last words?"

This caught Loyaan unprepared. He mumbled something to himself, he looked away and in the distance saw Ladan and his mother huddled together. He wouldn't let them down. He would face up to the Minister or whatever. Soyaan: a loved brother.

"What were his last words, do you remember?"

Loyaan was honest: "He called my name three times. He hiccupped and hiccupped and hiccupped. Then he started calling my name repeatedly, agitatedly. Those were his last words."

The Minister grinned. Then: "We were given a different version. We prefer that."

"A different version?"

"Before he called your name or the name of a certain woman. . . ."

Loyaan hurriedly interrupted: "What woman?"

A brief pause. Was it Beydan the Minister had heard about?

"Before he called your name or the name of that woman, did Soyaan — God bless his soul — not stumble on the words 'LABOUR IS HONOUR', just before he breathed his last? Did he not?"

Loyaan's hand, as though by its own will, searched for and found in the folds of his pocket the piece about clowns and cowards. His eyes searched for and found Ahmed-Wellie. "Labour is honour?" Why would Soyaan say that? Or did he?

"Did your brother Soyaan not stumble on those words?"

Loyaan would concede him a point. "He may have said that."

Sand ripples descended upon the participants from the sky. The cactus pricked Loyaan's hand as he administered a spadeful of sand to the heap above the tomb. More spades attacked the mound from the front, the flanks and every corner. The topmost and the lowest layers of the soil joined and became one with the dirt and the dust which stirred.

"That's enough," came the instructions from the most senior sheikh. "That's enough."

Prayers and prayers and prayers. Beggars asked for alms. The participants improvised generosities: hands blindly went into and out of pockets and offered the beggars whatever could be found. Twenty or so persons had suddenly appeared as beggars. Loyaan's noble hand extended forward to the beggar nearest him. The receiver stretched toward him a left hand. A weird specimen of a beggar, thought Loyaan as he took, with a grain of sand, the insolence of the left hand which the beggar had brought out to receive charity. The man didn't have the pose of a beggar. When all movement had ceased, when Loyaan's suspended right hand weighed upon the air and the beggar's left hand held what had remained of it, there crossed a flash of understanding across the man's face: he displayed the stump of his amputated right arm. Loyaan dropped his guard and smiled. His hand gave what his head approved of.

"I have only one arm," said the man.

Serious to the point of wanting to touch the amputated arm: "I am sorry, very sorry."

Prayers and prayers and prayers.

"I am sorry, but before we part . . . ," started the Minister.

"Yes?"

They were standing apart from the crowd, they had walked slightly away, with the Minister's finger resting on Loyaan's back. The Minister, for a while silent, studied Loyaan's face. It seemed he had something on his mind.

"Yes?"

He offered Loyaan a cigar. He put one in his own mouth. Loyaan shook his head. The Minister didn't replace the cigar, but held it in the air. He put the one which Loyaan had refused back into the packet, while muttering a declamatory something (Loyaan thought it sounded Cuban), and said:

"Incidentally, down at the Presidency we wondered — er . . . I am sorry, very sorry. I hope you don't mind my taking liberties — but down at the Presidency we wondered if Soyaan showed you or talked to you about a Memorandum he had been working on."

"A Memorandum?"

Keynaan was circling them, wanting to know what the Minister

48

was saying to Loyaan. He would come closer every now and then but didn't dare join them. Qumman and Ladan, too, lingered not very far from them. Whereas most of the participants had begun to move away from the tomb, some had picked up the shovels, others the pails. Some of the vehicles began to rev in the suspense of this long wait. Ahmed-Wellie went and stood by the car.

"A Memorandum, yes."

"What on?"

"Did he or did he not?"

"But what on? What was it on? Had he written it himself? Had he done it for the Presidency? Was it officially part of something he had been working on?"

The entourage of the Minister to the Presidency had closed in on them. But the men kept their distance, awaiting a wave of hand, a signal. The Minister brooded in silence. Then he said:

"Never mind what on. But have you seen a Memorandum?"

"A Memorandum entitled 'Labour is Honour'?"

This enraged the Minister. Anger surprises the powerful, thought Loyaan as he watched the Minister light his Cuban cigar, inhale the smoke and wait for the sedative effect of calm to reproduce itself on his expression. In between puffs:

"Due to a momentary lapse of memory . . ." he started, but stopped.

"Yes?"

He had changed his mind. "Never you mind about all that."

There was silence.

"But you will come and see me, won't you? We have a number of things to talk about. Please, come and see me. You needn't even phone in advance. All right?"

There was silence again.

"Soyaan: the martyr of our revolution. Yes. Come and see me. We shall speak about what we can do for him. And for you. And for the family. Soyaan served his country faithfully. My condolences again."

He went off. His entourage rushed in front of him, behind him and some fell into a trot as he walked towards his car. There was a great deal of commotion as the others got into the other vehicle to leave.

Chapter Three

Like an infant in the embrace of a garbage-bin, an infant barely a week old; abandoned; with the light of life seemingly spent like the cross-road hour of night and day; not a whimper; not a cry. A child of dawn, conceived, given birth to and abandoned at the crack of it. With its birth, it filled the cupped hands of dawn with a human responsibility. Will the sun receive it, will it find it a home?

Ladan asked: "Does it work, do you think?"

He did not answer.

"Give it back. Give it here," she said.

Before he handed it over to her, he looked at it again. All three hands were motionless, dead. There was no damage to the disc which was spotless, clean. He gave it to her.

She shook it a little too violently. Then announced: "It works, yes, it does work." She passed it back to him.

"Yes, it does."

The three hands had rolled into motion like a train into a tunnel with no exit. Like a child amazed, like a child excited, Loyaan watched the hands move, stared at them as they covered the same predictable circular course, with their nodding and ticking synchronised. He put it closer to his left ear. He could hear the heart of time beat.

"Keep it," she said.

He looked at her. She twisted her pained expression until the wrinkled folds on her forehead held firm. In the dim light, he hardly saw anything but the shadow of fear in her fixed stare.

"Don't you want to keep it?"

"What if I said I would prefer not to?"

"His used garments have gone to the poor in the neighbourhood."

"Everything that was his?"

"No, no."

"What?"

50

"We kept some. There are shirts and trousers which are new. There are those to which he was very attached. Aside from the watch, there is a tape-recorder and a record-player. We are going to keep all the expensive items."

Silence. The wind pushed the door half-open. Dusk's orchestrated shades of light and tropical darkness; the courtyard's reeling roar; the air in the room dry as the remains of locust-birds. She stood up. Her bones fell into place but creaked like half-tightened hinges. She went and closed the door. She returned. This was bad: a fortnight without any sports activities, she was thinking now. This must cease. She should call Sagal. *Mens sana in corpore sano!* But he said:

"Sit down. I want to ask you something."

Silence was her only prerogative. She waited.

"Was Soyaan . . . I mean did he, er, very often speak to you about his personal problems, his politics? Was he fond of talking to you about issues close to his heart?"

"Such as?"

His head was now congested with worry. Could he tell her of his discoveries, trust her with these secret findings? Would it upset her greatly if she knew that he deliberately withheld information from her? Endless questions, unprovidable answers.

"Do you think I am too young to be trusted with family secrets?" she challenged him.

She received for answer stammers of shock and hesitancy.

"Then ask and we shall see."

A long pause. Where would he start? Her upward glance made him reword his unarticulated thought. M to the power of 2? I/M and the projects underway? That piece on clowns, cowards and upstarts? She came to his aid.

"Soyaan hardly intimated a secret to anyone until after he had considered the consequences," she said. "I know, for example, of a long paper he wrote with the intention of having it published abroad. He hinted at the idea to me. I also know that he had a rich collection of unpublishable underground material. He once asked me to copy out titles."

"What underground material?"

"Some poems, some taped plays, that sort of thing."

"But you know of no Memorandums?"

"Memorandums?"

51

Something greater than himself appeared to have possessed him. Out of the ruins of an intimated fear two eyes stared startled, two eyes which burned brighter with the taper of anxiety — now dark, now vigorous and lively. He did not answer to the solicitations of his sister.

Suddenly, the room was very bright. Ladan had apparently switched on the electric light. The brown in his eyes had turned carcass-white.

"Yes, there is a Memorandum," she said.

"Do you know where it is?"

"I know of it because he told me he was working on a Memorandum for one of the Vice-Presidents. I suspect it was part of a project he had been assigned. What's all this?"

He wouldn't tell her about the dialogue he had had that afternoon with the Minister to the Presidency. Nor would he now show her the piece on clowns, cowards and upstarts. About Koschin — what about Koschin? Ought she not to know? There were also Ahmed-Wellie's horror stories about the hard-core among political prisoners.

"We found something," she said, "while emptying the pockets of the trousers I distributed among the poor."

"What?"

She put her hand into her pocket. She slowly withdrew a piece of paper in disastrous shape. With care, she unfolded it, making sure it didn't tear. She gave it to him.

"Thanks."

"There must be more of these somewhere," she said.

He didn't hear this comment. The kernels of his eyes grew dimmer as their shell contracted. Unbelievable. He read it to himself — soft, secretive, but unhearing.

"*Any person who spreads or takes out of the Somali Democratic Republic printed, reading, spoken or broadcast matter, or persons in the SDR who display, distribute or disseminate information aimed at damaging the sovereignty of the revolution of the Somali nation will be liable to death.*"

"Where did you find it?"

"Mother did."

"Where?"

"In one of his pockets."

Loyaan would have loved to let himself go, to explain to her what he thought had happened. Too many things had taken place in such a short time, yes, but nothing had escaped him — he was sure of that. Discomforted, he waited for her comment in silence. And indeed it came:

"There is another, this time in his own handwriting."

He was livid with himself for not having considered all this.

"Give it here."

If he had been with Soyaan, he might have known. He might have. He contorted his face unfolding the crumpled piece of aged paper, he acted as though he were unknotting some intricate lace-work. His mouth twisted, attentive, lips moved to formulate un-uttered ideas. . . .

"Any person who uses religion for the purpose of breaking up the unity of the Somali people or weakening or damaging the authority of the Somali state shall be punishable by death. (Article 12)."

Up went Loyaan's eyes and he saw tear drops coursing down Ladan's stained cheeks. He remembered a conversation he had had with Soyaan when he visited him in Baidoa. He had been in search of peace of mind in order to collect his wits about him. It was in fact the same day on which the ten sheikhs had been executed. "They wouldn't let the immediate family go anywhere near the dead bodies. I was there when they fired. I watched the bodies collapse like mined buildings. And the sky thundered a warning. But would he hear, would the General listen to anyone but his Russian advisers? The Grand Warder. The Grand Jailer of Somalia's Grand Prison." He had spoken with rage. He had employed all the talents at his disposal to describe the chaos. He spoke and spoke. But he had been with his twin brother. And at any rate, people talked and talked. That was all they could do. Had Soyaan got more involved in the past few weeks? Why had he had these two articles copied? Had he been writing anything? Did these have anything to do with the project he had been assigned to do for one of the Vice-Presidents?

Loyaan withheld from his sister all he had no need of telling her. He peered at her from under his withdrawn look. She flung herself into a fully-fledged state of no return. She burst into tears. He held her in his embrace.

"One in two: Loyaan and Soyaan. My brothers in twins."

Although that didn't make any sense to him, he decided he wouldn't ask for an explanation. She clung to him like a creeper to a wall. He rocked her to silence as one would a child. All was quiet.

The mere fact of their being twins supported the notion that there was greater room for comparison, thought he to himself. Twins suggest comparison much more easily, much more readily. The idea was inherent in their twinship. "In one, we look for the other. In the other, we assume, if we look hard, we shall find *the other*. Soyaan in Loyaan, now that the latter has died? Don't we look for a parent in a child? Don't we look for similarity in brothers, in sisters, in parents and children?"

Qumman, for one thing, saw them until late in their teens precisely as she had received them; she saw them exactly as she had carried them in her wounded womb: she conceived of them as she had received them, and thus had no choice but to think of them as one person. And she treated them as such. She would refer to them as if they were one and the same person. She would speak of them as one would talk about one's hands and fingers in the plural, the head and the nose in the singular. When one son was unwell and the other staggered away sick with the fatigue of loneliness, Qumman would name who it was that had been taken ill: just as one would specify which eye was sore and which wasn't, just as one would point at a tooth which needed to be extracted. She never taxed her wits with ancient and modern literatures which seemed to revolve around twins. She would content herself with this: Soyaan and Loyaan were a manifestation of God's love. And that, as far as she was concerned, was sufficient.

A man of a certain character such as Keynaan had been ("The Grand Patriarch rules, with the iron hand of male-dominated tradition, over his covey of children and wives": Soyaan to Loyaan) didn't have the material possibility of knowing how it felt to carry within oneself an egg which broke in two and gave birth to twins. From the initial instant of conception until the day of delivery when they installed themselves, Keynaan, as was his wont, did not pose to himself any of the cumbersome questions relating to the concept. He was incapable of giving credit to their one-ness even in foetus-formation.

As for Ladan: "Soyaan is the braille of my unguided vision; and Loyaan is the one who enables me to sow my noons and days with nightly stars." She would add that each twin complemented the other who supplemented him. She would then become long-winded in her loving epithets and mannerisms, would go on and on talking in mixed

54

metaphors and what have you. In conclusion, she would take a stand much more akin to that of her mother's.

Peculiar turns of phrase, say. Or gesticulations of a given nature. Nobody outside the immediate family circle could tell one from the other. For a long time no one saw the dissimilarities in these turns of phrase or gestures which were particular to one rather than the other. On occasions, they would search out the twin's hand: Loyaan's had a missing finger and that identified him easily. This confusion they created in people continued to trouble them until each became secure in his own identity. Then they appeared to enjoy the idea of pulling others by the leg: they exchanged clothes; they exchanged roles and views of life; they dated the same woman once; at one point, they even declared they had fallen in love with the same woman. Which was not true. It was for sheer fun.

At the age of twenty-one, the dictates of life began to single out distinct differences in their personalities, in their tastes and in their professions. At twenty-six, Soyaan qualified as an economist. Whereas Loyaan, a year and a half later, took a degree in dentistry.

Had their paths permanently parted? Had their similarities ended there? Could one search for Soyaan in Loyaan? Might one find the dead in the living? How acutely had the chisel of politics shaped differences in outlook? Loyaan: a dentist. Soyaan: an economist. "You count to thirty-two the teeth in my mouth, and I a million heads of cattle. . . ." *No, Soyaan, no. Not heads of cattle. Human heads. The yearly seasons of harvested heads which you present to the General. Rhetoric. Economics. Dentistry, Let us see now. . . .*

"I am a dentist, Mother. Not a general physician."

Her eyes turned a dubious grey. "Who ever heard of that?" she said. "The love of God. Five to six years in a foreign land. You return. You say you are not a doctor, you are a dentist. You are not a doctor, you cannot write out a chit for your ailing sister. I can tell you, my son, that I've never known anyone go to a doctor for curing teeth. What I ask is: why have I been told a lie?"

Loyaan had wrestled with all sorts of ideas.

"I was fooled. For six years, all anybody told me was that you would qualify as a doctor. And I waited for your return. A doctor for a son. I boasted: finally a doctor for a son. Hurrah. Not that I take any pills; these are poison. But I thought you would earn enough

55

money to give us independence so that we wouldn't need Keynaan any more. I thought we would somehow be able to forgo our means of financial independence. A tooth-doctor. What do you think will make people come to you?"

He didn't mean to be sarcastic. But he was.

"With this change in their diet, people will start having problems with their teeth. And if that doesn't happen we shall sweeten their milk-teeth with chocolate nourishments. The underfed have solid teeth erected in patient mouths. I am afraid we shall have to change their style of eating."

Silence. An anagram of received images which, in her head, she immediately replaced with the acquired one. Her inquiry into the reasons why they had told her a lie led her nowhere. And before her eyes lay her sick Ladan. With them was Loyaan. Ladan had lain in a stubble of pain and groaning. Qumman had stuffed things in her mouth to reduce the volume of her cry. What good would any doctor do anyway? It was the monthly pain of a circumcised woman's sufferance.

Mother had uttered a prophecy: "This country needs no tooth-doctors."

In the choir of the nation's sad song, Loyaan's loud lament; a million waves broke on the sandy shores of the nation's discontent, but Loyaan's dream wouldn't be washed clean. His surgery remained open from nine in the morning till ten in the evening. But no one came. No client holding a set of decayed teeth; no caller massaging a swollen jaw; no customer carrying in a separate box a set of golden pieces or fillings. His mother, triumphant, repeated a truism: "Africa's teeth are healthy; it is Africa's viscera that crawl with the fleas of insanitation. For local diseases there are no cures but local herbs. We have healthy teeth. See mine." She was fifty-five. "I never have the need to call on a dentist. Isn't that why there are only four dentists in Mogadiscio? Only four on the rolls. One at each of the only two hospitals in the city; the two others between them split the cosmopolitan Somali and the alien residents. You said that yourself," she argued. She had a suggestion. Loyaan should, like Soyaan before him, add his name to the end of the long list of regimented men and women. He should do his military service. He should, like every humiliated civil servant, sing the praise-songs of the General in return for a position, yes, a guaranteed monthly stipend. Every government employee underwent a military training whose duration depended on his or her performance. Every potential fresh recruit had to do a minimum of six months. The General had regimented the nation's manpower. *Attention. Stand at ease. Attention. Let us chant the chorus of his names. Let us.*

Loyaan filed an application for a job with the Ministry of Health. Not long after he had undergone the training (he clashed on several occasions with upstarts who were on the same course as he; twice he was booked as "anti-revolutionary reactionary" by the men from the Security: he now remembered). Then he was appointed as Regional Health Officer to the plague-stricken region of Baidoa.

It was just before nightfall when, restless, he came out.

The night had descended upon, but dwelled suspended in, the unsettled dust of dusk. It had come down and stayed light as a feather and breezy. Loyaan took short and thoughtful strides. The winged wind helped him fly off elsewhere, helped him migrate to a land of his past, the territory of his infancy. A fly-past of evening birds, and. . . .

Merca. The age of dreaming and childhood. The twins were nine. The muezzin had woken the dawn and Keynaan had got up to say his prayers. The twins awoke, too. They got up not to tell their beads but to tell each other about the dream each had seen and what had happened in them. Safe in the conventions of rules they had set themselves, every morning would start with the reliving of the previous night. Dreams and dreams. In Soyaan's, the father figure dominated. In Loyaan's: objects such as razor-blades and knives. With monotonous consistency, Keynaan would die in Soyaan's dream; he would meet his death at the armed hand of Loyaan. Also, with more or less the same regularity, Loyaan's weapons would come in handy to ward off all those wicked persons who had come to invade the twins' private universe.

Merca. The age of challenge and rivalry. And one day, in the flocculency of the sea, precisely at the place where they usually met to share these fanciful inventions of sleepy dreams, Soyaan suspected that Loyaan had cheated. Loyaan had erroneously repeated, verbatim, a dream of Soyaan's already two days old. Soyaan had reminded him of this fact. Loyaan, in defiance, rose to the challenge. They fought. They wrestled. They chased each other into and out of what they referred

57

to as "the wreck of history" (this consisted of an army tank and accessories abandoned by the Italians during the Second World War). They each had an iron rod salvaged from the wreck and they fenced. Loyaan dropped his. He picked up a sword-shaped metallic pedal as he sprang to his feet. A cut. Blood. Tetanus. No injections. Months later: minus a thumb.

Merca. Years later. The age of logic. And each of the two had decided what he would do, what profession he was suited to. Soyaan had abandoned the idea of becoming a naval engineer; Loyaan was no longer interested in becoming a pilot. No; he would qualify as a doctor. He decided on this because of his mother Qumman's near-fatal fourth confinement. He would qualify, and help his mother through future difficult births. *For a naval engineer, the frontiers of the sea are the limit, imagination runs wild, boundaryless; and you a nomad. I will be beside Mother, I shall mend the broken, I shall attend to the sick, the needy : I shall become a doctor.*

Mogadiscio. Years and years later. Soyaan had won a scholarship to Italy to study economics at the University of Rome. Loyaan had won his but would go to the University of Bologna to study dentistry.

"No one needs eight fingers and two thumbs."

Having said this, he laid out in full view his hands, furnished with eight fingers and a thumb. And he added: "That is what I call extravaganza."

Soyaan silently watched the sun's powerful brightness play miraculous mosaics on the waves of the sea. The sand where they were walking had turned powdery white from the constant tramping of feet.

"You would've become a pilot had you not lost a thumb. I remember the day when we had that fight. You used to say you wanted to become a pilot, and hence a hero."

"Not a pilot."

"What?"

"A surgeon. Remember my knives and razor-blades."

"No, no. A pilot and a hero."

"Wrong, wrong, wrong, absolutely wrong."

"Allow me to correct you—"

"I remember very well—"

"No, you don't."

"Yes, I do."
"Let me—"
"Listen! "

Quiet noises of the night: a child coughed; another called to its mother's skill. The night stood upright against the sky, a pillar of darkness. The murmur of the tropics meandered through the maze of the hour's mysteries. Loyaan's thoughts walked the untrod landscape of the unknowable. The weight of Soyaan's watch in his pocket, the watch which Ladan had given him, slowed him down; whereas his un-frisked brain-pockets felt heavier with all these untested ideas. In his trouser-pocket, there were two loose sheets of paper — one clearly in Soyaan's handwriting, the other typed. He would return home to mother and sister. He hoped the mourners would have left by the time he got there. He turned a corner. He followed another. A third to the left. A fourth to the right. In less than fifty seconds, he would be home. Quiet. Peace of mind. He was in dire need of a lavatory. Home in forty seconds. Or less.

"Loyaan! "

Leaning against a lamp-post and seated, there was the figure of a woman wrapped in tawdries. Loyaan approached. It was Beydan in her best of tastelessness, Beydan, Keynaan's other wife. He was at a loss for words, nor did he know what to do. Had she been thrown out of the house by his mother? Had something as disastrous as that hap-pened?

"What are you doing here?" *Quick, quick. What shall I do if Mother has shown her out? Quick, come out with a decision,* the voice inside him challenged.

Her silence wove a canvas of protectiveness. She maintained her calm. She was over eight months gone, might deliver any day now. Did she mean to impress anybody with this senseless tawdry in which she dressed her pregnancy? She motioned to him to come nearer so he could hear her.

"I had a frightful idea. That was all."

She was barely thirty. Keynaan was her second husband, this pregnancy her third, the other two children, girls, having gone with their father, her first husband. She wrapped herself in a shawl of showiness for this occasion because Qumman considered her a woman of inferior tribal breed. Words shaped on the corner of her lips, but

59

her mouth wouldn't formulate them into any sort of articulacy. He took her hand.

"Has my mother been rude?" he asked.

"No, no, no. No."

"Has anybody?"

"No."

"Why are you here then? Why haven't you stayed with the others?"

"I haven't been in. Not yet. I had a frightful idea, as I said."

"What frightful idea?"

"I thought your mother would throw me out if I went in."

Astride the tomb of suspicions, Loyaan said to himself, "This poor thing probably thought she would have a miscarriage if she were maltreated by Mother." The stars, when he looked up, were small as lemon-seeds strewn on the infertile soil of the sky. Hardly a wink. Barely a suggestion of brightness. He helped Beydan rise from the bundle of wastage to which circumstance had reduced her.

"Come on in and rest your bones."

He had clean forgotten he needed the use of a toilet. But when he remembered he held his thighs together. She supported herself on him. A leg at a time. Very, very slowly. Together they walked homewards.

"My condolences," she said.

Her arms were skeletal, her stomach preceded her, and her weak legs trembled. He could feel these. The blazing light which originated from the house raked up memories in both. But neither spoke a word. Poor thing! She had come to offer condolences. She feared she would be met with barefaced rudeness. Show her out. *Out of here, you witch. What would he do? Up on your feet. The threshold of hostility, mind the step. Prepare for the worst. Don't let life surprise you.* Their entry created a silence in the patio where some of the women had assembled. The patternless loom of shades, after a while, answered a known design: all those present, save Ladan and Qumman, turned their eyes away. And from that rubble rose Ladan. She came over and took Beydan's other arm. *Of such gestures are understanding sisters made,* thought he.

"Where do we take her?"

"Your room."

60

The deposits of a dusty smile on Beydan's face rose and fell as she greeted Ladan.

"I'll rest my tired bones and then go," she promised.

Ladan and Beydan and Loyaan limped past.

"My condolences," said Beydan loud enough for all to hear. "I've come to say only that. I've come with the best intentions. I can harm nobody with that. I mean no harm."

Her statement incited Qumman's burning look.

"I'll rest my tired bones and then go," she repeated.

A little later, it transpired that Keynaan was in the other room talking to the men. An acceptable compromise was reached: Loyaan would pay for their taxi to the bus station and their fare for their onward journey to Afgoi where they lived.

"I don't want to hear one single breath of contempt from you, Mother."

"Have it your way."

"Not another contemptuous breath. Please."

Ladan offered to act as the go-between.

However, just as Beydan was being helped into the taxi, Loyaan remembered he had fogotten to put to her an important question. He rushed out. He managed to get to her before the taxi moved.

"But tell me before you leave, please."

"Yes?"

He worked the words in his head. "When he came to your place and you gave him the meal, was he alone?"

"No."

"Who was with him?"

"A man."

"Had you seen the man before? Could you describe the man?"

"Yes, I had seen the man before."

"Was he ... er ... did Soyaan behave strangely — I mean. ..."

Ladan, Keynaan, Beydan and the driver all looked at Loyaan with their breath suspended. Their gaze converged upon him. He sensed the weight of their stare and that made him stammer an apology. He fell silent. Like a horse-breeder sending off his beloved stallion, Loyaan slapped the taxi on the bonnet, meaning: you can now go. At first, the driver wouldn't even start. Keynaan told him to do so.

Hoofbound, he followed Ladan who led the way. Inside his head,

61

a honeycomb of stirred agitation. Like a glass tipped downwards with a tsetse fly struggling to bite its way airwards, sense and logic strangled the unexpressed emotions with which his innards might have burst. Speaking to himself:

"Among them, an insignificant letter in an alphabet of mysteries."

"What is that you said?" asked Ladan.

He cut her short. He went straight to his room, saying: "See you tomorrow."

Wide-eyed with insomnia, he stood behind the window. A width of stars, a breadth of darkness, and no moon: the night. Could he close the doors of night, and therefore his eyes and sleep? He took several possible roads but came upon a cul-de-sac as before. Questions and questions. Whys and no wherefores. What had Soyaan eaten at Beydan's to have created such a disorder in his system, to have upset his constitution so? Would a post-mortem have answered all these questions? Why did the Minister at the Presidency make up the story about Soyaan's last words? Why "Labour is Honour"? Did someone else write the Memorandum with him? What role did the man Beydan had seen play in all this? Why did Ahmed-Wellie choose to tell him those stories? Why?

Loyaan then went to bed and lay on his back waiting for dawn to break.

Chapter Four

Like two cats in a brawl over a dead rat's meat — the evening silent except for their cries or an occasional braying of a donkey on heat. The cats wrestle. One of them falls. The claws of the other bite into the whiteness of the fallen rival's belly. There is blood, the cat's blood and the rat's. The cat licks its whiskers of triumph. It walks away majestically, leaving behind it a dead rat and a fallen rival.

"Wake up, wake up."

"What?"

"Let me tell you the latest, Loyaan. Wake up! "

He turned, and turning he groaned: "What is all this?"

In a tremulous tone, charged with emotion:

"The morning news, the morning news, the morning news! "

He sat up. As he rubbed his sleepy eyes, he thought: *Another army coup. Heavens God, no. Please. There is no General but this. Heavens, no. Please. No more military coups.*

"The morning news," she repeated.

"Yes, yes. Contain yourself now. What about it?"

But she wouldn't speak. As his concentrated look zoomed in on her, he noticed that she averted her eyes. What was wrong? His sheet had fallen off. He was naked.

"Sorry." He covered his indecency. He was fully awake. His jaws broke up with a yawn. He was a hairy man. The hair in his armpits had grown thicker with the humus of sweat.

"The news this morning opened with a speech given by the Minister to the Presidency. A minute of silence or a gesture of this nature. A few words of eulogy about Soyaan the Revolutionary."

The virtue of the unrecognised genius: he thought he could tell Ladan all the other things the Minister had said. He could perhaps quote word for word. Soyaan's last words were "Labour is Honour", et cetera, et cetera. "The Minister to the Presidency, on behalf of the General himself, wishes to present to the family of the deceased, the

friends of the deceased and to the nation a word of condolence."
But wait.

"That was the eight o'clock news."

He got up, having properly wrapped himself with the bedspread.
"Yes?"

"The ten o'clock news had the General's statement of con-
dolence. It was read by the Minister to the Presidency. It was brief
and to the point. This was a quarter of an hour ago."

"You could've woken me up."

"That is not all."

In his anxiety, he lost control of himself and of the situation.
For he said with pronounced venom: "And at eleven, the General
spoke in person and said this nation would erect a statue in honour
of the Son of the Revolution? Exactly at eleven. Isn't that so?"

"It is not half past ten yet."

He had picked up a pair of underpants and a T-shirt from a chair
just below the window in front of which he now stood motionless,
having seen a reflection of himself in its glass.

"I said that wasn't all," she went on.

He turned to face her squarely. "Well? Tell me, then." Too many
things happening too early in the morning. *I am not sure if I can cope.
I am not certain if my legs will hold, if the vertebra of my humour
won't break under the weight of life's tragic pressures, I am not
sure. . . .* But she was speaking:

"There is a woman just come."

"A woman?"

"A woman and a child she has brought along."

He missed the point. "Alms is all she wants: a mother with a
child."

Ladan shook her head. "This young woman has come, I suspect,
for a major remittance."

"A major remittance?"

"She doesn't to me look nor behave like a beggar."

Too many things happening at too quick a pace for this time of
the morning. A dawn laden with the burden of the days and the nights
which preceded it. A morning flooded with the muddy rivers of future
seasons. He stumbled into the pair of underpants. He flailed his arms
clumsily as he got into the T-shirt. Then his trousers.

"Describe."

"What?"

"Describe this woman to me."

"She is showily dressed and so is the child. She — why don't you come and see for yourself. She is in the other room speaking to Mother. The pretty child is with her."

For a moment, he hung in mid-movement as he stretched his hand to pick up a packet of cigarettes. Eventually he grasped the packet, but saw that it was empty: a pity!

"Did the woman say what she wants?"

"No."

He pressed his forehead. "Did she say who she is?"

"No."

He had a splitting headache, he was sure of that. "Is there anything I ought to know before I meet her?"

"No."

His tongue tasted unbrushed-sour. "Did she say what her name is?"

"No."

"No?"

"No."

"You're not any help, are you?"

"No."

They were silent for a second or so to recover from the shock of the frivolous. His tongue again: this time it felt sore. He held it against his palate: goose-pimples.

"She didn't say anything to you, then?"

"She said she would speak only to you."

Curtain up. Stage centre. Spotlight.

"Tell her I'm coming."

"My name is Loyaan."

"I know."

Was it the shock of recognition which traced the outline of a smile as he entered? He regarded the woman cautiously. An estuary of queries drowned whatever impressions she might have made on him. She didn't budge. A child, a few months old, was lying straight on her thighs and outstretched knees. She rocked the child gently, rhythmically, but looked up at Loyaan as he moved nearer to inspect, to see her from as close up as he could. He offered the child a casual

65

look. He walked away and reached the furthest wall at whose corner were hidden Soyaan's dirty shirts and trousers which would eventually be washed and distributed among the poor.

"Is there something we can do for you?" he asked.

Had he ever seen her before? Certainly he had never known her name. He may have encountered her at one of those populous parties one went to in Mogadiscio every now and then. They may have shared the same taxi. For she had the most familiar of faces. She was light-skinned — perhaps of Italo-Somali extraction. Very pretty. Small nose. Nearly as tall as he. She gave the impression of being a well-mannered person. Her gestures were those of an educated woman, a woman of class. (This description would have made Soyaan laugh. His politics of interpretation would have refused to accept it.) He liked her composedness. He envied her her calm. One day he might tell her so — if he ever had the chance to meet her again.

Her brown eyes sized him up. She remembered what she wished she had forgotten. Why was she here? Whatever had brought her here to this house? He would want to know.

"A pretty child. Very," was his comment.

Nothing from her.

"A boy or a girl?"

"A boy."

"What name?"

"Marco."

He still couldn't place her. He smelt his own sweat. And he tasted the mint flavour of the toothpaste he had used; he recalled that he hadn't rinsed his mouth out properly. But there were more urgent things awaiting his attention. There was the Minister to the Presidency on whom he must call to find out more about why the government was making all this fuss about Soyaan's revolutionary status now that he was dead. There was the challenge from his mother and his sister, a challenge to his so far unstated position vis-à-vis the General's régime. And there was this woman and her child. Soyaan . . . oh, no! He was going to be rude. He was going to ask her a straight question.

"Marco *who*, did you say?"

She rose to her feet. Marco woke and moved in her tight embrace. And she and paraphernalia paced up and down. She rallied all her forces to stay calm and unperturbed. The child shrieked, burst into a sudden cry of (was it?) pain. His legs kicked about as though he was intending to break loose.

Qumman and Ladan, who until that instant had sat quietly, began to stir. From mother to sister, from sister to the woman. Qumman couldn't hold it in any longer:

"Do you think he might want to make water?"

The woman was sharp and discourteous. "I know what he wants. After all, I am his mother," she said.

The air became tense. Loyaan's mouth tasted bitter again. Had he bitten his tongue? He had a better suggestion.

"Would you like a cup of tea?" he said to the woman. "I am going to have one myself."

Silence at first.

After a while: "Yes, please."

He let a few seconds pass. Then: "Would Marco like to join us, do you think?"

As if responding, Marco made a wriggling motion and shrieked no more.

"Milk for him."

Qumman stood up and announced: "I'll go and get the milk."

Ladan, however, improved on this offer, or so she thought. Waiting until her mother had disappeared through the door, she said then to the woman:

"While you and Loyaan talk, how about it if I take him and feed him?"

Another curt response: "He doesn't accept strangers."

This was received with an unwelcome quietness. No one spoke for a while. Loyaan had better find something for Ladan to do since he wished to speak to the woman alone.

"Is there nothing else you would like?"

She reflected. She said: "Cigarettes, please."

Ladan went to get some.

"Did you know him well?" Loyan said. A shot in the dark.

She didn't ask whom he meant. "Yes."

Then her hand fiddled with the fastening of her brassière. Did she want to feed the child? Her chest flattened as she loosened the hooks. She undid the front, and out came long breasts which she stuffed, one at a time, like a pair of toy teats, into the savage toothlessness of hunger, the cave that was Marco's mouth. One day her son would outgrow her, thought Loyaan, when the incisors of youth were sharp enough to cut the umbilical cord. . . . But he must not get carried away, he must not lose sight of what was at hand. So:

"How well did you know him?"

"I knew him as a man."

Her expression hardened. Had Marco bitten her? Wait.

After a pause: "I knew him as a brother."

"Ouch! I can appreciate the difference. Marco!"

It only now occurred to Loyaan that they both assumed they knew whom they were discussing, but neither had yet mentioned Soyaan by name. She hadn't offered her condolences, hadn't showered benedictions of the Merciful on Soyaan's soul (perhaps she was Catholic — in all probability, she wasn't Muslim). Maybe she had meant to tell him that Marco was. . . . The little man had fallen asleep.

Loyaan indicated to her that she could transfer the child to the bed opposite.

"What if he makes water on this bed?"

"What if he does?"

"If the bed is your mother's . . . urine fouls; urine, for a Muslim, is impure. She won't be able to say her prayers unless she washes and washes. What if he makes water in her bed?"

"Let him."

Gentle, graceful, she got up and laid the child on the bed. She placed a pillow on the outer edge, just in case he were to roll over. She stood up. Light. And yet as graceful as when she had had to adjust to the weight of the sleeping child. Loyaan was definitely impressed by her gentleness, by her grace. She had earned his unreserved admiration. He was prepared to allow her immediately into his private world. But she probably already knew more about him than he credited her with. Perhaps Soyaan had told her all that she needed to know. Gentle. Graceful. Well-mannered. And considerate. He was pleased that he could now characterise her. But what name, what name could he give her? He was enjoying the pace of the dialogue. Yes. *Seek wherein she hides. Find out. Uncover.* That was an essential rule of the game. She did up her brassière.

"You haven't told me your name."

"As if it matters."

"What?"

68

"Let us not waste precious time on that."

She lit a cigarette. She offered him one, her last. He lit his as well. Clouds of smoke whirled in the silent room. Marco's little snort of a snore stopped. Loyaan looked at Soyaan's watch on his wrist. Sometime today he should go to collect the Death Certificate. Sometime today he would have to present it to the Registration Office. He had other things to do.

"Do I understand that you've come here to tell the family that this child you have brought with you is Soyaan's?"

She choked on the cigarette. She coughed. She took a quick sip of water. He waited. There wasn't a word forthcoming, nothing from her, not a breath from him either. He must rephrase the question, he told himself. Unable to, he pulled on the cigarette.

"You understand correctly," she said finally.

He looked at the sleeping child with fresh eyes. As far as one could tell, yes, the child could be Soyaan's: the hands, the feet, the high forehead.

"I suspect you didn't bring anything to support your statement?"

"I'm sorry?"

"I mean, have you seen to the legal aspect of the affair?"

"Need I do that?"

The split in him towards her began to weaken the strong impression she had originally made on him. One must revere the dead, one must treat their wishes as though they were sacred. Unless. . . .

"Are you asking me to produce a certificate of marriage?"

"No, no. No."

"What then?"

An intellectual dilemma. Should he be dishonest with her and with himself? Soyaan hadn't needed any certificate for their affair or for the child. Perhaps it seemed necessary for the sake of his parents who, long before they heard the full story, would strike her off their list of possible — acceptable — choices: wasn't she Christian? Wasn't she half-Somali, half-Italian? His parents would certainly disassociate themselves from any position he took. But what about Ladan? Would she share his views, would she like this woman and accept her?

"I bore him this child. That is my certificate."

"And you loved him?"

69

The expression on her face was hard now. He hoped she hadn't misunderstood him. But she had. Her tone was as bitter as had been the taste on his tongue.

"That is beside the point," she said.

Ladan was in the doorway. She had knocked softly on the open door. He motioned her in. She had brought two packets of cigarettes, one for the woman, another for Loyaan. Ladan didn't wait to be told to leave, for she sensed the weight of the silence which she thought her entrance had caused. Afterwards he said:

"What do you ask in return?"

"I don't understand."

"A monthly remittance for yourself? A monthly something for Marco?"

"You misunderstand my intentions."

"Pardon?"

"I bore Soyaan a child of love. I've brought this love-child so as to share with you the love Soyaan left behind. I am sorry I couldn't come earlier. There were other reasons which I will one day explain to you."

He was proud of her, he was joyous. He stood her to her feet to hug her. But a voice deep inside him said, *Now, now, contain yourself. Use your head, don't lose it.*

She had a decent and very well-paid job. In addition to that, she had recently inherited her (Italian) father's wealth. So she could easily maintain Marco and her mother. Besides that, she could even provide financial help to Soyaan's family if (on account of Keynaan's matrimonial complications of which Soyaan had often spoken) they needed a generous hand. She was twenty-six. She was registered as an external student at the University of Rome, registered for a degree in law, and had already begun to research for her thesis entitled: *The Burgeoning of the National Security Service as an Institution of Power in Africa and Latin America.*

Loyaan found this all very interesting. He would talk of the last item last. One thing at a time.

"What's your name?"

"Margaritta."

Her profile: wrinkles of sunny smiles. Marco had woken up.

"Marco, *Marco mio,*" she chanted his name.

70

The one letter in an alphabet of mysteries and initials. Margaritta. Marco. *Marco mio. Margaritta mia.* M to the power of 2. There you are. An alphabet of mysterious pathways flown by a honey-guide.

Ladan and Qumman were both in the doorway. Margaritta was up on her feet. Marco had made water. But never mind. She would leave that very instant, anyway.

He walked her to where she had parked her car.

"I have many questions I've been dying to ask you," he said.

"Come and see me one of these days."

As they parted, she gave him her address and telephone number at work.

On his return to the room, his mother flew at him wildly. A string of abusive terms used only in reference to the *mistione* — half-Italian, half-Somali — community in Somalia. And:

"What did she want?"

"What do you think?" He raised his whole arm to stop Ladan from interfering, and to silence her possible indiscretions. It appeared the two had talked about Margaritta on their own. Qumman now had the floor and she covered it with a wash of colourful epithets.

"And on top of everything," she went on, "she wants us to give her bastard a name. She will squeeze herself into the decency and respectability of our home. Then she will ask for a daily allowance. And more, and more! When she is only a half-caste prostitute. Isn't that what she wants? To smear the memory of our Soyaan with the stains of her past? No, no. That won't happen!"

"Respect yourself, Mother."

She was in a state of rage which reduced her to a mine of nerves like electric wires. She was clearly suffering from a combination of exhaustion and hystero-epilepsy. He couldn't remember ever having seen her in that state before. What in heaven's name had happened? "Mother is a lioness protecting her cubs with any means available to her," Soyaan had once said. Why did she see Margaritta and Marco as a threat to her peace and the inner circle of her family (Keynaan by virtue of his marriage to another woman, namely Beydan, was excluded), why? What was it that had triggered this sudden emotive anger in his mother?

"Beydan's and that woman's child are the devil's breed, that is what they are. I don't want them here in my house, and I don't want Soyaan's name linked with that Christian either."

71

"The living must respect the wishes of the dead, Mother. It is clear that this woman bore Soyaan a child. I have proof of that. I can give you proof of that."

Ladan was the one who now spoke: "What is the child's name?"

"Marco."

Qumman pounced on that. "Now what kind of a Muslim name is that?"

"My dear Mother, a name is a choice made, a hope expresed. You named me Loyaan, you named her Ladan. The child was named Marco. I suggest we respect her choice. A mother is to a child more than a father is, you've always said. So. She is the mother; Soyaan, the father. Fathers are secondary — as Keynaan has been; as Soyaan must have been."

"No, not Soyaan." But she was calmer, she was a great deal less aggressive.

"What else does she want?" Ladan asked.

"We haven't talked over details. Though I can tell you straight away that she has enough money to maintain herself and her child. She has a job and other income, too."

Qumman's voice was markedly less hostile. There was no grating of rage in her throat, nor in her tone.

"The child's name and religion?" she asked.

"We haven't talked over details, I said. When we come to that, I shall tell her of your wishes. Is that all right? I suppose you would like to give him a distinctively Muslim name — say Moxamed?"

"How did you know?"

"Am I not your son?"

A pause. "And she has independent means?"

"I guarantee to you that the money Soyaan earmarked for your trip to Mecca will not be touched by Margaritta and Marco."

"What's her name again?"

"Margaritta."

The sun's rays filtered through the open window. There was a smile on Qumman's face. Loyaan remembered he had better go to town immediately to clear up the jungle of bureaucratic mess, or else. . . .

Chapter Five

Like a toy vehicle which has been a child's central concern for many days, the child's object of love. One day, however, while studying the outlines and the structure of what makes the machine tick, his eyes chance upon a nail sticking out. The child tugs at the nail, and pulls it out. The vehicle falls apart. The child, hours later, is seated in front of the disjointed piece of his original love. It transpires, when his mother comes, that he has misplaced the nail.

The sharp saw of the sun severed the sky in halves. The dust which had gathered, as if in mourning commemoration, erected a vaporous pillar of atmospheric pressure; the sawdust painted a brushwood of colours on the side of the heavens — heavy and thick now and again, hazy and vague a little later.

A road of asphalt stretched ahead of Loyaan, a road straight and smooth as seasoned wood. He walked and walked, his stare diffuse and unfocusing like a shaky memory, registering nothing in particular, being neither here nor there. Heavy as the stump of a fallen tree, the nerves of his brain had woodened. Soyaan: a mere leaflet which, on his dying, the foliaged face of the moon had dropped, as local myth had it. A mere foliole the season had no more use for. The green of a dew-moist leaf one morning, long, long ago, a letter from Soyaan . . . : "If you ever come to Mogadiscio and you go to the centre of it, you will now find new buildings, new high structures whose ribbons of inauguration have been cut with the very scissors which made the wrist of the nation's strength bleed and this country grow weak. The road on which your feet rest and which you tread, you must remember, is tarred with the very smear which blocks the pores of our body's breathing-space — how suffocating! New roads. New towering buildings. He crushes the anima of man, says Medina; he breaks the pride of one's dignity; he reduces women to mistresses of his prowess: He is, after all, the General. He constructs showy pieces of tumorous architecture, he gives to us monuments of false hope. He creates for the nation heroes of his own choosing. Name one

73

— and I will give you the rest. Anyway . . . the roadsides are decorated with neon signs illumining the sky of the city with the brilliance of his quotes of wisdom. Some of these sell to the masses, like any cheap commodity, a controversy of ideas which one is expected to buy uncritically — these being the General's wise sayings. To stay on, you break and praise. You do this in order to eke out an indecent living for the weaker members of the family, for mother, for sister and for the children. If you don't do this, you end up in prison. Your file at the security will grow fatter daily (I believe mine has). Or else you defect: anywhere else is better than this. I suspect, however, that things are worse in Baidoa than here. How have you fared? . . ."

"Magan allay!"

A beggar. Tatters of appeal, a hand outstretched, a face as famished as the drought which produced it. An aged, emaciated woman, and behind her a man, older and blind. She was the guide. He had a bank of coins tied to the loose end of his robe. Loyaan dropped a jingle or two into the tin. They thanked him. And as they moved, while he was still standing on the same side of the street, Loyaan saw the one-armed man whom he twice previously had encountered. But why, why would a one-armed man follow him everywhere he went? He reminded himself that he shouldn't become paranoid. He checked if he had misplaced the Death Certificate which the Office of the Municipality had issued to him. He took it out. He looked at it. He read it softly to himself. Soyaan: a mere page, which on Loyaan's request had taken the allotted space in the intricacy and spectrum of bureaucracy. He held the certificate in his hand, a certificate which had driven home a point: Soyaan was now *officially* dead. And bureaucracy had reduced the whole issue to a mere name on a piece of paper. Yes, a reference and a name. Things would have to be adjusted according to the registration number. Any reference to Soyaan would have to bear the reference number as given on the right-hand side of this certificate. To avoid bureaucratic delays, one had better quote the correct reference number.

Dottor Soyaan! A title before his name — titles, in this part of the world, being a legacy of the Italian love for pomp and flattery. *Dottor* Soyaan! *Dottore! Dottor* Loyaan! But what had *Dottor* Soyaan died of? Stomach upset and inherent complication of blood poisoning. Why had he said that to the clerk as he withdrew the certificate? Why had he said to the Minister of the Presidency that

Soyaan had died of "complications"? What did that mean — technically, medically, legally? He had no need to give reasons. Why? If only they had subjected the body to the medical ritual of a post-mortem, if only . . . ! He put the certificate back in his pocket. He stood on the side of the same street and waited for a taxi. A quarter of an hour later. . . .

"Here we meet again. Small world."

"*Ciao*, Ahmed-Wellie," Loyaan said, happy to see him.

Ahmed-Wellie cut off the engine of his car. "Can I give you a lift?"

"Yes, please."

"Where?"

"Home, if not inconvenient."

"If not inconvenient, if not inconvenient. Jump in."

The syndrome of greeting banalities; an exchange of other formalities, and how-are-yous repeated for emphasis. Ahmed-Wellie started the engine. Loyaan, after a mere second of hesitation (Qumman had warned him to be cautious; Ahmed-Wellie belonged to the same clan as the General — "as if it matters," had been Loyaan's comment), began offering a summary of the events which had taken place in the last twenty-four hours — omitting mention of Margaritta. Nor did he think it worth talking about the piece of paper on which Soyaan had copied two of the twenty-one articles which imposed the death penalty on any citizen who spread or took out of the Republic printed, spoken or reading matter, et cetera, et cetera. They stopped, waited for the red of the traffic-lights to change.

"And I suppose you've heard about the radio broadcasts. One at eight in the morning. The second at ten something. Perhaps a third at two o'clock."

A change of gear: the go-ahead green of the lights.

"And have you seen today's paper?" Ahmed-Wellie asked.

"No."

"There is your photograph and your name."

"What?"

"Easy — no panic: wrong caption, mistaken identity."

"My photograph and name — Why? Where is the paper? Show it to me."

He pulled up to the kerb. "It is in my bag in the back of the car."

"Where?"

75

"If you calm down, please." He pulled it from his medical kit in the back of the car. "A photograph, the wrong caption and mistaken identity."

"Is this what caused the delay in the paper's coming out today?"

Ahmed-Wellie played with the dangling car-keys. "Perhaps," he said as he turned the engine off.

Loyaan surprised Ahmed-Wellie by the calmness with which he opened the paper. He surprised him by the quietness in which he read it. He stared at the photograph which covered a quarter of one of the middle pages. He read the caption: "Loyaan Keynaan whose photograph appears above has died serving this revolution. God bless him and protect all those who loved him. Loyaan, Martyr of the Revolution, is dead but has left behind him a living legend of revolutionary vitality and loyalty to the highest of ideals. His last words were: *Labour is Honour*. May he be remembered thus!"

"The worst journalism I've ever read. No introductory paragraph, no explanation of anything. They come to a point before they start it."

His eyes offered a hint of his inner rage. Ahmed-Wellie was tempted to speak longwindedly about what he himself thought of all this, but withheld his opinion and remained silent. He started the car engine again.

He moved back into lane. He took the route homewards. Loyaan would say if he wanted to be taken elsewhere, he decided. Loyaan when he spoke said:

"May I keep the paper?"

"Of course."

Loyaan sat up properly, drew himself out of the confounded position of the feeble: he wasn't going to show anger. He wasn't going to lose his temper. They would have to try something else. The Minister to the Presidency might succeed in pulling a blanket of power over other people's eyes — not his! But what was the meaning of all this? Why did the General's régime wish to recruit Soyaan, a man already dead? Why was it that they felt the need to fabricate the story about his last words being "Labour is Honour" — both key nouns in the affair? Pray, what were the reasons for this? Loyaan wanted to make clear a very important point. Ahmed-Wellie turned a corner and, as he did, eased on the accelerator. They were in the village of Howl-wadaag, the village in which Loyaan's family lived.

76

Clouds of dust. Poverty. Walls which blinded one with their recent whitewashing glamour, walls which belonged to the upgraded tribals — those close to the General and his clique. Never mind. He would still make his point. He said to Ahmed-Wellie:

"I must somehow find a way of getting this across to somebody: Soyaan's last words were not 'Labour is Honour' as has been made out. He may have said that on another occasion. But it was not the last utterance he made. I was there holding his warm hand as it suddenly went cold."

"What was the last thing he said?"

"He repeated my name, he said my name three times."

"Yes?"

"That's all. He said my name three times."

They followed a bend, and another. Now the sun was in their eyes. Ahmed-Wellie shielded his with the sun-shade. Loyaan did not. The car slowed down again. Ahmed-Wellie asked:

"A fight over the dead soul of Soyaan, is that it, then, if put bluntly? They say his last words were 'Labour is Honour'. It seems that they will go ahead and decorate him posthumously. You say, and I agree with you, that his loyalty didn't lie with this dictatorship but with 'the humiliated', as he preferred to refer to the common man in this country. He is dead and cannot defend himself. It is a fight over his soul. What do you think?"

They were in front of the family house.

"Would you like to come in with me?" Loyaan wanted to know.

"I've asked you your opinion, Loyaan."

He unfastened the door of the car. He rolled up the window. He got out. He turned to Ahmed-Wellie, he bowed a courteous thanks to his friend.

"Thanks for the paper as well," he said.

A second later as Loyaan inserted the key in the door, Ahmed-Wellie's car engine's revving noise and gear changing could be heard. Loyaan went into the house.

"One hundred and eight."

"In coins?" Ladan asked.

"Yes, in coins."

And as Qumman re-counted the money in notes, Loyaan went and stood over them. Ladan looked up from the heap of coins whereas

Qumman rehearsed the number to herself lest she forgot it, and her tongue teased the dryness of her lips. Qumman shifted, changed the leg on which her weight had so far rested. She shouted as though she was in a cattle market:

"Five hundred and eighty shillings in notes."

"What is that?"

Ladan took and started to re-count the pile in notes. Meanwhile:

"And believe it or not, one single man paid three hundred shillings as his contribution," said Qumman. "Three hundred shillings. From his pocket. Your father was there. He told Ladan."

"Who is this man who felt so generous to a Soyaan dead and in his grave?"

She didn't catch the bitter irony in his voice. She turned to Ladan: "Did your father tell you who the man was?"

Ladan looked from one to the other. After a thoughtful pause: "No."

The sluggish heat of the hour set the tempo of Loyaan's heart-beat. He lived through heavy moments of agony. He spread the newspaper he had with him in front of himself. The first pages were lettered with the daily quotes of the General's wisdom. In the top right corner, there was the photograph of the All-Powerful retouched to make him look much younger and handsomer. The first and second sheets of the four-paged daily were dedicated to carrying in full a speech he had delivered the day before at the National Stadium. The first six lines of the big-lettered title were a summary of the tail-endedness of his hammered honoraries. Loyaan turned to the middle pages and faced the "wrong caption and mistaken identity" of a dead self.

"What is that?" said Qumman. "Why are you looking at it so?"

"Today's paper."

"What about it?"

He gave it to Ladan. "Read it to her. Do."

He went to his room.

Ten minutes or so later, when Loyaan had changed into a sarong and lay on a bed smoking his puffed lungs darker, Qumman outraged by his challenge entered without announcing herself, without knocking on the door, and said:

"What is wrong with this, tell me?" She waved the paper in the air.

78

He sat up. He was naked in the upper part and was hairy as Soyaan. He flicked the lengthened ash of his cigarette on to the floor. He let her continue.

"I am baffled, Loyaan. It feels as if I don't even know you."

"I am sorry, Mother."

Something had bruised her muscle of maternal strength surely. The wells of her eyes were irrigated with tears. Her eyelashes dipped in and out of that pool like chicks scratching the dust with their hungry feet. Her torrential reaction choked her throat with emotion.

"What is it that baffles you, Mother?"

"These random choices of yours. A woman with a child comes to disgrace the memory of your brother's dignity: what do you do? You accept her with open embrace, no questions asked, no research made, nothing, just like that. The government of this country (yes, the régime of this country, whether you like it or not — but that is another point) has offered your brother the honour due him: what do you do? With little thought and as though acting on advice given by enemies of this family, you refuse to behave sensibly."

"On whose advice am I acting, Mother?"

She wasn't going to let him interrupt her. "Are you sure you are doing the right thing? Are you sure Soyaan (God bless his soul) would have behaved in the same manner? Are you sure the child is his, and the honour not his due?"

He stubbed his cigarette out. "Acting on the advice of whom, Mother? Come to the point."

She wet her mouth, she let her lips receive the caress of the breeze, and then moistened them again. This would take energy out of both, she imagined, this conversation would help snap the umbilicus of their link faster.

"Do you know Ahmed-Wellie?"

"How do you mean?"

"Do you?"

"Are you asking, Mother, if I know what the tribal allegiances of Ahmed-Wellie are? I don't even know what tribe he belongs to. He may be related to the General tribally. So what? I don't care. The régime, if we come to that, bestows only dishonour on one, never honour."

Not challenging him on the latter part of the statement, she went on:

79

"On his spindle side, Ahmed-Wellie is related to the former civilian president. On his father's, to the (present military) president. How can you be as naive as that? Soyaan, too, trusted everybody. And she poisoned him."

Her masked heritage, her robed air of dignity: now the wind whistled away, the wind denuded her of those. She became inelegant. Should Loyaan go and hug her, cover her warmly with his clothed love? She would tremble, thought he, she would shiver despite the heat. He went to her, he embraced her, held her tightly, he squeezed out of her the following:

"I will go mad. Your mother is going mad."

"No, you won't."

"Your mother has indeed gone mad."

They remained embraced, although the very hands, which every now and again touched, started to milk the teats of the cows grazing on their fertile pastures. The pitchers which Loyaan used were more varied and could contain more. Qumman's were smaller, and more insular. She let his hand go. This sudden movement interrupted the flow, and he heard:

"Whereas he never mentioned that woman's name to me or to anybody I know of, Soyaan worked for the General, he worked in the Presidency. I am not convinced by your random taking of positions. The General has offered posthumous honour and perhaps a more lucrative gratuity for the family. There must be many things in this world I know nothing about. Allow me to use concepts with which I am familiar. The General. That woman and her child. Dr Ahmed-Wellie. Always trusting, Soyaan. And you, too. Stay away from that man.

"Who?"

"Ahmed-Wellie."

A pain such as that of haemorrhage: that was how Loyaan's entrails, when he pressed his stomach, pained. He listened to her eager voice comment:

"Cousins only twice removed, that man's father and the General."

"Things aren't that simple, Mother. Things aren't tribally straight either."

"I said I would use concepts with which I am familiar. And I say this: what harm can we do Soyaan if we accept this lucrative gratuity

80

for the family, what harm? In any case, the General would spend lavishly if not on us, on some other person, for some other cause in which he believes."

To himself: *Humiliate the living; make claims on the souls of the dead; bribe the living; pin stars of honour on the sandy breasts and on the head of the mounds of the uncomplaining dead. Decorate the tombs with the starred dignity of martyrdom.* To her, however, he said:

"A lot of harm, Mother."

"He is dead."

"All the more so, Mother."

"What?"

He was at a loss for words. He could instantaneously think of concepts that would render meaningless and insignificant the Somali proverb which, he felt, she would quote at him. "A dead man isn't as useful to one as his pair of shoes are." Besides, he had no intention of engaging her in the intricacy of Soyaan's politics, nor had he the wish to show her (and translate for her) his writings. Finally:

"Soyaan opposed this régime. He was against it."

"But he worked in the top office of the régime. He worked in the General's Presidency. He earned his money working there."

Try again: the voice inside Loyaan was giving guidance.

"Soyaan's grandest dream was to see the General dethroned."

"But that wasn't to be. And he is dead."

Another pause.

"That the child is his and the woman too, I can vouch," said he. "He once told me so himself. I have a letter he wrote to me. As for the posthumously awarded honour — well, he wouldn't have accepted it if alive, nor would the General have bestowed it on him. Just as he would've felt cheap if the identity of the man who paid three hundred shillings were revealed to him."

She put on her mask again. Ladan came to the door and wondered if Loyaan would like his meal brought in before it went cold. Qumman and Loyaan fell silent, both grateful for this very convenient cue.

"'Yes, please, I'll eat here," he said.

"Please."

"What?"

81

"Eat," Ladan said. "Please."

But he wouldn't. The spaghetti had gone dead cold. The fat had congealed. The lemon juice, in which a couple of ice-cubes had melted, had become undrinkably warm. The slice of papaya, the dessert of the day, had turned a shade more anaemic. A fly, singularly noisy, droned above the plate and drove Loyaan nearly crazy. Ladan picked up the fan in the room and whisked it away.

"Don't you want to eat?"

"Take it away, please."

No appetite. His tongue was a great sore infested with the germ of silence. His palate tasted his blood. His mouth soured into a salivary inarticulacy. No energy, either. The heat. The hate. *And life is this uphill walk of a million miles. When you're near the chimney of the hill, another pulls down by the tail-end of your reach.*

Silence. Then he lit a cigarette. The smoke awoke his dormant senses.

"Don't you think you could speak to Mother?" he asked.

"And say what?"

"Reason with her illogical turns of mind? Tell her she shouldn't sell the soul of her son Soyaan so cheaply?"

Ladan fanned in front of her. She looked like an abandoned ship anchored in the shallowness of the sea's coffin. "With Koschin taken away, and Soyaan dead — I shall meet no demands of anybody, I shall *will* not to see, reason or feel," she had said yesterday. Reason with whom? "I am blind as the General is to everything and everybody other than the path which illumines the power of his lighthouse. Soyaan: the braille of my unguided vision." She wouldn't go and teach any more. There was no point in any of that. No use in doing a year's National Service. Nothing made any sense any more. "Soyaan's death is the epitome of unreason. And Loyaan wants me to talk reason to my mother — who probably is as rational as he thinks he is — Mother who believes things had better be worked into different sequences and rhythms; Mother and Loyaan who've started speaking about formalities (what do we do about Margaritta and child whom we have on our bureaucratic in-tray, what do we do about the tribute paid to Soyaan posthumously and/or the gratuity to follow it, et cetera et cetera) when they no longer see any need for putting to themselves the question: dead, Soyaan dead, why?" He was now saying:

82

"If we cannot totally remove the hernia of inefficiency, Soyaan used to say, we might as well try to make the pimples of the body-politic bleed. We have a difficult problem on our hands. And I want you to help me, Ladan. Speak to her. Tell her all that you know about Soyaan, and what he stood for — politically! We should concede nothing which would dishonour his name. He lives in us, he lives on in you and me. If we sell his memory cheaply, his soul will belong to the highest bidder, to the General."

He wasn't prepared for the shock. She said:

"Please eat."

He threw the plates out of the window, one at a time.

Chapter Six

Like a child, perhaps consumptive, coughing convulsively — a lonely child. It crawls in the direction of voices which whisper, crawls in search of companionship. The voices, those of a man and a woman, hit the apex of a climax, which is followed by a moan from the man; then the shrieking hysteria of the woman shouting, "I didn't come, I didn't. It is unfair." The child's eyes fall on capsules and pills the colour of sweets. His uncoordinated movements of hand and mouth work miraculously and he swallows seven of these beauties. The clock strikes twelve.

It had lain low on the horizon. When grazing for a freer space, the moon had collided with a herd of clouds and had developed bumps dark as a wound past healing: it was then that it pussy-footed its way out of the gauze-thin pasture of cloudy bandages, and away from the herd. As though in tasteful colouring, the heavens were painted unhealthy yellow — the hour of twilight, the hour of indecision and change of guards. The sky however, met the challenge: it opened up little by little, like a cow her legs, as it accommodated the advances the moon made; it behaved like a willing cow in the company of an excited bull. The stars — frigid, timid — winked weakly but stayed put, afraid they might make the wrong pass and spoil things for everybody. The evening breeze, westward-bound, bestowed fondling caresses on the cheeks of Keynaan and Loyaan — father unlike son, God bless! It was chilly, but not so chilly as to make either return home to fetch a sweater or something warmer.

"Women are for sleeping with, for giving birth to and bringing up children; they are not good for any other thing," said Keynaan. "They are not to be trusted with secrets. They can serve the purposes Allah created them for originally, and no more. It pains me to see you work hard and fail. Again and again."

"I don't agree."

"You never married. You don't know them."

"I still don't agree."

And the two walked side by side, they walked silently with their

84

shoulders nearly touching. They were almost of the same height. But could they ever be of the same opinion? Could they share an idea, like two near-strangers might share a plate of anything, with hands coming into contact with one another every now and again, as their jaws munched, each with a morsel of something picked from the same source, the same plate and hence the same idea, could they? Or did it depend on what use each made of the lungfuls of oxygen inhaled, as they walked side by side, hardly talking, hardly noticing what was going on outside their own heads. Could Keynaan and Loyaan see anything eye to eye? Would they forget their differences? Would they exchange their shoes, would each be ready to place his feet in the other's and walk in them? Would their feet feel comfortable? Would the shoes pinch, would a heel come off, some nails as well? When once addressing himself to these differences, Soyaan said: "Not so much generational as they are qualitative — the differences between us twins and our father. My father grew up with the idea that the universe is flat; we, that it is round. We believe we have a perspective of an inclusive nature — more global; our views are 'rounder'. We believe that his are exclusive, that they are flat (and therefore uninteresting) as the universe his insularity ties him to." That was Soyaan to Loyaan. *But now, Loyaan, now : talk to the same theme, pray. Say something.* "My father sees himself as a miniature creature in a flat world dominated by a God-figure high and huge as any mountain anyone has seen. A miniature of a man before this huge mountain, and helpless too. When you confront him with a question of universal character, his answer is tailor-made, he will say: 'Only Allah knows, only Allah.' A miniature creature dependent upon his Creator to answer questions. Suddenly, however, he behaves as if he were the most powerful of men, the biggest. Suddenly, he is, as Soyaan called him, the Grand Patriarch. This happens when he is in front of his children and his wives."

"What did you do to make the women so upset, Loyaan?"

"What do you think?"

"Did you refuse to eat the food your mother prepared?"

"You are being very mean, Father."

"I could never upset them as much as you have. What did you do?"

"We disagreed. We saw that we viewed things differently."

85

"You discuss your ideas with women? You disappoint me."

Regardless of what went into their making, could the two share anything? Keynaan was nearly sixty, Loyaan not quite thirty. Someone had apparently already told him about Margaritta and Marco. Soyaan's child and his woman? Keynaan would not be rushed. He would take his time. He would wait and see. Legally it was within the male parent's absolute prerogative to act on behalf of a dead son or daughter or wife. In the absence of a male parent, then the nearest of kin, another male. Loyaan had no authority to confer the title of "widow" upon the woman who survived Soyaan; nor the title of "son" on her offspring. Soyaan would certainly not have married his father's selected bride — nor would his pride have allowed him to accept Keynaan's choice. But he was now dead — and the wishes of the dead needed defending.

"Women are like one's shadow, Somalis have a proverb," quoted Keynaan. "They follow at the heels of those who run away from them. They bully and boss and lead those who follow them."

"We disagree, you and I."

"You have no opinion on women."

"Oh, yes. I do. That is why I disagree with you. If I had none, I would shut up and accept yours or your generation's as gospel wisdom."

"You don't know them. You don't know your mother, for example."

Of course, he did. A shower of abuse from Keynaan, and cheeks wet with tears, poor Qumman. Whenever some superior officer humiliated him, he came and was aggressive to the twins and his wife. He would flog them, he would beat them — big, and powerful that he was, the Grand Patriarch whose authority drenched his powerless victims with the blood of his lashes. She would wait until the twins grew up, she confided to a neighbour. She would wait. Patience, patience. A third pregnancy which resulted in Ladan. And a near-fatal fourth. There were no pills a woman could take those days. Society, on top of it, required women to be tolerant, to be receptive, to be receiving — and forgiving. "Does one notice the small insects which die a suffering death under the eyeless heels of one's feet? Keynaan and his generation have never known women. Women are simply a generally generalised-about human species more mysterious than Martians," Soyaan would argue.

86

Keynaan slowed down. Loyaan came level with him.

"Shall we rest awhile and have tea?"

Loyaan saw a terraced tea-shop with chairs arranged outside. "Why not?"

The night drew on the face of the sky a constellation of stars which suggested to Loyaan (as it would have to any nomadic bard) the figure of a camel, a camel dragging its wounded hind legs up the un-walked pathways of a double lane of lighted stars. The darkness traced for Loyaan's untested imagination the confines of the camel's neck, its shoulders, its hump, its nose, and its forelegs.

"On a small pay which hardly varied, despite several successive colonial and national governments, I, Keynaan, served this nation in capacities low and high. For twenty-five years, I executed my duties honourably. Yes, Loyaan, honourably. I let you starve, I lived miserably and in poverty. Hence, when somebody accuses me of having had my hands smeared with the grease of bribery, I shall simply say—"

He was abruptly silent. For the waitress had come back with the tea: two cups, one white, the other black. Loyaan half-rose from the chair to pull closer a shaky table on which she could set the tea. Loyaan emptied all his change on to her extended hand. She smiled gratefully — perhaps she had never received so much at one go from one man unless he was hoping to take her exhausted, sweaty body to the creaky bed in the rooming-house in which she lived. Keynaan had the temptation to tease his son about the way she lingered near their table. But she was bound to misunderstand. A simpleton of a woman!

"For twenty-five years," he continued, "on small pay which hardly varied, I worked for the armed forces in one capacity or another. I fought battles. I won medals. I served in the hottest areas. I served in the most sensitive sections of this city. I performed the straightest of a policeman's duties, a baton to hand, with the same seriousness as I performed the most secretive of jobs such as those involving national security at top priority level. You were four or five when I joined the police force as a private. I was recruited and immediately sent down to this city. I'd served in all the regions by the time I retired."

"You were forced to retire, Father."

87

"I retired of my own accord. I couldn't take it any more."

Loyaan to himself: *sacked*. He was called in and fired right there and then. He was lucky he wasn't court-martialled. He was lucky the machinery of justice had no independent means of functioning with the oil of ethics universally shared. Power was invested in the long neck of the gun with which it was protected.

"Retired. I've been given a pension, too. If fired, I wouldn't get any pension."

"My interpretation of the events differs from yours."

"What do you know of what goes on inside the forces anyway?"

"One of your cases died under torture, Father. The story leaked. One of the junior officers who had *worked* the man told on you all. It created a scandal. The General feared it would end in a tribal mutiny, that the tribe from which the dead man hailed would take revenge on this government of tribal hegemony. To prove that his own tribesmen were innocent, the General had all accusing fingers point at you and the other two, all three of you in the service of his hegemony. Having exposed you, he was left with no choice but to sack you. Pension, what pension? A mean sum to unlock your rheumatised tongue and make your rusty jaws function so you can praise him."

Loyaan now held a cigarette between his lips and an unlit match between his fingers. He wasn't quite sure if when lighted the stick would stay firm, if the fire would catch the right end of the cigarette. He was shaking, his hands were trembling. His teeth bit his tongue. The accumulated anger of a quarter of century made him drown in a river of regrets and rage. *Retired? Sacked, discarded like a used French letter, you symbolise filth on the inside, muck on the outside, you are like a used French letter reminding one of one's powers of abuse and waste. Not retired honourably. Nobody does that any more in this country, nobody. We are all clowns, clapping applause whose touching result is to raise the General's self-importance and per-sonality-cult.* Ah, what a relief; he could light his cigarette. He had a puff. He saw that the waitress had returned and had brought two cups of sugared mixture at the urging of Keynaan. *Not retired honour-ably. You married the woman whose husband died under torture. That was what you did. You married Beydan. Will that wash your guilt-ridden soul in the laundrette of Beydan's tears? How serious is your wish to be exonerated in the presence of the God whom you so often invoke? Listen to him.*

"The commission appointed by the General has freed me from any blame. I was called in this afternoon and told so. I can have my job again. The same as before if I so wish."

But before Loyaan had time to form his thoughts into the shape of a reasonably logical response to his father's challenge, the cavities of the night opened up. Suddenly, the place was flooded with a stream of throaty voices, men and women, some in green uniforms, some in plain clothes, men and women on their way to the Orientation Centre in the area. From the centre (as if to welcome the fresh stream) came the drumming of the latest revolutionary beats. This was one of the most populous districts of Mogadiscio. "There are thirteen cells. This city is broken into thirteen cells, of which all but one is of manageable size. The Security deems it necessary to break this sandy city into these, have each house numbered, the residents counted — and everybody screwed! The General has the master-key to all cells, whether numbered or unnumbered. He is the Grand Warder, remember. Every civil servant and his family must register with the Centre nearest him. Thrice weekly, civil servants should report themselves to the Centres at which they are registered. Thrice weekly in the mornings, civil servants must attend a programme of orientation organised by the Revolutionary Council for all Ministries. If any person is found missing on two counts out of six, he or she loses his or her job. What do they do out there in Baidoa, Loyaan, I wonder?" Soyaan had written in a letter to him. That was about three years ago when the Centres had just started. Now it was to them that people went, not to mosques any more. People immediately their number exceeded five found it expedient to sing the General's praises. For it was against the law of the land to have an assembly of more than five persons unless they were at an Orientation Centre or unless they were there to chant the chorus of the General's ninety-nine good-names. *Hold it there. Don't get carried away, Loyaan. Address yourself to the challenge which has come from your father.* There was this voice which spoke through him — and to him. So:

"Did you hear this morning's news?"

He took a sip of tea.

"Yes."

Loyaan dragged on his cigarette and filled his lungs with smoke he wouldn't exhale, he decided.

"Soyaan never said that. Nor did he die serving the General's

89

idea of revolution. I was there with him when he hiccupped his last. And I have proof that he opposed this régime's dictatorship until the last second of his life."

" 'Labour is Honour': these were Soyaan's last words."

"But you were not there, Father."

"Does it matter?"

"Yes, it does."

"I was there when he said it. I will say I was there when he said it."

"He said my name three times. You were not there. I was. He said my name three times just before the warmth went out of his hands."

"Why would he say your name three times?"

"But you were not there. You weren't there when he hiccupped his last."

"I was there. You weren't."

"WHEN?"

"Don't shout."

A pause. A furtive look to this and that side.

"When?" asked Loyaan.

"I answered that very question in an interview which will be published in tomorrow's daily. I also gave them the right photograph of Soyaan. Yes, I offered the right photograph of the Martyr of the Revolution and an interview. A photograph of mine as well."

Loyaan stared at his father. He could not take his eyes off him. To what depths would he not descend to discredit his own son Soyaan?

"Did you give the interview on condition that you got the job again?"

"No."

"But you know it is dishonest of you to say that Soyaan died serving the General's régime? You know that he opposed it by whatever means were possible and within his powers. You know that."

A cloister of the night's pillars of darkness. The camel had disappeared, so had the pathway up which it had dragged its wounded hind legs. The Centre had come to life: they could hear declensions of the General's ninety-nine given names. The waiters came, this time at Loyaan's beckoning, and went to fetch sugar-powered cups of spicy tea, the speciality of this tea-shop. Outside, the night had

90

spread its leaves of opaqueness, like a fallen tree its withered branches.

"I know one thing for sure."

"What?"

Keynaan contemplated his son. He then said: "Two Security men have interrogated Soyaan's secretary/typist and reported that she typed the manuscript of a Memorandum. She would not reveal its exact contents even under torture."

The waitress brought the two teas and set them down. She took away Keynaan's and Loyaan's (untouched) cups. Meanwhile, he paid her another generous tip. She wiggled her bottom as she went, perhaps to excite him. But was he ready for that sort of thing? No. He lit a chimney of unsmoked cigarettes. His throat went drier. He soaked it with the tea she had brought.

"Where are they holding her?" he asked.

"That I won't tell you."

"Have you no dignity? Have you no sense of honour?"

"Empty words."

"What do you know of what these words meant to Soyaan?"

"Don't you provoke me!"

Two women came and sat near them. They were in the green uniform the revolutionary guards of each district wore to distinguish themselves from the rest of the populace. They were named the Standard-bearers of the Revolution by no less a figure than the General himself. They came mainly from the unemployable lumpen. Whoever stayed on the green corps as a volunteer for five to six months was guaranteed a job with the civil service or had his/her name added to the rolls of Security as an informer. Keynaan and Loyaan fell silent as they heard the Green Guard rehearse the National Anthem of Uganda. Tomorrow or the day after, Idi Amin would come as the honoured guest of the Somali Democratic Republic. A week or so before: Gadaffi. A month before that: Bokassa. *Garland these generals, these colonels with a necklace of haemhorraged intestines. Quench Numeiry's power-thirst with a Nile of communist blood*, thought Loyaan. *Issue to N— a Union Jack of powercoupons. To K—: a queen of elephant-pouches and hard tusks of currency.*

The waitress disturbed them by asking what they would like to have.

"We shall have to go and have a meal somewhere."

91

"Then I shall catch my bus back to Afgoi. Yes. Let us."

"Let us."

They took a taxi; then each a chair in the quietest corner in a restaurant not very far from where eventually, when they parted, Keynaan would catch a bus to Afgoi and Loyaan another taxi homewards. They placed their order with the waiter: rice and curry for Loyaan, spaghetti and Coke for Keynaan. As the waiter shouted the order to the kitchen, Loyaan said:

"It is his soul they are after."

"Whose soul?"

"Soyaan's, of course."

"The soul is God's domain, not ours. Don't confer upon mortals and generals powers which belong elsewhere. And what does it matter whether or not he opposed them when alive, now that he is dead? Have you forgotten the Somali proverb, 'A dead man is not as useful as his pair of shoes are' ?"

His mind began immediately to review the events of the past twenty-four hours in a hurry. His mother. Ahmed-Wellie. Margaritta. Ladan. The one-armed man who shadowed him — or was he getting paranoid? The brief piece found in Soyaan's pockets. The two articles copied in Soyaan's own hand and found in his pockets. The photograph and caption: mistaken identity. The press release of the Minister to the Presidency. And Keynaan.

"Has it ever crossed your mind that the Security Service had a hand in his death? Has it ever?"

"No, it hasn't."

"I think they might have."

"How?"

"You tell me. You know their methods. You were an inside man."

Haunting eyes. Not a blink although he stared and stared at Loyaan. Nor an instant of hesitancy. He saw what he wanted: Loyaan's downcast look.

"You surprise me," he said.

"How do you mean?"

"You really do."

The waiter came and set the wrong order before Loyaan. They exchanged plates. Loyaan passed the Coke to Keynaan. In silence, father rolled his spaghetti with the fork and spoon purposefully placed

92

under it; in silence, Loyaan salted the rice and curry of which he now took a mouthful.

"You are full of self-importance, each one of you."

"That is not answering my question. Has it ever crossed your mind?"

"No young man of your age that I know of has ever appeared as 'dangerous priority' on the list drawn up by the Security. No young man of your age, you hear me? The General fears no threat which might come from you and your lot. You have no common ideology for which you fight. You have no organised protest. Skirts. Air tickets to Europe. Posh cars. These are what you are after. The Security provides them. And you are no threat. Not one young man of your age from the civilian quarters—"

"Who does the General fear?" shouted Loyaan.

Two or three clients near them looked at them. Keynaan allowed the voice to die down, and the eyes to be averted and directed on to the meals in front of them.

"The General fears tribal chieftains or men of his age. Not you, nor Soyaan, nor anyone of your generation. You have no common ideology and no principles. You work for the interests of the countries in which you received your academic training. Some for western Europe, some for Russia."

"He fears men of your age?"

"He has some in prison; he appoints some as ambassadors; he bribes some with the portfolio of banana sales; he forces some to retire; he has some of them tortured. But why should the Security want to get rid of Soyaan? Granted he was a young man full of the ideals of youth and rebelliousness. Granted, he had a certain popularity and had developed the primary sensitivity that any future leader might need. But why? Tell me."

Loyaan was at odds with his own self. He looked up and away from his plate. A spider had spanned the air and a spreadeagled fly was caught in the woven trap. Loyaan heard the tinkle of spoons and forks, touching in the background. But he was remembering the story told him by Dr Ahmed-Wellie, that story of the blindfolded politician whom the Security had tortured. He also remembered one of Soyaan's heart-reaching appeals for somebody to do something for Koschin. Should he now ask his father to do the favour of finding out where

93

they were keeping him? Or should he wait until another day — possibly when the tides were low, and there wasn't so much at stake?

"Your mother blames Beydan," Keynaan was saying. "You, the Security. Do you know what that means? Do you know what I take that to mean?"

"Tell me."

"In essence, you and your mother hold me responsible for Soyaan's death."

"Can you explain yourself better, please?"

A mouthful of spaghetti down the gullet. A sip of Coke to wash it down.

"I represent the Security, and Beydan is but a mere shadow of the symbol your mother hates most. I didn't allow you to have Soyaan's body submitted to a post-mortem. Then there are the stories of him having said this instead of that. You hold me responsible for his death."

"Don't talk nonsense."

"Yes, you do."

"My mother's is an unfounded suspicion concerning superstition. Mine can be proven. I have documents. I have his writings. Not proof that they killed him. But that there is a good reason why they could have wanted him removed, taken out of circulation like a banned book."

The waiter again. Would they like something else? Dessert? Tea? Anything? Nothing for Keynaan. For Loyaan, whose plate was only teased but not eaten, a *macédoine* please. Keynaan's turn:

"I knew of a summons to have him removed one dawn a few months ago. But the man whose jeep was to collect him came and informed me of it. I went and appealed to the General the same night. I vowed to the General that I would speak to Soyaan."

"Do you see what I mean?"

Keynaan would not. He continued: "Soyaan was being used by other factions. Unwittingly he got caught in the intricacy of tribal politics which he could not understand. He did not know that. He had no means of knowing. He was trusting. He had a wrong set of friends. Ahmed-Wellie is one such person of whom you should be careful."

"Did you tell him so?"

"Yes."

94

"What did he say?"

"He said: 'The weed in the sea the salty water does not see'."

"What does that mean? Did he explain?"

"Did he ever!"

There was a brief pause.

"Why are you being dishonest to him deliberately since you knew his position? Why?"

The waiter had brought the *macédoine*.

"I breathe life into his name. I make him honourable. I give him life again. A school will be named after him, perhaps a street. He will live longer than you or I. You hold me responsible for his death. I believe I am responsible for the spiritual revival of his name. We disagree."

"You are mad. You are out of your head."

He looked at Loyaan in utter anger. The man could kill — surely! That fixed gaze would frighten anyone who didn't know Keynaan, anyone who had not been introduced to it as early as Loyaan. Yes. Loyaan was with Soyaan, and the twins were fighting over a ball. Towering above was this massive figure, their father, who snatched the ball from them and cut it in two. When he had just walked away but was still within hearing distance, Soyaan said, "I will kill him. When I am old enough to use a knife. I will." The blade. A lost thumb. The age of challenge. The age of growth. That of maturity. And Qumman: she would wait until the twins grew up, she would wait and then leave. Soyaan did not kill him. Neither did Qumman leave him. Soyaan died mysteriously before him; Qumman waited too long: he left her for another woman instead.

"I am the father. It is my prerogative to give life and death as I find fit. I've chosen to breathe life into Soyaan. And remember one thing, Loyaan: if I decide this minute to cut you in two, I can. The law of this land invests in men of my age the power. I am the Grand Patriarch."

With this heavy in the air, he walked out in the direction of the bus station. Loyaan paid the waiter. He came out and hailed a taxi. He wondered if he could guess what words his father had used in his interview with the only daily. He wondered what colours Keynaan had painted the pictures he gave of Soyaan — the standard-bearer of the General's revolution.

Part II

In the figure of the father the authoritarian state has its representative in every family, so that the family becomes its most important instrument of power.

WILHELM REICH

One guards only the absent in oneself.

PHILIP O'CONNOR

Chapter Seven

Like a baby born at the crack of the whip of dawn, a baby nameless, a baby that moans near the ladder which leads to a fisherman's dhow, with the cock crowing in the distance, calling the vanishing apparition of the night, calling to the frogs in the marshes; and life at a standstill, the sand blind, and sharks grazing in the greenless weeds in the bottom of the sea. The baby cuddles to himself a sea-shell dry as the sand which has made it heavier. The baby looks at a stone house which he can see in the reflection of the water in the lagoon.

"A carrier of the Revolutionary Torch; the Standard-bearer of Scientific Socialism; an advocate of Justice and Social Equality; a Believer in the General's interpretation of the country's needs: Soyaan Keynaan, Allah bless him, died two days ago. He died a premature death. He died serving the Revolution. He died, and his last words were praiseful of the General's policies: 'Labour is honour and there is no General but our General.'

"As has been the custom and is known from experience, the Revolutionary Government honours those who die serving her honourably. The Revolutionary Government, indeed, has pinned ribbons of honour on the bosoms of those who have served this nation's interest. Although it must be remembered that no reward and no remuneration however great and however generous can substitute fully for the vitality of the Hero of the Revolution.

"The Supreme Revolutionary Council has decided to name a street after Soyaan, the Hero of the Revolution. And on his tomb will be inscribed in gold the words: "Labour is honour and there is no General but our General'."

Loyaan was drenched in the sweat of shame and powerlessness. He held the paper in front of him as though it were a mirror of horror and dishonour. Soyaan's photograph had a caption underneath it with apologies to the readers although it didn't explain why. No doubt it had to do with Loyaan's photo which had appeared the day before: a mistaken identity. Then there was the interview given by his father which took up the available columns of the middle page. Keynaan sang a litany of the General's praise-names and at some point added:

"Soyaan saw himself in the light and through the eyes of a visionary, and considered himself a revolutionary of a given order. Every now and again, the youthful rebelliousness of his character came out and manifested itself in ways which were averse to the things he felt deep down inside. He was and remained to his last second an exemplary revolutionary who believed, without reservation, in the leadership of the General. A man of great potential. He was a man of grand qualities and when these were not put to use he could speak up and say, at times, the most unwarranted things; he was capable of speaking through the voices of others."

Elsewhere, a little further down:

"Revolutionaries have enemies within the ranks from which they are recruited as well as without. Soyaan had many of these. He loathed to be interpreted badly and to be misunderstood. He hated the false in man. And he fought it the hardest he could.

"As for his last words, I was there by his bedside when he said them, when he spoke these words of wisdom. I was there. 'LABOUR IS HONOUR AND THERE IS NO GENERAL BUT THE GENERAL'. Those were his last words. My family hopes these words will be remembered. My son, my daughter, my wife and I hope that our beloved Soyaan will be remembered by these words; that a monument of golden memories of these words will be constructed in his honour."

A fabrication of lies. But how could Loyaan correct them? He turned to the other pages of the paper. He sat in a stubble of perspiration and self-contempt. What would he say to his friends, to Soyaan's? Had he the face to confront anybody? Had he the power to correct this statement released by his father in the General's media? "My son, my daughter, my wife and I . . . !" Good heavens! What about this: "I was there by his bedside when he said them, when he spoke those words by which history will remember him, those words of wisdom, I was there. 'LABOUR IS HONOUR AND THERE IS NO GENERAL BUT OUR GENERAL'." Loyaan balled his fingers into a fist. "He repeated my name three times!" he shouted now. That was

100

all. But to whom could he say this? To Ahmed-Wellie? To Margaritta? How shocked were Soyaan's friends? How low had the mercury of their enthusiasm dropped? Would they have any esteem for him now, in particular those outside the country, those who were out of touch? What could he do to right this wrong? He must above all things prove that his father had fabricated these lies. But how? Perhaps he could provide people with a written statement which would disprove it. But how, how? Find the Memorandums first. Call at Margaritta's. Remember, meanwhile, the poor typist whom they had removed from circulation because she knew a great deal: she was the one who had typed the Memorandums. Where would he be able to find her? Also he must think how best he could publish Soyaan's "Clowns" piece, he should find means of circulating it confidentially among friends. He should consult Ahmed-Wellie.

There was Ladan half-leaning against the open door. "Would you like some tea?" She held a cup out to him from that distance.

"Have you seen the paper?"

"Would you like some tea?"

Loyaan stood. He saw how jaded she looked. Although it was past nine o'clock, at least she hadn't gone to school to teach. He approached. He said, a cigarette in hand:

"Speak to me, Ladan. What do you think?"

"Of what?"

"The papers."

With both hands, he accepted the cup. She had abandoned herself to the grim mood of apathy in which she lived the past few days. Her long hair had fallen into the tangled locks of unkempt sleep, her hair which she wouldn't comb nor wash with shampoo. Nothing mattered any more.

"I see nothing. I hear nothing. I think nothing. I am nothing."

Closer: she looked frightened, she appeared more prominently whey-faced than he had originally thought. He set the cup on the table by the door and took her hand. He pulled her closer yet again. They hugged.

"Soyaan is dead. And you are not," she said. "So please."

"Yes, yes. I shall take more care."

They remained embraced for a long time, neither moving. Through the corner of his eye, he saw that the cigarette had gone very near her robe. He released her gently.

101

"Have you told Mother?" he asked.

"Do you want me to?"

"What do you think?"

"Do you want me to tell her?"

Time he went to the office which registered the dead of the city. "You decide."

He would nerve himself for the worst. He would hold his head high. He would not break — no, not so easily at any rate. A voice inside him told him: *You must help encounter and finally fuse the wires of antagonism and the mass of unutilised human electricity; you must help encounter and then fuse the talents of Soyaan and Loyaan; in you must encounter the forces of life (Loyaan) and death (Soyaan); in you must gather and encounter the beginningless end of an afterbirth : lick it while it is still moist, warm, alive.*

"*Ciao*, Abdullahi."

"*Ciao*, Loyaan."

Loyaan had just got out of the taxi which had pulled up to the kerb. Abdullahi was the fifth friend whom he had greeted since he had hit town. And Abdullahi, like the other four, appeared to suddenly think of something and hurried away. Had it really come to that? Was he being avoided like a leper? Had he suddenly begun to beget monsters of unimaginable provenance? No one wished him "condolences". Neither would any of these speak about the paper of which they had probably heard if not read. Would they understand if he were to whisper an aside to them? "It is my father's doing, not mine. And Soyaan never said that. I was there. My father wasn't." Would that work? If he only could hold a press conference. *Ladies and gentlemen of the world press.* . . .

"*Ciao*, Fatuma."

"*Ciao*, Loyaan."

The woman was gone. She waved goodbye before she formalised her hello with a handshake. Gone. Like the five before her. He was in front of Azan Café. He walked in and ordered a capuccino. He stood by the counter. He leaned against it, his eyes fixed on the entrance. There he saw a number of friends who dispersed in all directions. The epidemic of the caste-shame which his presence had brought — was that why they were avoiding him? Was that all they could think of?

102

"*Ciao*, Loyaan."

"*Ciao*, Ali."

A grin on Loyaan's face. Ali didn't ask. He waited for Loyaan to speak. But Loyaan wouldn't either. Ali, a tribal upstart appointed by the General to replace a well-qualified university administrator, when he, Ali, had never even set foot in any institution of higher learning. Ali would stay with him, greet him. He was of the same clan as the General, and a clown, too. Ali's hand patted Loyaan's head somewhat patronisingly. *"My son, my daughter, my wife and I hope that our beloved Soyaan will be remembered by these words: that a monument of golden memories of these words will be constructed in his honour."* A smile from Ali, the upstart, and from Loyaan:

"Give the dead more than his due, and the living a hero to worship."

A quizzical look from the tribal upstart. Whereupon Loyaan continued:

"In the *autunno* of Prague, they weren't leaves which fell but heads. Remember 'fifty-six, remember Budapest. The methods haven't changed. The universe is round and not flat. It is oval-shaped like an egg awaiting a hand to break it in half like a rubber ball."

"What is all this?" asked Ali, the upstart.

Loyaan was gone.

"Your name?"

"Loyaan Keynaan."

"Whose death certificate have you come to withdraw and sign for?"

"My brother's."

"Name?"

"Soyaan Keynaan."

"When did he die?"

He told her when.

"What did he die of?"

"Have you not seen today's paper?"

"Of course, yes. Of course."

She pulled a drawer. She brought out the paper. She read it softly to herself. Her heavily made-up face became weightier and unmoved. She folded the paper and put it away, back into her drawer. There was a long pause, and:

"Shame. A young man of his education and intelligence. . . ."

"Yes?"

"Shame."

She wouldn't commit herself any more for now. She was in her early twenties, nails neatly varnished, hair tinted and faultlessly combed. She sat behind a weather-beaten teak table on top of which lay, as though temporarily, heaps and heaps of files stacked to one side. In front of her, there were two cupboards which, once opened, appeared never to have been closed again.

"He did not say that."

"He did not say what?"

"Soyaan did not say, 'Labour is honour and there is no general but our General'. He did not. I was there."

"No?"

"He did not."

She picked up her leather bag from the floor. She took out a pretty little handkerchief with which she gently dabbed at her oozing, sweaty nose. She replaced the handkerchief in her bag.

"I knew him, you know," she said.

"Did you?"

"Such gentleness. I liked him."

"You did?"

"His secretary and I are cousins. Distant cousins. Do you know Mulki? They came and took her two dawns ago. Poor thing. That evening I remember he gave me a lift home. First, he dropped Mulki home, then me. I remember it very clearly because Mulki had her youngest sister circumcised. He opposed that with such passion. He gave a long, learned lecture when driving Mulki home, a learned lecture on 'political aggression to women'. He fell to such gentle silence, like an infant asleep, while escorting me to where I lived. No fingers energised with the pushiness of lust. No shall-I-see-you-again. He didn't speak a word, not one. I asked Mulki about this."

"What did she say?"

" 'He is special'."

"Did she mean there was something going on betwen the two of them?"

She narrowed her eyes, as though concentrating finely on re-

104

touching her nail-varnish. Her hand again felt in her handbag. She took out a nail-clipper and began to file her nails. She said:

"He treated her as one would a sister. No, no. He had a mulatta as his friend. And he was very different from all these *parvenus* who show off their wealth and women. He led a very private, quiet sort of existence. Mulki knew of it. She told me herself."

Mulki. She wouldn't tell them anything even under torture, Keynaan had said. Where could she have put the Memorandum that the Security was searching for so desperately? What were the things Soyaan said in the Memorandum she had typed for him? Could Loyaan risk asking this distant cousin of hers if Mulki had confided in her? Had she told her what the Memorandum was about? Would she have talked to her about the Memo since she had talked about Margaritta? *Come on. You have nothing to lose. Rephrase it first. Yes. Re-word the question in your head*, said the inside voice to Loyaan.

"Why are the Security interested in Mulki, do you know?"

"Why have the Security imprisoned all the male members of Mulki's and my tribe? There are over three hundred of my tribesmen whom the General's men have taken away and imprisoned."

"You don't think it is because Mulki had knowledge of some document Soyaan drafted or wrote and she typed and in which the Security are interested? A document strongly worded, a document which condemns the General's régime unequivocally. Do you?"

She accepted the cigarette he offered.

"The General fears that the men of Mulki's and my clan will stage a coup to overthrow him."

"I am not sure if I am with you."

He lit her cigarette for her. She gave him time to light his.

"Isn't Soyaan the man the General's régime has named a street after because he died serving the interests of the Revolution? Isn't he the one whose last words were, 'Labour is honour and there is no General but our General'? I personally find the whole affair too embarrassing."

"But he did not say that. He did not, I am telling you. I was there."

"Ours is the only tribe which has resisted his fascist rule. No other. See how we've suffered. Mulki goes to prison. Our men, too: ten distant and close cousins of mine. Every other tribe has succumbed. A great let-down."

"But Soyaan did not say that."

"Your tribe is known for that sort of thing. Your tribe easily succumbs to anything," she said accusingly.

With a wave of the hand, he dismissed it all as nonsense.

"Please announce to the Director that I am here," he said.

She now made him wait. She made him feel more humiliated. She let a woman enter the Director's office and come out. Then a man. Another woman went in while she made him wait still. Should he just walk past the secretary and enter without knocking? But it felt as though white worms had invaded and begun eating into the wooden foundations of Loyaan's well-fenced strength. His head registered demolishing noises and the creaks of cranes pulling down constructions, and workers' voices of disturbing disquiet. This was far more complicated than the conflict which had existed between the "flat universe of Father's calculable dimensions and the oval-shaped one of solar and lunar evolutions and revolutions". For hidden behind the balled fist of power (spoke the voice through Loyaan again) a moustache had been sketched; a sickle red as the blood of the bull it had slaughtered; the hammer exposed as the nail which no more held firm since a whitlow infection had played havoc with the finger's foundation. *Speak this mouthful of wise socialist thoughts. Repeat it after me. Paint your walls the colours of Moscow. This is but a ball game. Clear the jungles. Turn them into stadiums of gathered masses whose shouts eulogise you. Have this Tartar delight. Bury your head like a cat its waste; let your people remain blind, like an ostrich with sand in its feathered eyes; be light like the wind; sing the Internationale. Follow, yes, follow the General.* The voices in Loyaan suddenly ceased to make sense even to him.

"Would you like a cigarette?" asked the secretary.

"Yes, please." The day had turned brighter and warmer. "Thanks."

"*Prego!*"

The Director's door opened. He said to his secretary: "Next? Who is next?"

"*Jaalle* Loyaan."

All members of Somalia's *privilegentzia* either knew one another or of one another. The Director of this department had known Soyaan personally but only of Loyaan indirectly. The voice of the *suggeritore*: "Members of the *priviligentzia* who work for this régime fall into one

106

of five categories — and here I exclude *a priori* the *parvenu*, the un-masked clown, i.e. the *arriviste*. First: there are the misled techno-crats who believe that politics is, in essence, the false utterances politi-cians make in the presence of trusting crowds and hence wouldn't wish to have anything to do with it themselves; they prefer to stay away. Secondly: there are the bureaucrats who have no political ambitions nor social awareness but who reason thus: 'I have a wife and children. It is for their sake I serve this régime in order that I have a means of earning a living; it is for their sake that I prostrate myself, that I accept to be humiliated.' Thirdly: there are the most interesting and the most daring of the lot, i.e. the saboteurs, men like Soyaan, women like Mulki, again men like Dr Ahmed-Wellie, like Xassan. . . ."

"Hello, Xassan."

"Sit down, Loyaan. Please."

"The fourth and fifth categories. . . ." But the voice of the *suggeritore* began to fade out. Xassan's blazing bulbs of inquisition which focused on Loyaan's face made the multi-visioned voices vanish, for the moment at any rate. Xassan looked down at a file on the desk between him and Loyaan, then up and at Loyaan.

"All this is very embarrassing," he said.

Loyaan nodded his agreement. The word again. *Embarrassing.* The secretary had used it too.

"Has my secretary not told you?"

"What?"

Xassan raised his skeletal weight off his chair. He walked over to the other side of the desk. His hand rested on Loyaan's shoulders, Loyaan who wouldn't even look up at him. Silently, he returned to where he had been previously. Under five-foot-eight, Xassan appeared over-burdened with registering lists of the dead of the thirteen districts of the city.

"I told her to tell you that I didn't want to see you."

"No, she didn't tell me anything. But why did you not want to see me?"

The job of his office consisted mainly of preparing files on govern-ment civil servants who died natural deaths. Xassan's office would prepare an affidavit to be signed by a dependent member of the deceased — a wife, a child or a mother. This original document would go to the Security Services; a carbon copy went to the Directorate of Personnel, a third to the dependants or claimants of rights thereof.

The certificate would enable the carrier to liquidate, do away with or reclaim all properties in the name of the deceased.

"I told the secretary to tell you that it is not our prerogative to issue you with the certificate. I told her to pass on this message. I don't know why she didn't tell you."

Loyaan's voice was anxious: "Why can't you issue it to me, pray?"

A bit too theatrical to be believed, Xassan finally said:

"Soyaan is from this day onwards state property and will be treated as such. They've come for and have taken his file. I worked on the file last night. Soyaan: a property of the state."

"Property of the state?"

"Yes. He is the property of the General."

"How do you mean?"

"They are rewriting your family's history, Soyaan's and the whole lot. Like the Russians rewrote Lenin's, Stalin's or that of any of the heroes their system created to survive subversion from within or without. They will need your co-operation, I am sure."

"That they won't get."

"I wouldn't be so certain."

There would be more contradictions and more gaps in Soyaan's life than there were in Lenin's or Brezhnev's or the General's or, for that matter, Stalin's. It was one thing to account for the reasons which had led a given man to do something; it was another to make a dead man account for the life imagined for him by another. What if Loyaan made Soyaan's writings public? What if he showed how ridiculous they were by proving that Soyaan had been till his last moment a man against the régime? The voice: *Calm down. Don't lose your calm. You should telephone the Minister to the Presidency and arrange to see him. Ask for an explanation. Why this, why that? Why was Soyaan declared state property? Don't jump, don't shoot before you've isolated and studied the target.*

"Heroes are state property. So are those executed by firing-squad. We don't deal with the files of either. The ten sheikhs recently executed, for instance. We don't even have numbers for their tombs. We don't know where they are buried, if they were."

"But Soyaan has a number."

"A revolutionary hero, an anti-revolutionary reactionary. . . ."

"Where are we, Xassan? Is this not Somalia?"

108

The telephone rang. Xassan answered it. A chorus of "ha's" and "ha's". He replaced the receiver. It was a long time before he said anything. When he spoke:

"That was the Minister to the Presidency."

"What did he want?"

"He asked if I had seen and spoken to you."

"What did you say?"

"I said I had."

"What did he say?"

"Nothing."

Loyaan wondered but didn't dare ask the Director if he could use his telephone, call up and arrange an appointment for tomorrow with the Minister to the Presidency. Xassan had the sensitivity to have anticipated this. He pushed the apparatus closer to Loyaan and by doing so he half-raised himself from his chair. He then got up.

"Don't say you are calling him from here. But use it."

"Do you have his number?"

Xassan gave him the number, then went out to give him the comfort of privacy when talking to the Minister to the Presidency. Loyaan dialled the number. He spoke with the secretary to the Minister, and then to the man himself.

"I have an appointment with the Minister to the Presidency for the day after tomorrow," he said to Ladan. "I called him and arranged one. I believe he has the answers to my questions."

"Soyaan as state property — this is the most ludicrous thing I've heard."

Was she half-laughing? Had Ladan suddenly changed, her face, her features? She was the rags of her old self which had caught fire, she was and became very interested in the details of conspiracies and who said what about whom. Yes, yes, she had eaten. So had Mother (she had gone to call on some relatives; she wouldn't be back until late in the afternoon). The taste of his salted words lingered on the periphery of his tongue weighed down with insipidity as he took mouthfuls of the fish and the rice Ladan had made for him. Soyaan had loved sea-food. He would have feasted his appetite. (It was here that Loyaan's memory swam away back to days when Ladan was barely two. How the two had loved her. How the twins had protected her from those murderous looks of Keynaan and the — at times —

indifferent attitudes of Qumman to a girl. They would invest in Ladan their hopes, they would trust their future with her. They used to take turns telling her fables from faraway lands, the sagas of Iceland and Norway, the Nights of Arabia, the stories of Tagore, the tales of Ukraine and those of China. They fed her small brain on figures round, complete and open-ended. They trained her young mind with the aid of circles, squares and trigonometry. She was like them — except she was a girl. *The world is an egg and it awaits your breaking it. Clear the mistiness of the white off your eyes and the yolk is yours — yellow and sick, yes, but yours for the asking, for the taking.*) Ladan was half-laughing, half-challenging him: Ladan was Ladan again.

"What do they want?" she said.

"They've got what they wanted. Father helped them get what they wanted. They badly needed his testimony. It is his soul they were after. And they bought it. What I don't quite get is the role the Minister to the Presidency plays in all this."

"Neither do I."

He saw it large and huge like the clear details of a brilliant idea, he saw it against the rough unevenness of the surrounds. He saw the nervous butterfly with one wing already gone and the other wounded. It entered, and licked its own head as though it were a fly washing itself in the cleanness of a thought.

"It is his soul they are after," she then said.

"If we let them."

The combed dust, the sunshine, the shade, all life's comforts and discomforts. *These are mine and I shall use them,* said the voice inside him, encouraging him on, giving him the impetus needed to struggle to save the soul of Soyaan since he couldn't save the body.

"What will you do now?"

"I shall go and see Margaritta."

"Margaritta? When?"

"After five. I shall go and see Soyaan's queen, Margaritta. Maybe she knows many things most of us don't."

110

Chapter Eight

Like a child in a cot being rocked to sleep by a woman who sings a lullaby in a language foreign to his ears; the child with eyes half-closed, his mouth moving as he sucks a pebble — not listening to the song, but feeling the rhythm of the lullaby. The woman stops rocking. The child opens his eyes. Both hear a cow's mooing and a goat's bleating approach. The woman resumes the rocking; the child bursts into a hysterical crying. The woman gives the child her milkless breasts. Quiet a second or so. Enraged — the cry again. He doesn't even accept to play with the pebble or have his hunger filled with strange breasts.

He walked up and down roads with no names. Would one of them be named after Soyaan? And which one? Up and down, the roads dusty, the village poor, the alleys narrow like a bottle's neck, alleys which ran into and ended in dusty dead-ends. To the left, a blind curve. To the right, a mosque with a well and men that streamed in or out, telling a rosary of wishes to Him who knew all their secrets before they even uttered them. They surely were telling Him how unhappy they were under the General's régime, thought Loyaan. They surely were reminding Him of His responsibility towards the families of the ten sheikhs recently executed — the sheikhs whom He should have avenged earlier. Goats. Cowsheds. Other prominent landmarks in villages of Mogadiscio, the non-cosmopolitan sections of this city. In this village there were no huge, monumental placards bearing the General's portrait and boasting in statistical quotations the progress and success of the revolution. These would have been "a contradiction in terms". Besides, when once or twice they had a costly portrait painted and brought here, well before the night had turned its back on the city, the eyes of the General had been pierced and anti-Soviet slogans had been scribbled on it. This village was purged the following day; three hundred boys and girls were taken for interrogation. Of the three hundred, about fifteen had been held in custody. They were still there. Untried. Tortured nightly. "Why have you written those anti-Soviet slogans? Who was it paid you to pierce the eyes of the

111

Father of the Nation? American Imperialists? Who? Names, names, we want names." *Now, now . . . don't you get carried away. You are looking for Margaritta. Address yourself to the issue at hand. Yes, Margaritta. First things first. Find her house, first. Then talk to her. And talk sense. You mustn't let yourself get emotional. It doesn't help anybody. It doesn't help the cause.*

Maybe he should ask the shop-keepers in the area if they knew Margaritta or her mother, Loyaan thought. Describe? A tall, beautiful woman, with large breasts, half-Italian, half-Somali, and with a child; and a villa, her own. *Can't you do any better, Loyaan?* challenged the voice in him. Ask. They know no better, anyway. Unless you play the game by its rules: identify the person by tribe. And the computer in their heads would be set into motion. If they didn't know the person you wished to contact, the villagers would give you the address of another clansman or clanswoman who would become your honeyguide, buzzing ahead of you until you are shown the honey-suckle you're looking for. But what tribe was Margaritta?

"Excuse me, please."

He stood before a group of women who were sitting in front of their mud huts, enjoying the cool breeze of the evening. Not very far away were a covey of chicks and their mother-hen: these took fright and ran for cover.

"Yes?"

You can't withdraw now that you've gone thus far. Ask. Look them in the face. Don't be shy, don't be ridiculous. Come on. Ask. Re-sift your thoughts.

"I am looking for a young *mistione* woman whose name is Margaritta. She has a small son. There is her mother whose name I do not know. The villa is hers. And the son is a few months old."

Consultations. The four women looked up at him and were silent. He had given them too much information. He had probably confused them. Why tell them that the villa was hers?

"Megrita?"

"Margaritta? Her son's name is Marco."

Further consultations. One of the women whispered loud enough to the others that perhaps the *mistione* woman this man was looking for was the daughter of that woman (she mentioned the name of a tribe) who was hard of hearing. Did they know the one she was talking about? The one with the car and the child, eh? They nodded their

112

heads. She gave the directions. It was past the Orientation Centre, two lefts, a right and another left. A gate still wet with green paint.

"Also would you kindly tell me where I might get bars of chocolate or things like that for the child?"

"There is a shop as you turn into the street this woman's house is on. You can't miss it."

"I thank you very much."

The night hadn't begun to light a festival of tropical stars. The moon remained ensconced in the twilight-tinged colours of the evening. The air was pleasant, a cool oceanic breeze with a slight touch of monsoon, and the odour of rain. The sky: a veranda of blueness, a canopy of safe-return, a covering for those flights of birds which went westwards in their journey home as they heralded the coming of the end, the coming of the hour, *his hour*. Loyaan came out of the shop. He had a chocolate box in his tight grip. His wisdom teeth tasted and told of that sense of betrayal common to moments such as this. He asked: is this the right thing to buy for a child of Marco's age? The green gate was right in front of him now. There was no return. He pressed the bell. And he waited.

"They came and searched the house. They had a warrant properly signed. They arrived just as the sun emerged from the sand dunes. There were three of them. One stayed behind in the car, the other two entered."

"What did they find?"

"Don't you want to know what they were looking for?"

"All right, what were they looking for?"

"Have you not come looking for it yourself?"

"What have I come in search of?"

"You tell me. What was it they came looking for?"

"No, you tell me."

"What have you come in search of, Loyaan?"

A pause. With his right foot, he pushed the gate inwards. She got the message all right. She opened the door wider. She let him enter further. She gave him all the time necessary to survey the place, to take everything in, and to say this:

"Shall we talk things over, please?"

113

The night finally came down, a robe wrapped in veiled darkness like the black-scarved puritanism of a Muslim. The muezzin's call of *Akbars* was chanted as though from a bulletin written with Allah's water of ablution. The night finally descended down the trees in Margaritta's garden like an abstract thought — vague like the sky's waistline; and uncontainable like the secrets of a woman. Bats chirpy, noisy and attention-seeking. And above Loyaan's and Margaritta's heads, hanging down from a tree as though keeping the fruit company, there was an electric bulb. It was on. Moths, fragile and skippy, circled about it like flies around a corpse dead long ago; like children who feast when to their village comes a vehicle; children touching, running away from it, playful, touchingly joyful. Dare he ask, speak now?

She had given him a rocking-chair and placed him in the spot that had been Soyaan's favourite. But did he know? She wouldn't tell him if he did not. She wouldn't if Soyaan hadn't. That meant she had something all her own, like a secret one was privileged to hold on to. She was sorry that Marco, "on account of a small indisposition", couldn't join them. Her mother had come and shouted a greeting from a distance but immediately withdrew. Low tables. Drinks of one's choice. Maids. Marco's maid, a girl still in her teens. But because of his indisposition the maids were there in his room today. Quiet the night. Soft the breeze. The moths moved about in frenzy. The *mayooko* buzzed in their ears. They sat in silence. Loyaan felt he had been through this before. He sensed he had known all this. Something in him told him that he had sat in the same place, that he had used the same rocking-chair, that he had drunk from the same glass. But had he ever known Margaritta? Had he known her in all the manners a man knows a woman? Had he? A voice within him: *remember who you are, remember why you are here, remember. Remember your responsibility.*

"Your father Keynaan has been a great embarrassment, hasn't he?"

The word again. *Embarrassment. Embarrassment.*

"Yes, yes. He has been. Yes."

"Somebody rang me at work this morning and suggested we could use it. A mutual friend, someone who thought I would be delighted to learn that Soyaan was knighted a hero of the Revolution."

"Who?"

"Somebody who thought the world would be interested in hearing about Soyaan being knighted."

She held her hand in mid-movement, meaning: would he like ice with his whisky or would he like it straight? He was undecided when she dropped some into it and bent to get some more. Soyaan's indecision about whether or not to have his whisky straight was something she had been used to. He pulled the glass from under her threatening ice-cube in the teeth of the picker.

"And what did you say to this man who rang you at work?"

"I was very polite."

"You said ANSA Rome wouldn't be interested in buying the news item — nor would other agencies. You said that ANSA Rome wouldn't think that Soyaan's name warranted the expense of the telex and other news facilities. You said, in short, that Soyaan was not well known anywhere. Isn't that what you said?"

"How do you know?"

The younger of the maids brought in, on saucers, some salted peanuts imported from Italy. She placed a saucer before each of them. Barefooted and quiet, she retreated.

"I asked you: how did you know?"

"I asked you: isn't that what you said to him?"

"Him?"

"Yes, him."

"Well, in that case. . . ."

He could have sworn he had had this conversation before. He could have sworn he had whisky *liscio* under the same tree long, long ago. Although his seventh sense told him that she had little faith in him, that she had not quite reached the point where she would put her trust in him completely. A he and not a she. If so, was it the Minister to the Presidency who had called her? Come to think of it, it was this very man who once made reference to "a certain woman whom you, Loyaan, should contact or who will contact you". Did this not occur long before anything else, long before the naming of a street after Soyaan, long before he became state property?

"I rang him a second after you had rung off."

"Him who?"

"The Minister to the Presidency."

"Is that so?"

He was silent. The night, instead, stirred as if from a brief sleep.

115

The bats awoke. The moths behaved as if agitated. There came and went a cat of enormous ugliness. Then they also heard Marco's cry. As this died down, Margaritta's mother's hard screaming filled their ears. She was giving instructions to one of the maids to wash the child's linen and to the other to bring in the cot and the toys.

"Yes. You rang the Minister to the Presidency. Then what, Margaritta?"

"I don't know how much of Soyaan's political commitments you've been made familiar with, how much of his 'other' life you've been told about. I know that he talked about you as one would of a younger brother, a man less mature politically, less conscious of social and political pressures — a younger brother in every sense. He used to say for instance that you were so organised and so methodical you never lost anything. 'Who loses one thing has a better chance of finding another thing long lost and abandoned. You must lose something in order, while searching for that very thing, to find another thing long lost and abandoned.' Anyway, I don't know where to start, I don't know what you know and what you don't, and I certainly don't want to bore you with repetitive banalities."

The sky, or what he could see of it, flaunted, like a peacock, its starry-eyed exhibitionism. The moon dwelled in a ringed pen, encircled by its young, some bright, some less bright, some conspicuous and some less so. Margaritta's face was lit up as she put the flames of the matchstick she had struck to the cigarette in her mouth. A long lungful of smoke, then:

"Did you know, for example, that he had been the man who reported on anything to do with the Soviet experts and in particular the civilian technicians, the teachers, the doctors, plus, of course, their 'retainers' — that is, all experts from the Eastern European socialist bloc? He was answerable. He spoke no Russian — an insurmountable difficulty, certainly. But he had a team of Somalis who spoke the language as well as a Somali speaks any foreign language. He had another team of Soviet experts who informed on the others and who, in turn, informed on Soyaan and his 'un-Soviet activities'. *Morale della storia* : he had thin files, a file on each Soviet expert in this country, thin files which, feather-like, flew with their weightlessness, while the Soviet Embassy here had thick files on every member of the team, so thick that when, undetected, Soyaan walked into the office of the Minister to the Presidency and saw one in Russian code

116

on another colleague of his, he couldn't lift it off the table. Now, now, look, don't read me wrongly, I am not drawing any conclusions, neither do I want you to. I just, well, let me see. . . ."

The moths became jumpier. The mosquitoes buzzed louder. The breeze was cool. When their glasses were empty Margaritta shouted to one of the maids to get them more ice. She poured *un dito* straight into his glass, then added another.

"In this country, rumour rules. O.K.? There is a rumour, for example, that one of the Vice-Presidents is pro-Western. Of course, it didn't mean anything to Soyaan, nor will it to you either, I hope; but social reality makes tribal allegiances an exigency one cannot live without. The Vice-President is your mother's tribesman. So. This Vice-President, rumour has it, was the one who initially hired Soyaan to open files and report on every Soviet expert in this country; on every Cuban; on every East German. Rumour has it that it was this very Vice-President who had Soyaan transferred from the Directorate of Planning to the Presidency."

"Go on."

"But the General, in a convenient reshuffle the Soviets asked for, was given the chance to nominate the present Minister to the Presidency to the post. A Russia-trained officer, good friends, good contacts, et cetera, et cetera. Within a month of his being appointed the files became thinner and less interesting, less intriguing."

The maid came in with a jugful of ice. She also brought them a new set of saucers heavy with salted peanuts. She placed one in front of Loyaan and another in front of Margaritta. She took away the empty saucers and the empty jug. She withdrew.

"How do you know of all this?" Loyaan asked.

An ice-cube in her drink. "Prepare yourself for a thickening plot."

"I am."

She raised her glass to him before taking a sip.

"My mother is Somali, remember. It means that I, too, have Somali clansmen. And the Minister to the Presidency is the son of one of my mother's distant cousins. As a matter of fact, he and I grew up together in more or less the same surroundings. Well, that is not quite true. Let us say he used to come to our house and my mother used to fill the skeletal remains of a never-parting ghost with nourishing food and life."

"Was he ever your lover?"

117

"You are being indiscreet."

Both let that pass.

"It was he introduced you to Soyaan?"

"Not precisely."

"He talked about him again and again and you finally. . . ."

"Something like that."

"Like what?"

"I went with the Minister to the Presidency to a party at which I ran into Soyaan who remembered (unlike you) that we had met years previously in Italy."

"Unlike who?"

"Yes. Unlike you."

"In what way?"

"To return to the topic at hand. . . ."

"No, no. Please."

"What?"

"I am interested."

"Soyaan's telephone was under control, his movements had been bugged . . . what is it now? Don't you want me to continue, to tell you more? Well, don't you?"

Loyaan suddenly got up.

"This drink is reaching my inhibited veins of Islamic puritanism and breaking down my defences. I need something to eat. I need a full stomach before I can cope with this."

She looked up at him. "Let me see what is in the fridge. We can make something here."

"No, no. Let's go and have a meal out."

"A meal out?"

He crushed the cigarette under his heel.

"Let me treat you to a meal out."

"Really, Loyaan."

"Unlike Soyaan. . . ."

"Yes?"

"Come. Let me buy you a meal out. Please. Come."

A little girl of barely four, with not a stitch of clothing on, entered the restaurant and went straight to the table at which Loyaan and Margaritta were seated. She picked up Loyaan's glass, and, with one single choking gulp, sent the fruit juice down her noisy

118

throat. Margaritta and Loyaan silently stared at her, whereas the waiter came down upon her with a subordinate's unjustified fury. With one wise move, lifting her hand, Margaritta managed to arrest the man's raised arm: she told him to leave the little girl alone. The little girl, for her part, walked out defiant and silent as when she had entered. She behaved as though she had done nothing wrong. She looked at the furious waiter just before she disappeared into the howling dust and wind of the night.

Loyaan and Margaritta were impressed.

"I met Soyaan and you the same night in Bologna years ago when we were students, you in Bologna, Soyaan in Rome, and I in Padova. I had come to the *dibattito* entitled *'Marxismo e il continente nero'* held under the auspices of the Consiglio Regionale dei Communisti Milittanti. You were with a woman — Italian, small nose, pretty face, wearing glasses — and she was glued to you. Soyaan had come alone. I was with my former husband. There was Medina. . . ."

"Medina?"

"Medina, the journalist. Her brother Nasser. There was Ahmed-Wellie, there were all the student activists, there was Xassan Guante, Razak, and all those who during those hot months occupied the Somali Embassy in Rome. Soyaan had taken the floor that night. The walls and halls of wintery Bologna echoed with the urgency of his voice. He stood out as being the most sensible of all those who rose to make the mikes register and magnify, to mechanical reproduction, the immediacy of the senseless phrases which they uttered. Do you remember snubbing me?"

"Who were you with?"

"My former husband."

"You have been married?"

"Yes."

"Who was your husband?"

"Italian."

"And where is he?"

"Where Italians usually are: in Italy. We are separated, have been for the past six years, and he lives with another woman, I presume in Rome. Why do you ask all this?"

"The child. Soyaan. This other man."

"The Minister to the Presidency?"

119

"No. Your former husband. Now you've brought in a fourth and more complications."

"I bore Soyaan my love. Not my husband. I bore Marco. He is mine now as he will be when courts review matrimony, concede or don't concede divorces. I see no complications."

"If you don't, I don't either."

At this point, who should come but the waiter. He arrived wearing a smile. He balanced the plates on his extended arms: *zuppa di pesce* and a slice of bread for Loyaan; a *scaloppina alla Milanese* and a mixed salad for the signora. Would the signore like to order the *seconda?* The waiter brought them a typed menu protected in polythene from the destructive humidity of Mogadiscio. *Capocetto Nero*: the name of the restaurant. One would think one was in a province of Italy — the way the food was displayed, the style, the table-cloths and the manner in which they were changed. Loyaan wouldn't look at the menu for now. He would later. What of the signora? Would they like *vino sciolto?* Or Chianti? Or Barbera? What? The waiter, despite the strong Somali accent when speaking Italian, made the minds of Loyaan and Margaritta travel back to Italy for a moment. Each was in a different world. Each kept different company. They lived in different cities as well. Loyaan waved the waiter away. As for Margaritta, she squeezed her lemon, she cut up her *scaloppina alla Milanese* into manageable mouthfuls; he ate his *zuppa*. Then:

"What was your reaction to the news about Soyaan being made a hero of the revolution and a street being named after him? How did you react to Keynaan's interview in the paper?"

She leaned backwards a little as if taking a fresh look at a painting she had seen previously. Her features contracted, her face concentrated, but she was silent for a long, long time. Then she bent down and took a slice of cucumber which she put on the same plate as her scaloppina, salted it and then ate it. She set her fork down, but held the knife in her hand.

"I went back and re-read the Memorandum."

"What Memorandum?"

"The one you're looking for."

"Of course."

"I am not *them*. You have no reason to play any of these hide-and-seek games with me. I am not *them*. So don't fear. There won't

120

be any knocking on your door before dawn-break. And I am an Italian citizen. And I work for ANSA. All right?"

A passive nod of the head acknowledged that. She went on.

"I am talking about the Memorandum which the Minister to the Presidency mentioned to you on the day of the burial. I am talking specifically about one of the Memorandums which I have in my own possession. All right?"

"One of the Memorandums?"

"Yes, one of them."

"How many are there in existence?"

"Let us say I know of two."

"And where is the other one?"

"Don't shout."

"I am not shouting," he shouted.

"Sorry."

"Where is the other one?"

"This conversation is getting out of hand."

"I've heard that before."

"You will hear it again."

Calm down, Loyaan, said the voice within him. *Have a hold on yourself again. Calm down. Count to ten. One. Two. Three. Hell! Meanwhile: touch. Reacquaint yourself with the physicality of the room. Take a spoonful of your soup. Remember. You are in a restaurant in Mogadiscio. You are having a conversation with Margaritta. Who is she? Look. Don't fear. Look. Is she real? On whose side is she? Listen.*

"Soyaan wrote several brief to-the-point memos. Brief, why brief? There were practical reasons. Being semi-illiterate, the General and the members of his oligarchy wouldn't even start reading if the memos were long: and he avoided, wherever possible, using the jargon common in literature of the left. He also wanted to discipline himself. He wrote some of these under stress: there were those assigned to him personally by the Vice-President I mentioned earlier. Now those were officially solicited and I wouldn't know where they are."

"Where is the other one?"

"Don't you want to know what they are about?"

"If I see them I can read them unless they were written in Russian code. I suspect that Soyaan was incapable of doing that. His Russian was practically non-existent despite his numerous visits there."

121

"Talking about Russian visits, do you recall who led the most important Somali delegation that has visited the Soviet Union? Do you recall Soyaan's first visit to that country?"

"What was so important about that?"

"It was during that visit that the first mention of this project filled Soyaan's gaping map with the curiosity of its juiciness; to research into something of national use, that is what he always wanted. Now who led the delegation?"

"The same Vice-President, supposedly pro-Western, yes?"

"Right."

Fork against knife. The waiter came to solicit their interest in the food displayed since the kitchen was now closed and there wouldn't be anything hot. Only coffee or capuccino. Seeing, however, that neither had quite finished the plates placed in front of them half an hour before, the waiter retreated, promising to return when called.

"You mentioned the existence of two Memorandums. You've said that you have one of them in your possession. Do you know where the other is? Do you know where I might find the other?"

"I am not quite sure."

"You are not quite sure?"

"I am not quite sure if the person who I think might know where it is is a person whose name I should mention at this stage. A good friend of Soyaan's and mine as well."

"What is this person's name, please?"

Her eyes were hard, her look rigid. She stared at him. She angrily pushed away her plate, she crossed the fork and knife like soldiers their guns when resting.

"You behave like those French policemen near St Michel who the moment they see an Algerian-looking fellow stride up to him and with one hand outstretched shout like a mendicant what they wish to have — except they don't cry, 'Alms, please,' but *'Document, s'il vous plaît.'* They believe it is their right to do so. . . . Name, please. With your hand flattened on the table, looking me in the eyes: 'Name, please.' "

The voice within him helped with some advice. *Calm down, don't say anything. She is not angry with you, nor does she have a good reason to be. She is having a quarrel with Soyaan.* So: apologies.

"I am sorry."

" 'Name, please'," she mimicked him.

122

The trace of a genuine smile which she hid away like a child the pleasure of wetting-shame, eyes down, but her face relaxed. She picked up the fork and with it took a slice of tomato which she salted and ate. She put her hand into her bag. She selected a ballpoint pen and a piece of writing paper from the mess of powder-pads, tampons and odds and ends of a woman of her background. She wrote the name down on the paper. She passed it to him.

"Thanks."

But why was she being so cautious suddenly? *Look at what is in front of you, idiot. Spell it: Ibrahim. Say it to yourself. Ibrahim.* Had she confused her long vowels with the short ones? Had she wrongly transliterated the Somali vowels?

"Ibrahim?" he asked softly. "Do you mean Ibrahim nicknamed Il Siciliano? I don't know him personally. But is that who you mean?"

"A most gentle man."

"And you think he has it?"

She looked to this and that side as if suspicious. She could certainly trust him, couldn't she? Besides, he had heard the name before. Was it from his mother or was it Ladan? What did the man do? Where could Loyaan find him? What was his role in the pastiche?

"The secretary/typist whom the Security have imprisoned and tortured: did you hear of that?"

"Yes?"

"That is his sister."

"Then that is Ibrahim, Il Siciliano."

"Yes, yes. That is him."

Time to recover from the shock. Then: :

"Ibrahim, Il Siciliano. Of course."

"He is Ibrahim Musse Ilmog."

They were the only two in the restaurant now. They got their bill without even asking for it. Loyaan, despite Margaritta's *femminista* cries of equality of the sexes, paid for the bill. He tipped the waiter generously, too.

"Now where do we go from here? Aren't you going to give me the Memo?"

"There is something else I wanted you to see."

"I want to see the Memorandum."

"Not tonight. It is in my bank locker. I haven't got it at home.

123

I shall go and withdraw it tomorrow. No, but there is something I want you to see. I'll give you a lift home later."

"What?"

"Let us go."

In a car, moving speedily homewards, Margaritta:

"Africa, for nearly a century, was governed with the iron hand of European colonial economic interests: these ran Africa as though it were a torture-chamber. Africa has known the iron rod, the whip-lash, thumb-screwing and removing of testicles: Africa has been humiliated one way or another. I am not saying anything new if I add that whether British, French, Belgian, Spanish, Portuguese or Italian, the colonial mafiadoms which, on behalf of the civilised world, administered the colonies barbarously, savagely, never considered it expedient to allow the sub-human subjects under their administration the same democratic rights as they themselves had, both in their own countries and in their privileged positions as rulers, viceroys or governors. For the colonies, they created a small élite that, in a world of make-believe, behaved as though they were on a par with their European classmates, their university colleagues. But wait.

"The sixties in Africa were years of colourful neckties, cheery smiles, group photographs; the sixties were 'civil'. Plane-loads of experts. After-midnight parties. 'Civil liberties'. Parliamentary elections whether with/for/without political persuasions. It was an African who now warmed the seat of the European with the peoples' discontent amassing day after day, night after night. Africa: a text-book reproduction of European values and western thinking. The pages of the sixties were not always written with the glowing letters of hopeful felicities and naiveties that false independence produced in people. There was no equal distribution of responsibility; there was economic dependence on the multinational, the return of the former European colonial as the UN expert, et cetera, and a discontinuous interruption to the history and methods of colonial rule. Came the seventies. Army coups. Barefaced dictatorships. We see Africa 'taken back' to an era she had lived through before, the era of European dictatorship, concentration-camps. Africa is again a torture chamber. Africa is humiliation. 'Africa,' Soyaan used to say, 'embarrasses me.' What has become of the élite who recreated these false hopes in the hearts of the African masses? Some have served and are serving tormented years of detention. Most have left their countries. Jobs with UNESCO, FAO; jobs in the oil-rich Gulf States."

She slowed down. She turned a curve.

"What of countries which still are run 'in the false democracies of the sixties', countries such as Senegal, say, or Kenya?"

"One a colony of France, to all intents and purposes, the other a large concentration-camp administered by a Kikuyu oligarchy and the British settler-master."

Another sandy curve. The car skidded a little. Margaritta nearly lost control of the wheel, but regained it instantly and therefore sighed. She changed gear.

"Are you saying that Africa is the same or nearly the same torture-chamber as it was when the colonials were here? Or are you saying that African dictatorships are but a re-creation of the same methods and things these career-soldiers learned from their colonial masters during the toughest struggles?"

"Or something like that."

A blind bend. Margaritta slowed down. She flicked the dipper, helped it dip faster with her hand. That perhaps was the last turn they would go into, for she had come to a complete halt and got out of the car. She opened the recently painted green door with care, she returned, and switched off the engine.

"We've arrived."

He followed her in, making no noise.

For Loyaan the rocking-chair and for Margaritta the one she had before they went out to the restaurant. But she had entered the house (he said he actually preferred they sat in the garden where the drinks were) and come back carrying with her the framed photograph of her Marco a month old. Small as the fist of an adult, Marco was curled into the size of a ring-finger. She dismantled the frame. She showed Loyaan the inscription Soyaan had scribbled on the back of the photograph, his handwriting spare and tiny. Loyaan read and re-read the salutary greetings of Soyaan to "My son, my love, my only and only one". Such small writing. Loyaan was having difficulty reading it.He distanced the writing from his eyes. The light-bulb shone brightest when quietest, he thought. He read:

On the hill the city lights leap up

But here in the fields the quiet dusk folds down
A man lies in a ditch. He listens hard. . . .
They are coming, and he can run no further
    He will die.

They have taken away his whip and gun
He will die, this cursed son. The first pursuer
Is here. The darkness is ready to give him up
He has, at most, a hundred breaths to draw. . . .
The man's body will rot under lime, and that soon
But the parades have taught his uniform to march.
The hunters close in: do they feel the danger?
When they wrench his body to pieces, will they hear
A sigh as his spirit is sucked into the air
That *they* must breathe? . . .

        And who shall save *them*
If after all the years and all the deaths
They find a world still pitiless, a street
Where no grass of love grows over the hard stone.

He checked the date Soyaan had made the inscription: three
months ago. And on the extreme end of the top margin there was the
omniferous Hindu symbol M. M to the power of 2: Margaritta and
Marco; Margaritta and "my love, my son, my only one". I/M and
comrade-in-project: Ibrahim and Margaritta: comrade in my project?
Or did the letter M here stand for the names of Margaritta, Marco
and Ibrahim's sister? What was her name? Mulki? *"He will die, this
cursed man. The first pursuer is here."*

    He has, at most, a hundred breaths to draw. . . .
    But the parades have taught his uniform to march. . . .
    When they wrench his body to pieces, will they hear
    A sigh as his spirit is sucked into the air
      That *they* must breathe?

Had he chosen the poem randomly? Did these religious and
military metaphors contain more than the intrinsic significance that
one might get on the first reading? What had happened three months

126

ago? Why had he chosen this particular date? Why had he under-lined the *they*?

"It was when the ten sheikhs were executed. The very day."

Loyaan gave a grunt of delusion. He said nothing until after he had put the photograph back in its frame and re-mounted the frame. He faced the still eyes of Marco, again the size of a knuckle. And:

"You knew him personally?"

"Who?"

"Ibrahim Il Siciliano, you pronounce his name."

"Yes. He is a good friend of Ahmed-Wellie's as well."

His voice trembled with the urgency of the secret he was hiding from her. For Loyaan now began to suspect that Ahmed-Wellie might . . . no, never mind that now.

"And his sister?" he said suddenly.

"What about her?"

"Do you know her name? Do you know what 'M to the power of 2' means?"

"N like in Nimrod?"

"No, M like in Machiavelli."

"What is all this about?"

"Do you know Mulki?"

"No, I don't. Why? Something to do with the interview?"

With one swig, he gulped down his drink.

"In what way can we convince Soyaan's friends that he died faithful to his principles?"

"People are wicked inside. I cannot look my friends in the eyes."

"Very embarrassing."

"Soyaan initialled a mystery of alphabets on certain pieces of paper found in his trousers and shirt pockets. A mystery of alphabets like 'M to the power of 2', like 'I oblique M' in connection with a project. Curious things, yes. But they seem to have meaning. For a start, we can demystify his alphabet of secrets."

"Explain."

"Like M to the power of 2. Mogadiscio-Moscow."

"M to the power of 2?"

His tongue was fattening in the greasy pool of drinks. She poured him more as requested. She added another *dito* into hers. They raised their glasses in a toast.

"Margaritta and Marco."

"Loyaan and the family."

The drink had clearly got to his thinking nerves and incapacitated them so suddenly that Margaritta was caught unprepared for it. She must take him home now while she could. So she stood up and stretched her yawning arms and opened her mouth. She suggested she accompanied him home in the car before either fell asleep. She had him rise. She supported him out of the chair (she was almost as tall as he) and finally into the car. His neck loosened into the shapelessness of sleep as soon as the vehicle moved; his head swung like a pendulum timing the unslept hours of previous nights; his tongue, heavy as a fattened bull, snored the unspoken, uncensored dreams of these tormented days and evenings. When she braked brutally too quickly, he fell forwards, forehead first.

"We're home, and the lights are on," she said. "Can you wait on your own until the door is opened, or do you want me to face your mother and your sister and have them curse me and all that?"

"Do you think I am drunk?" he said.

The window opened. Then the door. Qumman. Then Ladan. The two women moved in on the car, each coming slowly, with their hands shielding their eyes.

"Who is it?" Qumman's voice rang with fear.

Loyaan opened the door of the car, but his left leg tripped on his right, and he fell over. That was an ugly scene for Margaritta. She opened her door and got out. But before she walked around to help Loyaan rise, she heard:

"We can do that ourselves. Rest in peace. And good night."

The lights burned as they had burned before his return all that night. Qumman and Ladan couldn't bring themselves to sleep because they were worried. Also: Ibrahim Il Siciliano had come and waited for not less than five hours. He had refused to share any secrets with either mother or sister. Alone, he had chain-smoked and read and waited. Had *they* removed Loyaan? was the question which crossed the minds of all three. Thank God he was back.

He was too drunk and too sleepy to be told of this important visit.

He started, and woke up lying in sweat just before dawnbreak. He was being pursued, he was being chased by a one-armed beggar in green tatters, wearing a starry uniform of some sort. The one-armed man had a gun in his unamputated hand, and there was another man with a dog on a lead just behind him. The three chased Loyaan up and down the stairs of a huge building. And while running away from these, he had seen framed the photograph of the Minister to the Presidency and it took its place next to the portrait of the General. He had shouted a name before he started and woke up lying in sweat. He had shouted the name Ibrahim. Now that Mulki had been tortured, now that she had refused to co-operate, the men of the Security had come for Ibrahim. He would face a firing-squad, someone said. "No, no, he won't," had shouted Loyaan. "You shoot me instead."

Qumman and Ladan took turns sitting by his bed worriedly until the sun woke up.

Chapter Nine

Like an old woman past her hundredth year, an old woman lying on her belly on a bed under the open sky. Very near her is a small child playfully fiddling with a wreck of naked radio wires. She hears the child's gurgling delight as he crunches and munches the wire and is herself content that the child is. Behind the two, a few hundred or so yards away, in a westward direction, there is an open-mouthed grave. Beside it, there is a burial-mound.

Loyaan was now standing in front of an imposing building which had been the pride of the Ministry of Constructions. With it, the Ministry had gained the confidence of the General; its Minister was honoured, offered a medal of a star. With this colossal monstrosity, it was proven that a local could build just as ugly a thing if opportunity came his way. From start to finish, beginning with the blueprints, during the planning stage, during the filling of the foundation, the plan was taken to and shown to the General for approval. Naturally nobody told him that Mussolini's era of ENI-constructions and Stalin's had served as points of departure. The architects and the engineers shared amiable dialogues with him. This was commemorated with a group photograph which appeared in the only daily paper. The Head of the Team accepted, without qualification, all the changes suggested by the General. Of course, he knew better. Hear, hear! See and behold the General standing in front of the Learned Gowns of the Department of Jurisprudence, Groomed Academes and Members of the Diplomatic Corps. Listen to his Maiden Speech. This is the Judiciary Year. Hear him stammer. Hearken and listen: is he mad? How can he talk of justice when in the same breath he mentions institutions such as the Security Services or the Security Courts? Listen to his voice like a sensitive tuner to the machine when testing a tape for scratches and you will sense his fear, you will understand why he stammers when talking of social justice.

Agh! The pain in the head, the hangover of last night. How embarrassing for Margaritta as well, how embarrassing for all. Was

130

that his migraine come back? How the pain hammered and split the head in two when it hit, when it arrived, how it hurt. He was half an hour early for the appointment with Ibrahim. To be precise, he was thirty-six minutes early. Why, he felt the weight of his and Mother's embarrassing silent stare which said: "How can you expect me, *naif* that you are, to embrace Margaritta and accept her child as Soyaan's and she as his woman?" He held his head in his hands, He now sat on a bench there.

In the sunny background, the building gave him the impression of having just sprouted that instant out of the rubble and waste all around. For just behind it, down the slope, stretched an asphalt street separating it from the stone houses which had merged with the brown earth that would eventually swallow up everything. The stone houses of Shanganni, it appeared, had withstood the weather and the whims of powerful governments and men. He got up. He lit a cigarette. He smoked his veined lungs and enjoyed the feel and the spread of the drawn smoke. He walked away from the building — seeing it in the reflection of its glassy windows, imagining it as a giant ship about to sink in wavefuls of storm and dust. Loyaan headed in the direction of the sea.

The sea foamed, it frothed, it flirted with the sun which teased it. The sea roared. It made Loyaan rehearse a line just half-recalled. And in the distance, way down waveful of events: the twins. There were ships flying foreign flags, big and small boats carrying bananas and other merchandise, ships which had dropped anchor. And out of the blue clearness of the waters emerges Keynaan, the tyrant: in his right hand, he grips a club at its butt-end; in his left, the rubber ball which he has torn in two, the rubber ball upon which the twins had together drawn a complete and an illustrated mini-atlas. A world with no frontiers. A world of their own fantasies. "I don't want you to believe everything these whites teach you. I want you simply to get some kind of certificate so that you can get jobs as clerks with the government. Just that. 'The world is round. The sun is stationary.' What nonsense is that?" Could they make him understand? How could they communicate to him that the world had been made to stand on its head? How could they make him understand that at school they were told they had no history? Garibaldi. The Tower of Pisa. The Duomo of Milan. Crispi. Il Duce. They were told that Merca had no history since it didn't have monumental buildings in which children sought the

131

hidden ghosts of their historical antecedents. What irreverent condescensions! What lies! Merca had no documented history. Mogadiscio had none. Well, not until . . . here we are, hear us out (had said the teacher), not until the Arabs came. Of course, there was a cluster of mud huts which eroded and were eaten by the white ants which came out of the sand dunes surrounding this coastal city. What indiscretions! That voice again, the voice from within, Soyaan speaking through and to Loyaan: "Riding the powerful waves of the sea came the *Daters*, bringing with them a pharo of lighted visions, chanting a call of prayer, opening their throats singing the muezzin's dawn chant. The Daters. The Tyrants. The Crescent. The Cross. The Red Star of Blood and human sacrifice. What did they want? Monuments erected on the ruins, the country's rubble? Why did they so much want us caught in the wind of warring interests?" His memory ferried to and fro, cutting across unmeasurable time and space, fetching from the sunken ship precisely that which would serve him, *his cause*.

Time, it was time he went back to meet Ibrahim Musse, nicknamed "Siciliano". Behind him, Hospital De Martini, once the only hospital in the whole country. Yes, Dr Ahmed-Wellie worked there with a team of Chinese doctors. How it dulled Loyaan's mind when he thought of the unhealthiness of its health policies. The contradictions of this country's compromises. A city with no more than four hospitals in all. One for the Military. One for the Police, And two for the general public: one of these was De Martini. Definitely not a hospital fit for anything. The Ministry of Constructions had suggested they demolished it and built another. The Chinese said they would, if requested, provide aid and construct a maternity hospital. The smell of the sea, meanwhile, merged with that of medicinals and chemicals. An inch a day. The sea fed on the unmaintained foundations of the only hospital the colonial government had provided for the ailing thousands. "A tomb, not a hospital," would say Qumman. "I have faith in the Almighty. His word heals. His hand blesses. I have trust in Him. True, Ladan was delivered on to the cupped hands of the hospital's nurses. But I was in labour. And you know what they did? They gave more stitches than I needed." Well, well. That was enough for now. He would return to call on Ibrahim prompt as a kept promise. Then he would go to Afgoi and visit his step-mother Beydan.

The Ministry of Justice & Religious Affairs. And Loyaan took the flight of stairs by surprise. The stairs surrendered themselves to his hurrying feet which stirred patches of sand in the corners where walls greeted one another, encountered one another as they had agreed in the clichéd nursery. He nearly collided with several religious dignitaries, sheikhs whose white cloaks made the place look drab and dull. The sheikhs conversed in loud voices across which echoed their unspoken perturbances. Recently ten colleagues of theirs had faced a firing-squad. They died religious martyrs. Their deaths were mourned in secretive quietness. The immediate families of the religious martyrs did not receive the corpses of their dead. These families staged unceremonious mourning sessions in private; prayers for their souls; the curse upon the General secretly addressed to the Almighty. Now these sheikhs were the clowns, the arrivistes: they were those who were willing to search for and find in their concordances references which legitimised the tyranny with which the country was being ruled. Turn into a Soviet inspired Marxist-Leninist state, a country with a hundred per cent Muslim population. In one hand, the Blue Book of the General and Lenin's writings in improvised translations; in the other, the Holy Koran. In one instant: "We have blind faith in Allah's doctrine"; in the same: "We are Marxist-Leninist and Mohammedan."

"Ooooops. I am sorry."

Loyaan had collided with two judges in dark gowns. One of them recognised him. His face looked disturbed. He stopped. They shook hands. The judge murmured something Loyaan couldn't hear, something which sounded like "Condolences". But he held a brief-case so tightly Loyaan thought the man suspected he might snatch it away from him. The other, however, stood apart, backed away rather like a Caucasian child retreating from the frightening black man's extended arm of friendliness. They were silent now still standing in the landing. Through the corner of his furtively moving eye, he could see posters, portraits of different sizes and derivations. There was the General's portrait recently retouched to make him look younger and handsomer.

"Ciao."

"Ciao."

Up another flight of stairs as he read in haste the writings on the walls, as he puffed and panted. Title-plates on closed doors. He read them one by one. He controlled them myopically. What was Ibrahim Musse's title, he wondered now? Why titles and not names? Was it because nearly all senior officers were acting-this or acting-that? Was it because before the letter which appointed any civil servant to take up a certain office was signed the General would change his mind and nominate another to that very position? He would stop to check. He would go on. He would read another. A peon in khaki came to him and shouted rudely:

"What are you doing going from one office to another like that?"

"I am sorry."

The peon looked Loyaan up and down. He suddenly became gentler: "Can I do anything for you, *jaalle?*"

We are all comrades once in the court of the General.

"Yes?"

"Dr Ibrahim Musse, please." *Mark the title. Mind who you are talking to.*

"If you follow me."

Long forehead. Large, squat nose. Lovely eyes. A man of medium height. Age: a year or two older than Loyaan. He returned to his seat behind the writing-desk on which he had a file open. He told his secretary to leave them but give him a free line: he wanted to ring an outside number. He excused himself. He dialled a number and waited. He spoke a monosyllable. He replaced the mouthpiece. Had he delivered a coded message to somebody? What had he said? He hung up and dialled another number just as discreetly. Another monosyllable. He closed the file which had lain open in front of him. What monosyllabic mysteries were these he delivered to those waiting ears? Little by little, small as eye-drops, a pool filled: Margaritta. The poem. The mystery of the alphabets Soyaan had initialled on those pieces of paper found in his pockets. M to the power of 2. Ibrahim Musse. Where was his sister? Did he have the Memorandum Soyaan and he had written together? Where was it? Where else did he fit in all this? He had come to Qumman's the previous night. Why? Why did he give an appointment in his office? What did all this mean? What monosyllabic coded messages did he deliver to those waiting ears?

"Ibrahim, I. . . ."

His arm raised: "Later."

He dialled a two-digit number, perhaps internal.

"Is that you?"

A pause.

"Could you come for a second, please?"

134

He addressed a benevolent smile to Loyaan.

"A second."

The secretary walked in, her hips, etc.

"Can I have this retyped with all the right insertions in the right places, please?"

She took the file from him. She moved to leave.

"And by the way. . . ." She turned. "I am going out for the rest of the day. O.K.? You don't know where I am and whom I am with. Get that ready for tomorrow first thing. Prepare the other files as well."

"Yes, *jaalle*." And she went out.

"We, too, can go," said he to Loyaan.

Once outside the colossal building, neither had the least idea where they could go to have some peace while they talked. In passing, Loyaan had mentioned that he intended to visit his step-mother in Afgoi sometime in the day.

"I've had a thought," Ibrahim then said.

"What?"

"I can give you a lift to Afgoi. It is only twenty-nine kilometres."

"Don't go out of your way, please."

"No, I am not."

"It will give us time to talk."

"That is the idea."

He took out a bunch of keys and opened the car door. He went round to let himself in. He got in and without speaking started the engine. He pushed open the door Loyaan was nearer to.

"All right, let's go."

"The Memo Soyaan and I worked on, the one my sister typed, if you want to know, is titled 'Dionysius's Ear'. It is not a long Memo. Maximum eight typewritten pages. Dionysius's Ear."

"Dionysius, the Syracusan tyrant?"

"That is it."

"And where is it?"

"What?"

"The Memo?"

"Patience. Patience has never been your forte."

"Nor my virtue."

135

They were past Mogadiscio's checkpoint. In a ledger, every vehicle entering or leaving the city was registered; so was the number of passengers and their names, reason for the vehicle's leaving or re-entering the city. Patience. *Patience*, suggested the voice from within. *We are in and have been in a state of emergency the past few years, the period tense, the prisons nearly full, and more prisons being built, such as the one the East Germans have nearly completed. Patience. "Wear not your conscience on your forehead," somebody was fond of saying although I cannot remember who. Patience. Prudenza paga. Don't exhibit more of yourself than you should*, concluded the voice.

"But why Dionysius?"

"The Syracusan tyrant had a cave built in the shape of a human ear which echoed to him in polysyllables whatever the prisoners whispered secretly to one another. Soyaan and I saw a similarity between this and the method the General has used so far. The Security Services in this country recruit their main corps from illiterates, men and women who belong to an oral tradition, and who neither read nor write but report daily, report what they hear as they hear it, word by word. They report verbatim what they think they heard when they walked into a shop. They need no warrant to arrest anybody. Everything is done verbally. Instructions are given on the phone: 'Before dawn arrest so-and-so.' Most of these are not even traceable to their origin, for there are no written warrants. And when a junior security officer requests that he be supplied with a written and signed warrant, the answer from the superior officer is: 'We shall have had it prepared and signed by the time the man is in custody.' You can bet that won't be done. A very peculiar phenomenon here. We've found that two third of the prisoners have no files, that over two thirds of them are serving indeterminate prison sentences. We have indeed discovered that the only privileged prisoners are those with thin files of three-page reports concerning hour of arrest, reason for arrest (i.e. high treason), et cetera. We say in our Memo that the General (with the assistance of the Soviets) has had an ear-service of tyranny constructed. The Memo is divided into two sections: there is the Introduction written entirely, and documented, by Soyaan; and there is the Appendix which was done by me, and which gives a list of detainees who have been forgotten by the officers who originally imprisoned them; the appendix also provides a list of those illegally detained because of confusion arising from mistaken identity."

136

"And where is it?"

"If you let me give you the full report first, please."

"Sorry."

Silence. The speedometer clocked ninety kilometres an hour. Ibrahim indicated to Loyaan that he should use the safety-belt. Loyaan preferred not to, and chose not to wear it. The wind held the car back. But it tore against it, forcing it to break noisily.

"There is also another Memorandum which Soyaan wrote under the insistent solicitation of one of the Vice-Presidents. The idea of this was to prove scientifically how uneconomical it is to let so many of the nation's intellectuals and professionals languish in prisons when in their places we employ Soviet technocrats and Cuban sugarcane experts. A great many of the nation's professionals, intellectuals and technicians have left the country for fear they would be imprisoned, tortured or badly treated. This too is a well-documented statement which Soyaan made."

"What is its title?"

"He showed it to me in its first draft, asking for comment. I haven't seen the final draft. But I know what has become of it. I know who might have the only copy in existence."

"Who?"

Ibrahim brusquely braked; there was a camel right in the middle of the road licking the grass-remains off the road. A herdsman was calling lovingly to his beast. They gave the herdsman time to lead away his love with care, talking to it as to a child. Meanwhile, Loyaan had lit a cigarette. Meanwhile, Ibrahim had changed gear.

"Who?"

"Margaritta has it."

The mention of this name kindled lamplets inside Loyaan's head. Inside him now burned with a slowness akin to candles, and in silence too, a number of heinous thoughts which fed on the wax of accumulated guilt. Margaritta. Mother and Ladan. And the scene of a dream in which whales were being served morsels of lacerated testicles of political victims. What horrors! What nightmares!

"Have you spoken to her?"

"Yes, I have."

"What did she say?"

Prudenza! He wouldn't tell him all that she had said. He wouldn't show him any of the papers the family had found in Soyaan's pockets,

137

either. Nor would he share with him all those confidential things he had been told. A friend of Soyaan's, yes. But so was Ahmed-Wellie. And Qumman had suspicions he might be up to something wicked. *Prudenza paga!* Just as he hadn't told anybody anything so far. Let everybody interpret things as they wished. Although one particular thing must be made absolutely clear: Soyaan never told the beads of the General's praises, either in public or private. But why was he made and created a Hero of the Revolution? *Address yourself to this query, Loyaan.* Why was he knighted, given the title? *Ask. Come on. Ask for opinions. No harm done. Go on. Don't fear.* Why?

"I don't think I have a clear answer myself," said Ibrahim.

Come on, insisted the voice within. *Push him a bit more. Have him say some more. Make him commit himself. Let him say what is not clear to him. Let him speak his thoughts.*

"We belonged to a clandestine group, Soyaan and I, a clandestine movement of opposition which is composed of intellectuals and professionals who've taken an oath — *per modo di dire* — to serve not the interests of any superpower but this nation's. We decided on our first meeting attended by the full membership of the movement that we would adhere to certain principles: first, we wouldn't call ourselves a movement; secondly, we would meet once a month to report on the progress made in whatever we were working on individually or collectively; thirdly, any research gathered and compiled in the name of the movement would carry nobody's name or initials. We were ten to start with, ten young intellectuals whose names would mean something to you if I were to mention them; but I choose not to, although I can tell you that you know almost all of them by face and name. Some have spoken to you since Soyaan's death. Some are out of the country. Some are in prison. But the important thing is that we are vigilant and that we are all the more conscious politically despite what has happened, despite Soyaan's death. Anyway. . . ."

Wreaths of sand and dust. The sun had gone higher up its ladder and burned hotter. The tyres of the car skidded down a path trodden a million times, the speedometer eating up mileage-minutes and seconds nonchalantly. On either side of the road a forest of thorny bushes although, with proper planning, the land would be cultivable since the river was only ten kilometres away.

"One cannot disguise the fact that our people have been made

138

suspicious of one another, that this régime has given a two-handled sword sharp at both ends to each of us. Must everything be re-interpreted according to the code of clan-, class- or group-interest, must everything be seen in this light? Nothing escapes the close scrutiny of the security system whose planted *ears* have sprouted in every homestead. This country hasn't a tradition of protest movements, trade unions or organised groups of any kind. There is no tradition such as there is in Egypt, Ethiopia, or Sudan, of student movements which can help form or unform governments or shape public opinion. So people, inarticulate with fear, prefer not to speak. 'I have a wife and children to take care of,' one of them would say to you. 'I have an aged mother and a family to care for, to maintain,' another would tell you. 'My neck is not longer than yours. Extend yours. But I won't. I have open mouths to feed. To feed these open mouths, I need to close mine. When not closed, my mouth helps me to masticate not formulate thoughts.' You hear these or variations of these. So. Soyaan and I drew up a list of ten intellectuals whom we thought we could trust, whom we thought we could engage in collaboration with us. And what did we ask of these ten whom we invited to our meeting? 'We seek your collaboration,' we said. 'That is all. What do we want you to do? We want you to collect information for a common pool. We want you to research with us. We will disseminate the information received in that manner, we will eventually publish our findings, we will distribute them gratis in cyclostyled format, we will start with the General himself,' we said. 'We can foretell,' we added, 'that the written word, more powerful than the gun, will frighten them. In the chaos ensuing from that, and just as they start their purge, we will announce our clandestinity and publish a leaflet of our intention, and you will see that more people will adhere to it. Then we will baptise it as a movement, we will give it a name.' "

A pause. Tyres hissed in the heat of melted tar. What was the article that his mother had found, copied in Soyaan's own hand, in his pocket? Article 17 or was it 18? *Any person who spreads, distributes or publishes reading, spoken or broadcast matter damaging the sovereignty of the revolution of the Somali nation will be liable to death.* Loyaan puffed on his cigarette and listened to Ibrahim who said:

"Three meetings at most, and we split. One group was headed by Medina and the other by Soyaan. Medina held on to the belief that

139

the General was the Master of Grand Irrelevances and Irreverences (in capitals) and that no intellectual in his senses should take him seriously. She believed, and so did those who had joined her group, that whatever publishable research we gathered on the workings of his régime wouldn't help anybody have a clearer picture. *A priori*, Medina considered the General a Grand Fool, and that science hadn't the capacity to analyse the workings of the minds of idiots. Soyaan and I were of a different opinion. We held the view that there is a pattern studyable, that there is a logic behind almost all that the General has done, that the minds of fools or idiots have already been studied anyway. We held the view that the man wasn't a fool, and wasn't a Master of Grand Irrelevances and Irreverences. If we take our General seriously, if Uganda took Idi seriously and didn't consider him a bully or a buffoon, if the people of the Central Republic took their Emperor for what he was worth, if . . . ! But before we knew it, somebody had called somebody else something. Pro-Soviet. Pro-American. Pro-this. Pro-that. 'How long will he last, do you think? Before we research and write on him, you will see, he will be no more,' said Medina. We said. 'They said that of Haile Selassie and of Franco.' We were split right down the middle. Five of us against five of them. Soyaan, myself, Samater (Medina's husband), Ahmed-Wellie and others. Two months later, Samater decided he wouldn't adhere to our group after all. Medina had nagged at him day and night, I suspect."

Now they had farm land on either side. Acres and acres of maize. A government farm. Moving about in small and large groups there were about twenty persons in green uniforms. They were standing placards with writings at strategic points for every passer-by to see. Words of welcome for the honourable president visiting the country, surmised Loyaan to himself. He didn't say anything. Neither did Ibrahim for a while. Then:

"Dionysius's Ear was our first collective effort. The one Margaritta has, I believe, is the second. I am working on another myself. Ahmed-Wellie is also doing some interesting work on torture in the prisons. We wondered if you would like to join us. Ahmed-Wellie and I wondered if you would like to take Soyaan's place."

Without giving a thought, Loyaan said: "Yes, I would love to."

That got him a genuine grin from Ibrahim. But what could he do? What could he do to contribute? He had more or less compromised with the authorities of his region when there. That kind of

140

compromise helped him make amends where things were amiss drastically. He was no intellectual whose pen-power severed and demolished false bridges like Soyaan's. He was a simple dentist when one really came to it. He was too inopionated. "Mine is a known departing point: I have a mouth and a known number of teeth to start with. Soyaan: no. Begin from the beginning. Tell Ibrahim about the things which were found in Soyaan's pockets. The article — 18 or 17, one can check later, and does it matter anyway? The short piece about clowns et cetera. Bits and pieces of papers here and there. Tell him about the poem on the back of Marco's photo. Tell him about Margaritta. Tell him whatever there is to know. Trust who trusts you. There is nothing to fear. Begin from the beginning. Don't omit the Minister's asking for the Memorandums. In brief. But everything. Go on. Start. One. Two. Three. Go." But he could not bring himself to trust Ibrahim with the secrets. Just as he wouldn't fully trust Ahmed-Wellie any more.

"I have my suspicions," said Ibrahim after a long silence. "We gather from what has happened that death must have been as much of a surprise to him as it was to us all. I was very close to Soyaan. I knew him well. He had projects. He had future plans. But how? What precisely was it that killed Soyaan?"

"There was no post-mortem to enable us find that out."

Ibrahim slowed down. Groups of women were sitting in the shade of a tree. Others were rehearsing songs and dance steps, they were dancing joyously in the middle of the road. The car came to a complete halt. The women were in colourful dresses, flowered and fresh as the roses of dawn. It was Loyaan again:

"The Master of Grand Irrelevances? No, Medina is wrong. The man kills. The man has designs on our lives. The man can eliminate a person and then take possession of his soul and have him discredited in the eyes of his friends and those with whom he worked, those he protested with. I shall ring Medina to say a few things to her. I will ring her when all this is over. . . ."

Ibrahim said: "That interview given by your father has shocked me greatly. How could he have allowed himself to do that? How could you? Could you not have spoken to him?"

"I tried."

"Forgive me, but it must be said: the man is an embarrassment."

"The man is worse than evil."

141

They were at the entrance to the town. Above them, an arch called Revolutionary Victory. Pasted inartistically on its cardboard pillars and on its front were portraits of the General and the visiting statesman. In the shade of the trees on either flanks were traffic policemen chatting away with one another. One of them waved them on. There was no need to register number-plates, name of owner of vehicle, purpose of travel at the check-point of Afgoi. Move on.

"Well, well. What about Mulki?" said Loyaan.

"She was informed of the risk involved when she accepted to type the manuscript. We told her, both of us did."

"Which one did she type?"

"Dionysius's Ear."

"And she won't speak?"

"No fear of that."

"The KGB-trained torturers know how to make a person surrender all secrets, I am told."

"Now that Soyaan is dead, she knows it is me they are after. No, she won't speak. But will that stop them from coming to me?"

A roundabout. Flowery and green. The local government welcomed one to the town in Somali, Arabic, Italian, French, German and English. Ibrahim drove elegantly without speaking. Loyaan remembered that Margaritta had promised to bring him the Memorandum she had. What about Ibrahim's? *Go on. Ask where it is*.

"Where would you like me to drop you?"

"May I ask you where the Memo is?"

"You'll get your copy in due course. Soyaan's own copy, that is."

He told Ibrahim where he should be dropped.

Chapter Ten

Like a foetus, formless as the white of an egg, fluid, cream-coloured like sperm, yes, intestinefuls of a future breath — perhaps a child, perhaps a miscarriage. Like the unboned foetus caught in the membranes of maternity. . . .

Before Loyaan lay a system of footpaths, white like the scaled skin of a leper. A system of footpaths which wound, turned as though in circles. Footpaths which led to dead-ends. A mud hut would, occasionally, choke the easy flow. A cow-shed littered with a variety of dung would, on other occasions, strangle the continuum of the footpath's unfolding. He saw these as symbols. He saw them as white stains of sickness on the face of the brown earth. The corpse of a dog dead a week. Tapeworms of decay and disharmony. And yet he walked indifferent to the smell, thinking: "Empty at my touch like a soap-bubble, everything reducible to nought, nothing. Inexistent at my remembering, like a dream." Light was the white sand which his feet stirred, narrow the path into which he now turned.

The place was noisy with children hiding in the game of the seeker and the sought. At the cross-paths, strategically right in front of a squat hut, stood a beggar chanting alms-songs. The beggar was about eighteen, at the maximum twenty years old. He was well-built physically; there was nothing wrong with him, that is. He was neatly robed in white. He had a tin in his right hand. When Loyaan came level with him, the beggar shouted a little louder as though in defiance, as though he was urging the occupants of the house to hurry up, to decide faster and respond positively or negatively, to speak, if they wanted the set response: "We have nothing to offer you today, only God has"; or "May He give you His generosity in abundance". Yes, before Loyaan stretched the footpath, straight as a line drawn by a child's hand, a line uncertain, curving where it shouldn't, ending abruptly. Behind him, the beggar's chant, a beggar as muscular as a boxer, eighteen, at maximum twenty. He was a devoted student of the word of God, a young man dedicated enough to enlist as a pupil, attached to a grand imam, the leader of a small group of the Wandering Scholars. These varied in number from one region to another. Sometimes you saw ten of them, sometimes twenty. They would all be dressed in white robes. Almost all of them good-looking, and neat as the purity which they represented. But since mosques weren't as rich as churches, the imam when in towns with his Wandering Scholars would disperse his pupils in all seven directions. They would then call at the homes of the town's residents and collect food and money. They would take what money they hadn't used back to their imam whose placement would guarantee an honorary priesthood of a wealthy family in town and who therefore would be fed well. Another beggar, handsomer than the other, tall, and well-groomed. But lame. This one chanted differently: his accent sounded local. His clothes were dusty and travelled. This was the lunch hour, and beggars were gathering tinfuls of alms to silence the goddess of hunger. A third, a fourth and a fifth. The town was full of them today. Why? Had it something to do with a religious festivity? Suddenly . . . of course, he knew now. Before any head of state visited a town, the Local Government and the Security swept away these ugly sights and kept them at bay for the whole period the foreign dignitaries were in the country. This happened a few days before delegations heralding a visiting dignitary came, a month or two before OAU or Arab League meetings. Beggars began to leave Mogadiscio's city centre in order not to be swept away in a van to prison. They retreated to quieter places, to the city's peripheries, or a town like Afgoi. And before these delegations caught up with them they would have left Afgoi. However, such torturous treatment was reserved only for professional beggars, not those gently-robed pupils in white. Look who's there! Or was he seeing visions? The one-armed beggar was there. *Empty at your touch like the wind. Inexistent like the houri of a Muslim's dream of heaven.* But why did the one-armed beggar follow him everywhere? What was it he was after? A left turn and a right turn. "Let him follow me," Loyaan said to himself. He struck a matchstick. He lit a cigarette. He sat in the shade of a fig tree by the river. *The first pursuer is here.*

He etched the sketch of a drawing on the earth with his fingers. A silent river. A modest river. Shabelle. Like a man drugged with chemicals, the river lay still, calm, quiet. The birds in the trees on its banks hopped from branch to branch, frantically jumpy and chatty,

144

chirping and mating and loving. In a sea-bound serenity, the river's water stayed firm under the caressing touch of the moving wind. Further down, there were women washing, beating their washing against stones dark with the tropical sweat. *Life is a great swim away from the nodal tide, the killer wave,* he thought. *When one has gone over the hump, prepared oneself for a welcoming reception of the water's lap, another tide leaps upwards like an enraged fire and one is caught in it, breathless; this occurs when one is at one's weakest, and one is burned in this enraged fire like a passion — the flames of life's waters.* There: a parable of princesses in the freshness of heaven; thousands of nights; Baghdad-thieves; and the lamps of Aladdin; the victorious sword of Saladdin. *Life is a swim away from Allah's rhetoric of unmaintained promises. The river which flows right into the oasis of my desert, the river which irrigates the miraged waterlessness of my faith. Biyo.* Water-in-life.

He unknowingly had drawn a circle, like that of a moon, on the earth. Right at the centre of the circle he buried the stub of his cigarette. *This is the leafed moon,* thought he. The leaf of the one who has died falls the instant the soul returns to its creator. A dry leaf. A lifeless leaf. Anaemic yellow, and sick-looking, the colour of jaundice. *Biyo:* water for the Somali is life. *Bio:* organic life in Greek. See the symbol in the myth, see the falling leaf in the precipitating wind, weightless, its mother-tree willing to part with it — like chewed sugar-cane stalks which one spits out, ugly like sawdust, discarded like something no longer of any use. But was Soyaan surprised by death? All these unfinished plans and projects told the story clearly. It is the element of surprise in an accident which kills one, the shock of its violent suddenness, the shock of its unexpected abruptness. And yet it didn't appear as though it was accidental — it seemed his death was rather instrumental in making the régime react nervously, create him a hero, silence Keynaan with money and a guaranteed job. Would we have known any better if a post-mortem had been performed? What had he eaten at Beydan's? Was there nobody with him? If so, who? Did he say anything to her, anything which might lead someone somewhere?

Loyaan got up. He put his hand into his pocket. He took out the envelope which contained the money he had brought for Beydan, the money Soyaan had promised he would give her. He walked the fifty yards in such a hurry he made it seem much shorter. He replaced the envelope in his pocket seeing that there was yet another muscular beggar chanting in front of a closed door. *God is an economic proposition,* thought he. *God gives, God takes away what He gives.*

He knocked gently on Beydan's door.

The old woman who had opened the door let its handle go. She was pale with fright and trembled as though she had seen a ghost. Her mouth would not close and she stared at him in silence. When she spoke, her shaking voice reached him:

"For a moment, I thought. . . ."

"It is all right," he said. "I understand."

"What? What do you understand?"

As he pushed past her: "Let me introduce myself. I am no ghost: I am Loyaan."

He turned round.

"I know," she said, "I thought, for a moment. . . . "

"I understand," I said. "I am not Soyaan."

"My God!"

Silence. The sun poured its blazing vapouriness upon everything. This heightened the contrast between Loyaan and the woman both in looks and age. She was definitely over fifty. The furrows her wrinkles had dug shared the available space on her face with the wounded scars of time. Loyaan knew who the woman was. He had seen her before with Beydan. He remembered that she had escorted Beydan to the funeral. She was an aunt of hers. A very gentle-voiced woman. A widow two-thirds of her life, having had lost her first, second and third husbands in approximately eighteen months. "The witch", Qumman would unhesitatingly have said if she were here; she wouldn't shake hands with her even with her palms well covered with a cloth.

"Get in, get in."

"Thank you."

A hen as ancient as the woman, balancing itself on its rickety feet, took the lead and Loyaan followed it across the large dusty courtyard. The woman stayed safely a few feet behind him. Neither said anything until they came within a short distance of a row of huts built in the shape of a crescent, mud huts squat as were probably the men who had constructed them. The hen was joined by a covey of her chicks; Loyaan heard the woman say:

"Let me get you something to sit on, and meanwhile tell your

146

aunt that you are here. Stand in the shade, yes, the shade of that tree. I won't be long."

He squinted at the sun. He did as advised: he went in the shade of a tree and faced the row of squat mud huts in front of which were seated the women who lodged there. One of the women would every now and again dip her middle and index finger into a can which had originally contained some kind of tomato *purée* and would paint the nipples of her mammae with (Loyaan guessed — he knew it couldn't be otherwise) a concentration of myrrh and other herbs. She performed this ritual with the same care as a model might when varnishing nails or applying lipstick. Not very distant from her, there was a child of about three and a half years old, a boy, who had a charm of string round his waist and wore several amulets, three on each arm — six of beautifully worked leather — and yet another, like a necklace, around his neck. He also had an anklet. The woman anointing the nipples of her breasts was herself young. She did this to wean the child. Look and behold. The charmed, amuleted child now went and stood by her; from a close distance, he contemplated the painted mammae.

"Here," she said. "Do you want to be breastfed?" she asked. He nodded. He went to her and began suckling.

"Agh!" he spat and cursed. He was such an overweight child.

"Just a second," shouted the old woman to Loyaan.

"It is all right."

In a moment the woman returned to smirching her mammae, the child to his playing, and Loyaan to watching them at their game. Female breasts to this woman were a source of food, not of eroticism. Uninhibitedly, she nursed them as one would nurse a boil on one's genitals — but that only in private. Medium-sized her breasts, flat on her chest and lean — rather like a sunflower after sunset, weak, and hanging head-down like a sleeping penis. You could bet they were rock-hard once. Then child-delivery and three and a half years of breast-feeding had turned them soft like bananas too mature to stay unpicked.

"Loyaan?" cried the old woman from inside the same doorway. "Yes?"

"Would you like to wait there or will you come in?"

He wasn't quite sure what to say. She went on:

"She isn't feeling very well. But I can bring a mat out for her."

He approached saying: "I'll come then."

147

However, the old woman reappeared and told him:

"She says she would like to come out and sun her tired bones. I say the wind isn't good for her."

"I am sure the sun is good for her. Fresher air," he said.

"You wait then."

Before she re-entered the room in which Beydan was, there came a small shout; perhaps it was Beydan herself saying something. Loyaan did not hear that clearly.

"She wants you to go in," the old woman interpreted.

Loyaan hesitated.

"Go in, come on."

He would rather wait for her outside, actually. But:

"Hoddi, hoddi?"

"Hodeen!" came the answer far and feeble.

From the sound, he sensed Beydan needed a few seconds before she could be seen. He guessed that she was either putting on something or getting out of something.

"I'll wait for her outside," he told the old woman. "The sun will do her a lot of good. Do you need help to bring a mat or something out for her?"

"No, I don't."

"Then I'll wait for her outside."

"Will I survive this, I keep wondering?" she said touching her pregnancy.

"Of course you will."

"I wish I were as optimistic," she said.

And the old woman, her aunt, came and served him a cold drink, bringing two ice-cubes in an empty glass and an unopened bottle. She gave him the opener. There was to be no cause for Qumman to accuse them of bewitching him or poisoning his food. Loyaan was hurt, but said nothing aside from "thanks" as he poured out the Coke. He felt embarrassed by all this, he was at a loss for the right words to express his thoughts. *What am I? Who am I? Whom am I dealing with? What century is this? Of what era must I partake fully, actively?* Must he fully and actively belong to this century of technology, of SAMs, MiGs and satellites and KGBs and CIA espionage networks, or to one of Beydans and Qummans, one of wizardry and witchcraft and hair-burning rites of sorcery? It was then that he remembered something said by no less than Clemenceau. (Loyaan now had a sip of his drink, a sip coolly taken and relished; he let it linger until its fuzziness ceased on the edge of his tongue.) Said Clemenceau: "In one generation, Americans have had the most unique experience of the history of mankind; in only one generation, America has ceased being referred to as a barbaric nation and has qualified itself to be labelled decadent." What about Africa? What about Saudi Arabia? What about Iran? *What would Clemenceau's comments have been were he now alive to make comments about persons like myself, like Soyaan and like most of the people we've lived with, known and shared our days and nights with? What would he have said of us?* In search of an answer Loyaan looked in Beydan's direction. He could see nothing but stains on her exhausted physique, pains on her face, her frail figure. Her massive eyes powered as searchlights were focused on him. She was sitting on a straw mat in the same shade as he. She had been born a couple of years before he was, although the claims of pregnancies such as this and life with Keynaan had made their mark. It was not so much a question of a generation, linking or dividing persons in this continent. No, it was a question of cultural trends, what strands of cultural affinities hung down and reached one. In short, it was a question of how cultural discontinuities had woven Solomonic arabesques of difference between any given two persons. See now, see the pain on her forehead. See her support her frail weight on the hands which had until then lain under her. Watch her stretch her legs outwards. Look at her mound of a belly reach upwards to her chin as she sat up. What future was there for the unborn? What did the future have in store for the carrier of that future? Look at her move on her buttocks — just like the children of this village rubbing their bottoms clean against the sand after they have defecated. What did the future hold in store for those children? Haemorrhage? What about her and the unborn? Clemenceau. . . .

"You've come to speak of Soyaan, haven't you?"

"I've come to see you. That is the most important reason why I am here."

"No, no. You've come to speak of Soyaan."

"No, no. I've come to see you, and speak of Soyaan and other things as well. I've come to do all this."

"I had nothing to do with his death."

"I never said or thought you had."

149

"But your mother does."

"That is something between the two of you."

"She is your mother, after all."

He chose to remain silent. He chose not to continue. He had feared something like this would happen, had feared the conversation would go out of hand. *Regain your calm,* said the voice which during the past few days spoke to him whenever he was in dire need of being reminded of his moral, intellectual and ethical duties. *Stay calm and listen. Why have you come here? Haven't you come here to speak of Soyaan, what he ate when here, with whom he came if not alone, haven't you? Well. Do that. Don't condescend. Don't give her stupid, stony reasons with which to grind her hoe. Be gentle. Listen.*

"It is a delightful surprise to see you here. A very delightful surprise. Although I expected you would come sooner than this. What use are my responses to your questions now that the reason for Soyaan's death is of no grand interest any more? The newspapers and the radio have stopped talking about him. He is a dead hero. And do reasons matter once a person is dead?"

"Of course, they do."

"Your father is not of that opinion."

That shut him up. Another sip. He sensed the weight of those powered eyes of Beydan's which searched for an instant of weakness in him. She knew that mere mention of Keynaan's name would silence him. Keynaan. True: he tore in two the twins' illustrated ball of a globe; true: he destroyed their image of a dreamed universe. But what did he do to her? A sip of his Coke. Women are inferior beings, he unhesitatingly would declare. "Talk to whom? Listen to whom? Beydan or Qumman? You must be out of your head, son. The Koran said . . . !" Yes, I know, I know what the Koran said, when and why. "Please spare me that." For one thing, Beydan as a child, as a girl, was never given a globe to illustrate nor a world to dream. She was offered broken claypots to play with and bones to dress as dolls. She was bound leg and foot to a choice not her own. Her hand was exchanged for cash delivered. She was somebody's property. She was nobody. Men? The vintaged class of superior beings. Men could drop their anchor's weight anywhere they pleased. Their sail could flutter in the wind of their freedom. That is what the Koran promised men of equal birth. But the General himself, disbelieving the teachings of the Koran, denied men equal to himself the right to have their sails beat un-

150

tampered with in the openness of God's air. Think of the General as another infidel, quoting and misquoting Lenin in order to remain in power, think of him as a man caught in the warring winds, the criss-cross of storms, the dry monsoons, the weather as forecast by fortune-tellers his wives had hired. *Caught in the warring trade-winds and other economic interests there just like Keynaan, Beydan, and my mother and my friends. To rule, the General hoists the mast of his flagpost which he feels is secure more with the KGB than with the Koran.* . . . Beydan had something to say:

"What's-his-name has come several times. He comes to speak to your father. The two tell me to leave them alone. I'm sent out of the room whenever he is here."

"Who what's-his-name?"

"It escapes me now. The Minister's name."

"What Minister?"

"The one who's made all these declarations."

"*Him?*"

"He was here first thing in the morning. He came in a long car, chauffeur-driven, and there were two Security men with him. He entered our room without our having invited him. Power doesn't need invitations. They come when they please. They go where they please."

"Has he ever asked you questions?"

"Yes, he has."

"What?"

"He annoys me with those silly questions of his. He annoys me when he tries to show and prove to all present how ridiculous your mother is accusing me as she has done of poisoning Soyaan's food. Your father chuckles in a corner, pleasing the thrilled lunacy of this Minister. They both annoy me. In fact, before they tell me to leave them alone, I go."

He sipped his drink in silence. He needed something stronger, he thought. Whisky. Brandy. Something to go down to the core of his acute senses and cool his hot nerves. Of course, he couldn't ask for it. A plain woman who in all probability had never set eyes on a bottle of whisky, even the local brand made with the help of Cuban expertise in Jowhar. Mention of anything to do with that would perhaps scandalise her so much she would feel the shock and — who knows — might have a heart-attack or abort. But . . . think of other things. Not

151

about Keynaan whose meanness embarrassed anyone with any sense of integrity. Think not of drinks the Koran has prohibited. Think of other things. Look at the tree. Ah, a butterfly. See how it transmits flowery messages from one branch of the tree to another. Watch it flutter, with calculated moves, watch it. Let that induce peace, however momentary, however brief.

"He, too, should've died," she resumed. "Technically. . . . ."

"Who?"

"This what's-his-name Minister."

"How? Why?"

"Soyaan and this Minister came together. They ate the meal I served them, Soyaan less than the Minister. We gave them our own lunch since we didn't have anything else. But there was no need to tell them that."

"When they came to you there was no one else with them?"

"I didn't see anybody else. Someone might have been waiting for them somewhere else. But the Minister was driving the car."

"Could you describe the car?"

"I know nothing about cars. A red car. Smaller than the kind that Ministers are driven in, smaller by far than the one in which he came today, and there was no chauffeur either. Perhaps it was his personal car. He was thrilled with it."

"What else?"

"What else, what else — questions and questions! On the day the paper carried your photo by mistake, the Minister came here and asked question after question, wanting to know if there was something in particular I was likely to remember of that day. I said: 'Have your war and discuss your polemics outside of here. We are women, we are weak,' I told him. 'When we are widowed, we cry softly lest you or the General hear, lest the Security men return to take away those you haven't already imprisoned. Go and discuss your politics away from here.'"

"What did he do then?"

"Enraged, he dashed out. However, before he did that, he stared angrily at Keynaan for a long time. I hadn't heard the revving of his engine, when Keynaan began beating me. A woman in my state, what could I do but take what came?"

The sun's vivid brightness. The old woman, Beydan's aunt, came to inquire if everything was all right. She came treading on the

152

tail-end of her shortened shadow and left being followed by it. "Women are like your shadow," Loyaan remembered the Somali proverb: "They follow who leaves them, they run from who follows them." A generalisation, of course, like all proverbs. Would Keynaan go after Beydan if she decided to leave him? "We are women, we are weak. When we are widowed, we cry softly lest the General hears, lest you return to take away those you haven't already imprisoned." Well put that, he said to himself. She had experienced the worst there was. Her former husband had died in the torture-chamber. He had been Keynaan's case. The General compensated: he ordered Keynaan to marry her in place of the murdered husband. Loyaan also remembered a conversation he once had in Baidoa with a woman whose husband had recently been imprisoned. "It is the cold wind falling on your ribs which makes you feel abandoned, it the absence of warmth which renders life difficult." A sip of his Coke. *We are like women — weak and meek and helplessly powerless in the presence of the powers of the General.* His furtive glance upwards told him that the butterfly had flown away. A look in the direction of Beydan who was saying:

" 'I am thirsty like the sand of the sea,' Soyaan said to me that day. 'I drink and drink and drink, but am still thirsty. I shall have to see a doctor, I think,' he said. 'Thirsty like the sand of the sea.' "

"What did he drink when here?"

"We brought him the beer he asked for. He drank great quantities of it, at least two large bottles. The Minister didn't touch that. He asked for a soft drink."

"Anything else?"

"He was taking tablets. He took three or four of them when here. Small as malaria-tablets."

"Anything else?"

"He looked very tired. His eyes were red and he rubbed them every now and again. He looked very tired."

"Not ill?"

"He said he was thirsty."

"He didn't look strange, did he?"

"He chain-smoked, one cigarette after the other. They sat here, Soyaan on a high chair, the Minister on the stool. He chain-smoked and took these tablets and asked for beer for the first time since I'd known him. And he was very tired. I asked him if he was not feeling well. He answered that he was thirsty, that was all. He repeated: 'I am thirsty like the sand of the sea.' He added, however, that inside he was as agitated as the wavy sea."

A sudden pain made her hold her teeth tighter together. False alarm. Perhaps, a premature set of contractions. Should he do something? What? She stretched herself out and lay on her back like a cockroach whose legs struggle with the last ounce of life. She closed her eyes. He took her wrist and timed her pulse. Even if she had real labour pains, what could he do for her? Beydan wouldn't want to be taken to hospital. "They stitch you badly," said a woman once to him. "At Martini, they deliver as many as ten in half a day. The midwives are government paid. They get their stipend whether they deliver one or twenty and they don't care. Do you think you can wear those trousers stitched for the army? It is the quantity, not the quality which matters. They stitch you hurriedly and badly. They create complications. Whereas the old women, preferably one's own relations, do it with love and with care." The old woman was here precisely to do this job, was she? He let go Beydan's wrist. Her eyes opened. She lay motionless on her back, muttering a soft prayer, brief and to the point.

"I keep wondering if I will survive this," she said.

"Of course, you will."

He pulled his seat forward, so that he would be in the shade. The sun had changed position; it was not as fiercely hot. He waited for her to speak and say something.

"These fits come oftener because we didn't pacify them with the *Kur* rite since it coincided with Soyaan's death," she said. "These fits come oftener and sharper. Soyaan, God bless him."

She sat up, having supported herself on her shaky elbows and having had Loyaan help her. She moaned with pain. Then:

"Your mother was in Afgoi yesterday, did you know?"

"Did she come to see you?"

"No."

"Why was she in Afgoi then?"

"She didn't tell you?"

"No, she didn't."

She sat upright, as straight as she could. She found the pain unbearably more frequent. She put a pillow under her elbow and leaned her head against her cupped hand.

154

"Your mother came to Afgoi to consult a master-witch whom she paid handsomely from the money the mourners contributed towards Soyaan's funeral. Your mother engaged the services of this man to do somebody harm," she said.

"Who? You?"

"Possibly me, possibly somebody else."

"My father?"

"Possibly your father, possibly me, possibly somebody else. She paid this master-witch so handsomely he won't say precisely what she asked of him and whom she wanted to be got rid of."

"How do you know all this?"

"The master-witch she hired is related by marriage to my aunt, this aunt here. He gave her sufficient hints to make her understand. He also suggested what protective mixtures I should take to fight back and come out triumphantly. Your mother is prepared to do *somebody* some harm."

Sudden painful bangs. She cried with pain. The old woman rushed out to her aid. Loyaan rose to his feet and held himself back despite the temptation to try to do something or other. The old woman had placed a hand under Beydan's head, and with the other hand she made Beydan sniff at a root. She then carefully and slowly set Beydan's head on the mat. She rubbed the root hard against Beydan's nose. What root was it? Loyaan bent down and listened to her heartbeat. She needed a doctor, not roots nor master-witches. She needed a doctor. And Heaven's God! Look. Look. Dr Ahmed-Wellie had entered through the outside door. There coming in haste was Dr Ahmed-Wellie. Good heavens, how did he know of all this? This was a very curious coincidence. Why was he here?

"Unbelievable. What did you say? Please repeat it," said Loyaan to Ahmed-Wellie.

"Don't make me feel more ridiculous. Let us go. Let us get into the car."

"No. Please. Repeat what you said."

Ahmed-Wellie started the engine of his car. He was impatient as when he waited for Loyaan to come out of Beydan's and join him. He had in haste prescribed something for Beydan. Nothing to fear. She wouldn't abort. Eat well. Sleep well. Take long walks. And no congregation of master-witches would be able to harm her or her child.

"What did you say? Just repeat that."

"I'll repeat it on one condition."

"What?"

"That you enter the car and that we leave this place. It smells."

"Unbelievable. How could you?"

He switched off the engine. He was angry and impatient. He appeared jaded. He wouldn't wait any longer. He wouldn't allow Loyaan to laugh at him, to mock him. Ahmed-Wellie wouldn't. He started the engine again. It seemed he would set an ultimatum and leave without Loyaan. *You shouldn't exaggerate, said the voice to him. You shouldn't overdo things like that. Do it tenderly now. Open the door and enter and say nothing, don't even be tempted to explain yourself, just let things slide into neat form, let him go where he pleases; just sit quietly, silently.*

"Will you close that door, please?"

"Yes."

And Ahmed-Wellie drove off, making the tyres screech as he turned into a bend, he drove clumsily as though he was accident-prone. He didn't even stop and wait as the road-sign instructed him to. He accosted any crossroad, he took the roundabout by surprise. But what was it he had said to Loyaan as soon as they left Beydan's company? What "ridiculous" statement had he made? "Your mother requested a favour of me. Your mother requested that I, a doctor and a friend, made sure you didn't come home with a stomach upset like Soyaan's. Your mother asked me to come to Afgoi and escort you back to the house, safe and healthy as when you left in the morning. Your mother said I should warn you of the possibility that your food might be poisoned by Beydan." Now what was ridiculous about that? Mothers made awkward demands. Had she not said the same to Loyaan himself? To have come all the way and tell it as naturally as he had — that was ridiculous. Not ridiculous, actually. Unexpectedly shocking. Ahmed-Wellie should have been civil about it: he should have prefaced it with a derogatory comment — he didn't do that: this perhaps was the aspect Loyaan found most shocking. The car slowed down. They had reached the check-point at which they should register number-plate of vehicle, name of owner, number of passengers, reason for travel, et cetera. But there, there, the traffic-warden recognised Dr Ahmed-Wellie, smiled at him waved them on. A *sittay-manogto*, swaying with the weight of its passengers, came in near head-collision,

156

although unjustifiably, with their car. Alert, Ahmed-Wellie swerved away to safety and drove on, not stopping for an instant nor looking back. When he had regained complete control of wheel and rhythm, when the speedometer had begun to read a constant figure in two digits, Ahmed-Wellie said:

"I've also come to give you further developments."

Loyaan's thoughts, like the tongue of a good gastronome, had begun to consume what could be easily digested, and had tasted, in the palate of his memory, all that which he should have remembered. A menu of ideas. First courses. Second courses. And so on and so forth. Was Soyaan's food poisoned by Beydan? Why did the Minister not suffer from the stomach disorder as Soyaan had? No. Loyaan hadn't heard what Ahmed-Wellie said. He had made no reaction whatsoever, he hadn't budged from that quiet position into which he fell as the speed of the car gained its rhythm. To break that rhythm, the car slowed down.

"I've come to speak to you of other things," Ahmed-Wellie repeated.

"What?"

He changed gears. He drove in the second for a while. And:

"They've taken Ibrahim Siciliano for an interrogation."

"No."

"They have."

"When?"

"Soon as he left you."

"How do you know?"

He changed to third. He went faster. *When busy with anthropological inquiries of who poisoned whom, and who bewitched whom, the Security on advice from elsewhere, lift the curded cream of our best.* "I keep wondering will I survive this," Beydan had said. Would Ibrahim? Would they torture him to make him tell all that they were interested in? Would they crush his balls, would they screw nails into his fingernails? When he was unable to urinate with fear would they go and wake Dr Ahmed-Wellie, blindfold him into a car, confuse his sense of direction by driving up and down a sandy street, would they then produce Ibrahim as the patient: cure him? Did ethics enter here? You said no to them and therefore risked your own life stupidly and left another person to suffer for lack of medical care. You accepted the dictates of a human need, and dealt with your patient as if he or she were brought to you at your clinic in the hospital. They'd taken Ibrahim for interrogation when . . . ! *Don't lose your calm. Think.* What about his sister? Did Ahmed-Wellie know anything about her?

"Yes."

"What?"

"She broke under torture."

"She mentioned names?"

"Yes."

"And the Memorandum?"

"I don't know."

"You think that that is in their hands?"

"Everything is possible."

Hold it. Don't tell him that Margaritta has the other. The fewer people who know of the existence of such a document, the better. Definitely. One by one, they come and remove them, and we wait for them. We talk as though these are the most normal of things. "Do you know that the Security knocked at So-and-so's door at dawn and took him to an unknown destination?" Three months, nine months, a year. Nobody ever asked for the right to see a husband, a son or a brother. No one, when released after a year's imprisonment, requested a fair trial in which to be proved guilty of a crime or given compensation. Nobody was shocked to hear that So-and-so had been taken for interrogation. Sometimes, these interrogations lasted long. They might last as long as a year. At times, two years. Loyaan knew of one which lasted four long years of suspense when the imprisoned didn't know and was never told what crime he may have committed. Ibrahim. And his sister. They certainly wouldn't release her now that they'd taken him away for interrogation. Ahmed-Wellie was, however, saying:

"They came last dawn. They blindfolded me as usual. They drove round and round and finally took me to a place which smelt of engine-oil and rusty metal. I could be wrong, but I imagined I was in a garage. They led me by the hand and seated me in front of a figure whose face was hidden from me. 'Here you are,' said the officer who had taken me there. I was confronted with a woman's breasts. My good God, I thought. Was this Mulki, Ibrahim's sister? Through torture, the breasts had become black with wounds, and the woman's body had suffered the whips' lashes. They needed a nurse for this. Why had they

158

brought me here? Could this be Mulki? I waited for a chance to whisper a question. I waited for an opportunity to say something I thought she would recognise me by. There was the guard, mind you, and I could've got into trouble if he had either heard or misheard me. These are beasts you cannot play with. So I said: 'Do you have menstrual complications every time you have your period? And have you ever seen a doctor?' No answer. I thought it was her. I took another look at the woman's body, nude save for the mask on her face. I felt her breasts and it pained her as I touched them, as I pressed them here and there. Her breasts seemed used, sucked — like a mother's. I was certain about that. It was then that I asked: 'Have you any children?' She nodded in the affirmative. Relief. That wasn't Mulki, for she had no children so far as I knew. But this feeling of relief didn't last long. If she wasn't Mulki, if she wasn't Ibrahim's sister, if she wasn't the typist who had helped Soyaan, well, she was another, she was another person and had the same right as anybody else. She loved somebody, and somebody must have loved her. She was there, you could be certain, for a crime she hadn't committed, a crime nobody had taken the trouble to prove against her. The ethics-syndrome again. But what could I do for her? Prescribe the best medicine there is, give her a good diet at least so that she doesn't come out undernourished on top of it all. But they had another doctor to countersign my chit. There was a Russian doctor. (One of my Chinese colleagues at Martini, one day, pointed out to me the Russian doctor the Security uses for such clandestine things. I didn't think a Chinese would go as far as that, but this one did. He, too, was human. A favour for a favour: I was the one who introduced him to the mistress he has, a nurse.) Anyway, the ethics-syndrome. Against the ethics of political violence, the weak have no means of survival other than to collaborate, up to a point, with the powerful. It is while collaborating that strategies can be studied. I pressed her where it hurt most. She groaned with the ache of my touch which had obviously hurt her. Meanwhile I asked her her name. I didn't hear it clearly, but it had more syllables than Mulki's. They blindfolded me again. They took off her mask while I was still there in the same room for I could hear her sigh of relief as she breathed louder and freer. By then they had blinded me with the mask. And that was that."

"Had you never met Mulki?"

"Yes, I had."

159

"How come you couldn't tell more easily? You know, I don't believe you. . . . " and he trailed off.

"What? What don't you believe?"

"Never mind what I don't believe."

The car choked on the accelerator. In no time, however, he pressed the pedal with the accurate pressure of foot. Then he went on to explain meekly:

"The woman's height, the colour of skin being the same as Mulki's, the premonition I had that one day they were going to play a nasty trick and present me with a tortured friend; the fact that I didn't think the woman needed a general physician: these, I suspect, weighed heavily on my mind."

"But why *you?* Why *you* all the time?"

"I am glad they choose me whenever they come to think of it now, because I believe if they went to those irresponsible doctors who are politically unaware the situation might have been different. I consider it symbolic: that I wash the blood they shed; that I bandage the sores they open; that I nurse the wounds they inflict upon the innocent; that I cure those whom they make sick; that I end a chapter of pain which they start; that I close the hole they dig; that I mend the bones they break; and that I am the hope they do not promise."

"Do you think they know you are a member of Soyaan's and Ibrahim's clandestine movement, that you are a collaborator of theirs? Or do you think they trust you because (I must say the unsaid) you are of the same clan as the General?"

"I do not know. I cannot tell."

Blow after blow, thought Loyaan, *and they will finally omit Ahmed-Wellie and then come to me. Perhaps Margaritta before that. They will render me helpless first. One by one, they will take away, remove all my contacts. They will discredit me before that. They've discredited Soyaan and myself by publishing the interview my father gave.* How lonely he had felt the day the interview came out in the papers, the day when all Soyaan's and his friends justifiably felt themselves betrayed by what had appeared publicly in the government paper. In addition to this, they would exploit the differences which perforce existed between his father and himself, the disagreements which were monumentally there between him and his mother on the one hand, and between Beydan and himself. Like worms, they would eat away into his walls of defence, little by little, and at their own

160

convenience. Like ants, they would move in silently and with their swordy teeth munch away quietly at what protected him. Maybe he shouldn't depend on anybody from here onwards. Maybe he should work on this unaided from now on so that when the moment came, when they'd removed and imprisoned Ahmed-Wellie, say, or Margaritta, he wouldn't feel so lonely. *Tomorrow, it starts in the morning, my dialogue with naked power begins tomorrow. It commences with my appointment with the Minister to the Presidency. We shall meet man to man, he all the more powerful what with the stars on his shoulders and the office he occupies and the guard at his gate and the meaning his signature is given every time it appears on a piece of paper; I all the more powerless and lonely because I haven't Samson's hair nor the magic word of Sesame open-this, open-that, no treasures, and hardly a future like Beydan's unborn child. But like a circus-hand's, my fingers will weave a magic carpet and I shall walk on it all the way, a red carpet of power. We shall meet man to man. . . .*

"Where do you wish me to take you?"

They were at the check-point.

"Take me home, please."

Ahmed-Wellie pulled up to the side and got out to register number-plate of car, name of owner of the vehicle, number of passenger, reason of travel. When he returned:

"I will drop you home and go straight off. I won't stop at your place."

"All right."

"Home then."

Heaven's God, no. Why, life never ceased to surprise one. In front of the house there was Margaritta, alone, in her car. What had brought her here? The Memorandum? *I go from one to the other. I go from one car to another.* Ibrahim was out of bounds now. Ahmed-Wellie might well be taken away before the night's darkness brightened into dawn, who knew. *From one to the other, like a call-girl who hires her night out to the highest bidder. Ring. Come. Quick.* What had Margaritta brought? Bad news? Or the Memorandum entitled Dionysius's Ear? What?

"Why didn't you enter?"

"After that embarrassing night when I drove you home drunk, do you remember? I couldn't face either your mother or Ladan."

161

They exchanged cheeks.

"They would never be rude."

"No. Your mother has been rude to me, rude as only women can be to one another. Ladan is not there, either. So I preferred to wait for you outside."

"I am sorry."

"I forgot to mention that I once drove Soyaan home dead-drunk, too. So she probably associates me with evil; I am, to her, the infidel mulatta who entices away her children one after the other, seduces them, gets them drunk and gives them illegitimate children. Yes, I understand."

He couldn't think of anything to say. He held his breath in suspense. He remembered what he had been through; he re-lived, in the briefest time possible, all that he had gone through since the morning when he had gone for the appointment with Ibrahim, he remembered his meeting with Beydan, then Ahmed-Wellie's curious call at Beydan's and the things he had told him. "Qumman is simply a woman who feels threatened by Beydan and by Margaritta; Beydan because of her being the wife Keynaan prefers and also because Soyaan supposedly ate poisoned food at her place; Margaritta because she represents the type of woman Qumman's generation detests." "I forgot to mention that I once drove Soyaan home dead-drunk." Qumman detested young, educated, "liberated women", the Margarittas, the Medinas. Well, that simplified things, thought he.

"I am sorry for all that," he repeated.

A phlegmatic emotion blocked her throat, and her voice did not come until she cleared it. Meanwhile, he kissed her on the forehead, took and pressed her hand. When they stood apart:

"Have you brought it with you?"

"What?"

"Have you brought Dionysius's Ear with you?"

"That is why I've come."

She accepted the cigarette he offered her. She let her bottom rest against the car's bonnet and had her cigarette lighted at the same time as he lit his own. She puffed in silence on hers, while he dragged on his.

"Did they stop you while you were on your way here and steal it off you, is that what they've done?"

She shook her head: no.

162

"What did they do?"

"They did worse than that."

Should he laugh, should he cry, should he hit her. should he do something or nothing? *Why am I always late? Why am I always the one who hears last? Why am I the one who learns of things last?*

"Did they break into your safe?"

"Something neater than that."

"I won't be able to guess if you don't tell me."

He sensed his heart twist with pain. He felt incapacitated by the information he was in need of receiving. What would she tell him? He considered that perhaps the best thing was just to leave her, forget that she had ever promised him a Memorandum, forget for the time being that they had ever encountered, that she had known and loved and cared for and borne Soyaan a son named Marco. They had Mulki and Ibrahim. That meant they also had the Memorandum the two had between themselves. *They are fast, aren't they? They know how to cover their traces. They prepare their own alibi. And when I meet the Minister to the Presidency tomorrow, what will I say? What evidence have I up my whatever?*

"How did they do it?" asked Loyaan.

"They opened my locker at the bank."

"Bank? How could they do that? The bank has one key, you have the other."

"They forced it."

"How did they come to know that you had it locked in there?"

"*He*'s always known that I keep my jewellery and valuable documents in the locker at the bank. You haven't forgotten, have you, that the Minister and I were once lovers?"

"What did the bank people say?"

"They gave me another locker for my jewellery and the rest of my documents and they apologised. What can they do? We are in a state of emergency as we've been the past five years."

"Life never ceases to surprise me."

There was a long pause.

"I am sorry," she said.

There was another longer pause.

"How is Marco?"

"He is fine, fine, fine."

"Luckier than us. I wonder if you've made him realise that he is

163

at the centre of it all, the key to this whole mystery. Soyaan. The Minister to the Presidency. The poem Soyaan scribbled on the back of the photograph. You. Me. My mother. My father. Beydan. We've victimised the rest, I seem to think, we've got involved in something which is none of their concern."

"I don't think I am with you," she said.

He kissed her on the forehead. Leaving:

"I meet him tomorrow. When I've spoken to him, I shall let you know."

"Him who?"

"Who else?" The Minister."

And he was gone.

Part III

Like bastard children, hiding in their names
(...)
forests
Of history thickening with amnesia.
DEREK WALCOTT

Your breast will not lie by the breast
Of your beloved in sleep.
W. B. YEATS

No water is still, on top.
JAMES DICKEY

Chapter Eleven

Like an ant that moves up a slope, down a crevice in a ditch, until it comes upon another dead ant, halts and goes round it again and again. The living ant ceases moving, and looks at the ant which has died, perhaps thinking of dragging it away back to a nest, somewhere definitely safer. But a little further up, descending upon them, descending upon the field, from across ditches far and near, one hears, no, one sees the roaring of a river coming towards the field, the ditches and the ants, a running river whose speed is uncheckable. The living ant hears, and having heard ceases moving, and sees the water rushing towards her and. . . .

The place was quiet but for the noise of an aeroplane hovering overhead. The shade was cool. Trees rubbed blossom against blossom above the ground, these trees which shielded the sky; yes, the convex of a leaf, showing its green, would come into contact with the concave of another, way up, above Loyaan, above everything, near the heavens. The friction, the contact, the touch: these when they lasted lured the butterfly and the worker-bee. And the wind hissed through the openings in the branches, radiated a warm welcome. Trees in units. Trees watered in grouplets. Here an orderly. There another. There an army vehicle. Here the starred eagle, the insignia of power. Posters huge as death, prompt as Michael the Archangel, posters positioned in the most prominent places, the one at the entrance more showily painted with red, the colour of blood, of death, Lenin's favourite, Stalin's perversity, and the General's pronounced loyalty to the Soviet hegemony. The first cigarette of the morning, the lungs more receptive, opening up gradually like the pink of a peacock howling when aroused — no, pardon, the lungs crackling rather like aluminium roofing which stretches under the potency of the tropical sun. The plane again. A MiG-19 this time. A swarm of birds, frightened by the ear-breaking noise, flew from one branch which hung down only to take shelter in the forest-safety of the same tree's heart, where, crisscrossing like the legs of passengers in a crowded train compartment the womb of the tree lay exposed, a possible prey, a womb waiting. . . .

167

Just like me, thought he. He was made to sit here and wait. A soldier had asked him to do that. Did he have an appointment with the Minister to the Presidency? If he had, where was the invitation? Ministers here didn't give appointments on telephones. He would just have to wait. *But . . . !* "We have instructions." And he was frisked from the crown down to the nerves of his instep. His pockets were emptied. He was given a form to fill, a form unjustifiably too long for the brief encounter he expected to have with the Minister. Loyaan usually had problems filling in forms and made a mess of every one he completed. He would cancel something and write another thing on top. No, no, this wasn't neat enough. "Name. Father's name. Profession. Name of Officer you wish to see. Reason." For this, there was sufficient space to write an editorial on any topic. Was he to fill every line here? His hands under his chin. Frisked, his pockets emptied, his body touched, abused, and humiliated, he was made to wait. "Ministers here don't give appointments on the telephone. I am afraid you will have to wait until the person who took the form you filled in returns. Please take a seat." They called this a seat? Huge rocks roughened with age, huge rocks smoothed by the bottoms which had used them. *Don't lose your calm. Be the rock, hard, unmoving and uncompromising; be the one which survives the comings and goings of governments and dictators, foreigners or locals; be the rock, intense, containing all, softness in its sand, cold at night, hot when the sun is up and out — and bloodless when cut. Be the one which peeps out of the cracks of the rocks, like saxifrage, the geckos and lizards, grey whether small or large, earthly and ugly — unlike Lagos lizards which lie on the ground, head defiantly raised, tail flat and properly positioned for activity.* There was another rock further up, a rock wide at the waist like a woman from the Mediterranean. If only they could speak, these rocks, what things they had seen, what hands they had touched, what buttocks they had come into contact with. Greece and Sicily: history as chiselled out of the harshness of rocks, come the Greeks themselves, the Sicilians, the Normans, the Arabs, come Garibaldi and his red shirts. (The black shirts of Mussolini, the red neckscarves of Lenin, Stalin; the green uniforms of the General's Green Guards.) When last in Sicily, he remembered now, he had found himself in a cave of a tavern peopled with toothless ancient men who drew their pension in wine bottles, as they counted the cups just to kill time, as they counted waiting for death, the bringer of relief. Not

Soyaan, no. Nor Ibrahim. *And not me, certainly. Soyaan had plans, we have projects, we have a list of things to do, a list of unread titles, a powerful sun to heat our young blood, a moon to light our night.* To interrupt that without notice, without telling any person, well, to cease *being:* that was wicked.

"Matches, please, do you have matches?"

Loyaan looked up. A soldier, a private soldier, biting the filtered end of a cigarette. Loyaan took out his lighter, but would not press the fire-button until he had told the man that by buying the cigarette he had in his mouth, did he realise, he was helping the white régime in South Africa.

"No, I didn't."

Loyaan regarded the man with understanding sympathy. "It is South Africa owned."

The soldier shouted out the brand-name of the cigarette as though by doing so he would remember better next time, as though that would help him never buy it again, pacify his conscience, help, in his small way, fight for the liberation of the African ("The African," would insist Soyaan, "not the black man; be specific: the other is white, perhaps, if one is generous towards him 'Euro-African', but never African") in the South. What of that in the North, shackled with the chains of an Asiatic code of thinking, what about the African in the North?

"Here," he lit it for him.

The soldier kicked his heels together and thanked him. "I didn't know," he confessed.

He shouted the brand name of the cigarette to the surroundings, and the rocks echoed his cry. He would not forget. He would never buy another ever again.

"But I have a near-full pocket of it. What do you think I must do with it, *jaalle?* Must I throw this near-full packet away? It is my conscience now. What do I do?"

"If you can stop smoking altogether so much the better."

The soldier stood upright and away from Loyaan. "Now that is another proposition altogether."

"Why don't you?" Loyaan lit his own.

"Why don't *you?*"

"Habit. I smoke out of habit. But I will one day, I promise you. We outgrew certain habits such as the constant need for our mothers,

169

I will one day outgrow this habit of sucking the smoke of my own teeth."

"I am addicted like you."

"Addicted?"

"Yes, addicted."

The soldier kicked his heels together and offered a salute improvised in time to an officer passing by. The senior officer, a lieutenant-colonel barely Loyaan's age, stared at him. Did he recognise him? Loyaan had. He was a simple sub-lieutenant when the General's régime came to power. And now what? In order to feel well-guarded, well-protected, the General had of late appointed a number of his tribesmen to prominent, key army positions. He had lent oxygen to the half-dead of other tribesmen so that there were no genuinely strong rivals from other clans. What about all other potential rivals? They were in prison or living on hopes in exile where they were humiliated, where they were jobless. Loyaan, after a thoughtful pause said:

"One gets addicted to power, not cigarettes."

The dust which had risen gathered itself into boulders of vapourous heat and wouldn't settle. The soldier, it appeared, wasn't willing to continue the dialogue. His heels touched lightly, respectfully, and he retreated:

"Back to work while you wait. I am sorry."

You must groom it like a bride and love it like a god. You must fence it with care, you must lie about it, as one does about a person one loves dearly, you must protect it with false notions of grandeur. Power — oh, what a mistress — remains faithful. You can then wear it like a flower in your hair, or a medal pinned to your chest. You must be patient as a famous person, and corrupting as fame; you must be avaricious as hunger, and green as a novice. Loyaan thought this while he followed the soldier whom the Minister to the Presidency had sent down to escort him through the intricacy of power's columny corridors and the door of his office. Look left, look right. They had now entered the one-way traffic of power: all things led to and owed their origin to the main author of all, the General. Parked in the shades were cars with CD-plates. There were men walking on foot. Others were in cars. The foreign language most commonly used here was Russian. Loyaan saw Soviet technocrats taking strolls, quiet as their sandalled feet, sweaty in their un-starched khaki, unoriginal in their thinking, unforthcoming when asked a question. He remembered one such Soviet aircraft engineer with whom he used to play chess. He read while he played with this man who was silent as tennis shoes on tarred court. October, that dawn in October. . . .

"The Minister asked me to apologise on his behalf for the delay," spoke the soldier finally delivering the message. "He said he forgot to tell somebody to wait for you at the main entrance."

"That is very kind of him."

"I meant to say this when we met."

"Never mind, I understand."

Loyaan trailed after him, turning where he turned, smiling to himself whenever the soldier offered a salute to a senior officer who hadn't even noticed he existed, many of whom at any rate wouldn't return the honour. A row of one-storey barracks, a cluster of squat tin houses were to one side. These were built by the Italians before the First World War. Now they housed the wives and children of the army officers from whom the General had formed his inner group. The children played war-games, their mothers, in groups, sat out in the shade chatting not directly about politics and power but the spoils these had given So-and-so's wife ("He hasn't been a military attaché even a month but have you seen the things he has sent his wife? A mere sergeant six months ago," et cetera, et cetera) and this or that one's cousin. October-power. Viva Lenin, viva! Viva the hegemony! That dawn in October 1969 when power (a mistress of wicked ways) slept manless, unloved, when she was given reason to believe she wasn't the most beautiful of mistresses, when chaos reigned and the men of the sixties (Margaritta's thesis about Africa's post-independence liberal governments preceding the seventies of military power and torture returned to his memory) couldn't agree to whom the hand should go. Any way you shuffled, the cards remained non-trumps. The queen, nobody was quick enough to realise, had slept alone for a good fortnight; the courtiers had been undecided all this time; they were themselves as sleepless as she was: but never mind. Came a suitor that dawn in October, came a General the month would, a year to the day later, garland with a revolutionary wreath and fervour; who arrived demonstrating an ace (that of "the popular will"). He eloped with her and loved her secretly and tended her with whispery kisses and charm. That dawn in October, the twenty-first of the month to be

171

precise, four days after the other October, and nearly coinciding with Numeiry's. Viva October-power!

"We've arrived."

A two-storey building, nearly as old as the Italian colony, and in front of it a sentry saluted when the soldier who had taken Loyaan walked in. Typewriters ticking away, kettles singing as tea and coffee were made, the corridor absolutely empty with not a soul in sight. The soldier and Loyaan went to the end of it and turned right just before the stairwell. Two steps, and:

"Here we are."

An orderly in civilian peon-uniform jumped up from his seat. The escort said to the peon:

"He has an appointment with the Minister. Show him in, *jaalle*."

"Yes, *jaalle*."

Heels again. The escort turned to go: "Thanks . . . er . . . *jaalle*."

"*Jaalle!*"

The Minister indicated an armchair to Loyaan as he came round from a mahogany escritoire (having just stood up from the pretence of working hard at something, Loyaan told himself). He was short and soft-spoken; his voice, though, was confident; his stride, as he walked to meet Loyaan's extended handshake, measured. The office was spacious. It was furnished with Scandinavian taste in teak and wood-lined. It was designed, thought Loyaan, with Italian chic and colour choice. A round table was at the centre of this well-furnished room. On the far wall was a celestial globe of bright and dim bodies. On another glass-topped table, a globe of the universe. Portraits of the General, photographs of him with the Minister on the day he had taken the oath as member of cabinet.

"Please! "

"Thanks! "

Soft as a pigeon's feathery breast: the touch of the arm of the chair in which Loyaan sat. The tips of his fingers, for lack of anything else to do, sought meanings and clues in the miniature bumps they encountered going up and down, moving quickly, then slowly, with or against the current. In places, it felt as though there were rigid spots like those on a towel on which had dried drops of sperm. Nothing, no idea, not a thought. Loyaan and the Minister avoided each other's eyes. Then a cynosure of his wandering gaze: the globe.

172

Keynaan. Soyaan and Loyaan as children. The Memorandums. What Soyaan said or didn't say. The post-mortem. Whether or not Beydan poisoned Soyaan's food. The articles found in his pockets. The piece on clowns and upstarts. Margaritta. Soyaan as hero, being knighted posthumously and a street being named after him. The interview with Keynaan. The wrong photograph in the paper. The speeches. The act of condolence. The poem on the back of Marco's photograph. Mulki in prison, Mulki under the pressure of torture. Keynaan re-offered a job in the Service. Ibrahim and Ahmed-Wellie and their clandestine movement so far unnamed. The split in the movement. Soyaan's and Ibrahim's working together on the Memos. The visit to Beydan. The Minister's repeated visits, his being seen with Keynaan. . . .

"How are you, Loyaan?"

"I am well, thank you."

"How's everybody at home, mother, sister?"

"They are well, thank you."

"How are things generally?"

"Confusing."

"And what about Beydan, have you seen her lately?"

"I saw her yesterday."

"How was she?"

"Well, and weighty."

"I am glad."

Now where does one start? Answer: with silence. *Make him nervous, give him no chance to know what you've come for. He will speak. He will begin fidgeting in his throne of temporary convenience. He will tremble with worry. Start with silence. End with silence. Don't be rude, nor gentle. Be theatrical for a change. Lower the volume of your voice to that of a stage whisper. Act confident, a man sure of himself. Whisper the unspoken secrets of the nation's heart which beats with fright. "Are they here? No? They were at my neighbour's yesterday. When will my turn come? I have a wife, I have children, I have an aged mother-in-law and several cousins who've come from the countryside; I keep them in the city, send them to school. I cannot throw years of labour up in the air like that. My daughter goes to high school, so do my two sons. My wife is pregnant with a child." Whisper the un-staged theatre of fear.* That globe again. Keynaan again. Guess what:

"Your father was here early this morning."

173

"Oh?"

"Did you not meet him on the way here?"

"No," said Loyaan, not in the least surprised.

"He must've taken another route."

"How was he?" he asked the Minister.

"He was unhappy that he wasn't promoted immediately he was rehabilitated. The Service paid his salary arrears all the years he was not actively serving the state. Yes, he was unhappy about not being promoted to the rank of lieutenant. I said I will take it up with the General and see what can be done for him."

Silence. Bait thrown. A pause long enough to elicit Loyaan's comment, to allure his trapped mind to say something "against" his father. No, he wouldn't fall for that. The Minister would have to try harder, place more alluring bait on the hook. He didn't have comments to waste, but was grateful for the information received unasked for. Let the Minister cross and uncross his legs. Scratch his head for thoughts like a hen scratches the dust for a peck's bite. Offer cigars straight from the factory in Havana, fresh, healthy and mouthfilling. Loyaan wasn't going to fall for any of that. He would wait for him to continue. The tongue of guilt, like a bell's, would eventually sound a confession, if not today certainly tomorrow, if not tomorrow most definitely the day after. Loyaan was in no hurry. No appointments for the day.

"Only this morning, we received the Local Government's disposition about which particular street should be named after Soyaan. One of the back streets of the cathedral. Your father wasn't pleased with this. He didn't think the road was in the good view of the public. 'Must one search for his name in this unmapped city?' he says. Personally, I think that street is very important. It is in the city centre. What do you think?"

"Nothing."

"I want you to speak your thoughts."

"Speak my thoughts?"

"Yes. Why not?"

Silence. *You have no thoughts on this, Loyaan. You have none. Not until you've heard a good reason why a street is to be named after Soyaan; you have no thoughts on this. Stuff your mouth with one of your cigarettes. Get on with it. Don't take one of those cigars. Cubans might be acting on behalf of the KGB. Careful. A murderer returns to the spot. If you have the patience to just wait, take your time, light your cigarette and not say anything, you will see that he will speak. See?*

"I think we can, in the course of the year, put a motion to the Supreme Revolutionary Council suggesting that a square be named after him, a school as well. Your father liked the idea. And you?"

"It is none of my concern."

"I am sorry. What do you mean that it is none of your concern?"

A point of no return. Loyaan would now have to say something. *Take your time, though. Be the inconvenience he never imagined you could be. Look at him cross and uncross his legs nervously. Look at his anxious face. Power is in your hand. Hold on to it, don't part with it, don't let it out of sight lest it betray you, lest it feel unloved, lest it seek company elsewhere, like a pet dog whose tongue pants the pain of loneliness, like a cat which accepts the companionship of anyone anywhere. Alone with your own thoughts, yes. But not lonely. Nor isolated as the Minister is. Your word is your power. Your inner thoughts your company. They need you to join them. They need your*

approval of their absurdities, their illogicalities. They have Keynaan's. They didn't and couldn't have Soyaan's. Neither should they have yours. "Over my dead body," said he. Did they not get Soyaan's soul when life disposed of his body?

"You haven't answered me."

"Did you ask a question?"

"Why is it not any of your concern?"

"I am sure you understand why."

The orderly, without knocking, walked in carrying a tray of drinks, soft drinks such as orange in tins, grapefruit *pressé*, and ice-cold beer. What would Loyaan like? Nothing, thank you. But the tray was put between them. The orderly withdrew and closed the door softly behind him. The Minister poured himself the orange. He said to Loyaan:

"It was you who asked for an appointment to see me. May I ask why you wanted to talk to me, and about what?"

He wouldn't admit it but the telephone's ringing startled him. The Minister let it ring itself to silence. He had another sip of his drink. He waited.

"Do you know a girl called Mulki?" Loyaan asked.

"Mulki who?"

"Mulki Musse, a secretary/typist who this year is doing her National Service working with the Ministry of the Fisheries and Naval Affairs. Do you? Mulki Musse."

"Is there any good reason why I, a Minister to the Presidency, should know a secretary/typist/student who is doing her National Service on secondment to the Ministry of the Fisheries and the Naval Affairs? Is there?"

"Yes."

"Tell me."

The Minister got up. He went behind his escritoire. He pressed a button. He spoke to somebody, said could he/she please come with writing-pad, et cetera. A secretary? Was that who he had spoken to?

"Do you know a man by the name of Ibrahim Musse, nicknamed 'Il Siciliano'?"

"He works for the Ministry of Justice?"

"That is right."

"I know of him."

A woman in her late twenties armed with a writing-pad and a set of pens entered but didn't approach until told to take a seat and wait. Loyaan wouldn't go on.

"Please."

He looked from the woman to the Minister and back again. "What is she doing here?"

"She is my secretary."

"We are having a private conversation. Please ask her to leave."

"This is not private. We're having this conversation in the office of a government minister, and are talking about Soyaan, a man knighted by the Revolution. She is here to register what we say."

"Send her away." Loyaan got up. "For your own good."

"No."

He put his cigarettes in his pockets.

"Haven't they as yet installed the KGB bugging-system in all government offices? Can't you use hidden methods, a thing the size of a button glued to the ceiling or something? Send her away."

A movement of his head was sufficient to order the woman to leave the room. From the look of it, the Minister was very angry. Loyaan told himself that he did not care. Angry? He could boil in the cauldron of his rage, who cared? *But I cannot afford to lose my patience. I must stay calm. I mustn't lose my calm which, in effect, is*

176

my power. Smile now. There. Smile. Apologise? No need. Keep quiet for long enough and he will apologise for the misunderstanding.

"Sorry about that. I thought. . . ."

"It's all right."

Lid that up, cover it with your warmed hands. Pour yourself something. Coat your agitated tongue with the bitterness of that juice. Yes, do. Sit down. Take out your cigarettes from your pocket. Don't say a thing for a while. Now:

"When you and I met that afternoon at the cemetery, you asked me, I am sure you remember, if I knew anything concerning two Memorandums Soyaan had worked on. I remember I said that I didn't."

"Go on."

"That same afternoon — I remember this also as clearly as the day Soyaan died — you asked if he, Soyaan, spoke the words 'Labour is Honour' just before he breathed his last. I recall telling you that he did not; that, in fact, his last breath was spent on pronouncing my name. Do you remember that?"

"Yes, I remember that. Go on."

"You have since then made many things happen according to a certain plan. You have, for instance, made my father speak a false-hood, you've had him swear to the truth of what he has said, you've made him give an interview publicised in the only daily which is in your own hands. LABOUR IS HONOUR AND THERE IS NO GENERAL BUT OUR GENERAL. Yes, my father who wasn't at the side of the bed when Soyaan died swears to the truth of what you've reported in the papers. A street is named after Soyaan. He has become state property and everything that concerns his name must be addressed to your office. Today you talk of squares and schools to honour Soyaan's name with. May I ask, with all due respect of course, why my brother was singled out for this singular honour from all those who died during that week?"

"Your brother had the revolutionary zeal which distinguished him from the others who died during that week. Your brother and I collaborated on a number of projects. I knew him to be a man of great integrity and revolutionary fervour."

Like a fallen meteor, the light in the Minister's eyes became pale and weak. Loyaan's waiting silence worsened things all the more.

177

Search for these eyes of his just as Beydan had looked out for mine with her super-powered stare. Make him speak. And listen.

"I am sorry but I suspect you've been frequenting the wrong set of people who are of bad influence. There is a jealous set of persons who circulate the rumour that Soyaan was anti this régime. I know this to be untrue. Soyaan died for this régime, serving it."

"The wrong set of persons? A jealous set of friends? And you talk of bad influence as though I were a little boy or a little dog following the wrong lead. You talk of rumours being circulated. What is all this?"

"I've just paraphrased your father's words."

Loyaan for a second was bent on following that up with a mere sentence which would strike Keynaan's name off every list for good. But no. The globe again. He drew the curtain on that private portion of his experience. He remained unseen and unseeing for a time. Then:

"To begin with, my father wasn't there when Soyaan hiccupped his last. I was. I can prove that to anyone who is interested in bringing to an end this made-up story, I tell you I can."

"He wasn't there?"

"He wasn't."

"But in the interview he said he was."

"In the interview my father added that Soyaan said not only that LABOUR IS HONOUR but that THERE IS NO GENERAL BUT OUR GENERAL. Whereas Soyaan's writings prove that he considered the General a usurper, a tribalist, a fascist of the first grade, a Dionysius."

"Now that alters things."

"Sorry?"

"Never mind."

The Minister got up and went behind his escritoire and jotted down something on a piece of paper. He looked up and at Loyaan, his pen in mid-air:

"What writings of Soyaan prove that he considered the General a usurper, a tribalist, a fascist of the first grade and a modern Dionysius?"

"I have them."

The Minister leaned forward. "You have the Memorandums? Do you have the Memorandums?"

"The wrong set of people, a group of jealous friends. . . ."

Irrepressible anger:

"What is all this? Do you or don't you have the Memorandums?"

"If you calm down, Mr Minister, everything will become clear."

The Minister threw the pen across the room in rage. His face, when still silent, fell into wrinkles reminiscent of an ants' nest into which and out of which flowed unholy thoughts — un-whole! Would he press the button, and say: "Remove him out of my sight." The *dolfino* of the Generalissimo had turned white as the underside of a whale. Whereas Loyaan was thinking to himself that he didn't have anything to lose; that the Security wouldn't dare touch him, at least not until weeks, perhaps months had passed; that the power of the weak is in their weakness. Well, why not! He could even show, if necessary, all those bits and pieces of writings found in Soyaan's pockets, he could show them to whoever was interested in seeing them. Wouldn't the Minister be? Just as much as Loyaan would be interested in getting copies of the Memorandums. Just as much as Loyaan would do anything to save Ibrahim and Mulki from their hold. The Minister had by then come round and taken his place opposite Loyaan. The sun's vapoury rays drenched the office with a liquidy touch of warmth. The Minister rubbed his hands together, the Minister crossed and uncrossed his legs. It was Loyaan who said:

"If we return to the beginning, Mr Minister, if we start where the whole thing began, Mr Minister. . . ."

"Yes?"

"Ibrahim. Mulki. The Memorandums."

"I don't understand what Ibrahim and Mulki have to do with the Memorandums."

"Do you know them?"

"I know of Ibrahim, but I've never heard of her."

"Never?"

"Never of her."

"You've never heard of a Mulki, a secretary/typist taken away for interrogation one dawn by the Security, then tortured and made to speak? Do you mean you haven't ever heard of the person who told you that she had typed Soyaan's Memorandum entitled Dionysius's Ear? Never?"

"Never."

Perversely, Loyaan was enjoying himself now, he was laughing inside, and the pride he felt brightened his eyes. He believed he would see, before he left the office, the Minister just fade away — like a burning candle standing upright against the darkness, shedding fatty tears of light — fade away, just like that. He saw himself as the torturer, as the powerful pervert who puts the needle between the flesh of the thumb and the nail, screws it in harder, deeper, further and further, until it draws blood, not innocent blood, but just blood, red blood. *Drill it in, harder, deeper make it more painful, more dolorous, turn the ailing soul's cry into the scream of the tortured.*

"And you haven't heard of Ibrahim, nicknamed Siciliano?"

The telephone made them both turn. It rang itself to silence as before. Then:

"I still cannot see what these have to do with the Memorandums, with Soyaan, with me or you?"

Loyaan felt challenged like a torturer who couldn't make the tortured confess after the umpteenth piercing of the needle. Change method. Think of something which would work on him. Twist his testicles, saw them off, humiliate him. Mention names, drop them and before he had thought of picking them up, change topic, method, style.

"You know Margaritta?"

"Margaritta?"

"Yes, Margaritta."

Focus. Pincers. Knives here. See his mask drop. Watch him breathe unhealthily, watch him inhale and exhale with greater frequency, faster and in a disordered way. Watch him cross and uncross his legs, rub his hands together. The Minister then opened the box in front of him. He took out a cigar. He broke its polythene with the same cruelty as a rapist would deflower a virgin. But he took his time as he smelt the sweetness of its odour before he put it into his mouth. Hardcore. None of that had worked on him. No?

"I thought we were not having a private conversation," he said.

"We are not having a private conversation."

"What about Margaritta then?"

As hard a core as I've ever seen, hard as a kernel.

"The Security have forced her locker in the bank open."

"When?"

"Why do you pretend you know nothing of this, then?"

"I am not pretending anything. It is true. I know nothing of all this. I've never heard of Mulki. I know nothing about what has hap-

180

pened to Ibrahim nicknamed Siciliano. Nor about Margaritta's locker being forced open. But what have *they* taken out? Jewellery?"

"*They* who?"

"What?"

"Are they *they* to you? Very well: they've taken out what was in it."

"What? What was in Margaritta's locker?"

"You tell me."

"How can I? Margaritta was once a good friend of mine. Once like a sister to me. Then we shared intimacies, what a man and a woman share. I haven't seen her though for quite some time now."

"Do you remember talking of 'a certain woman' whom you suggested I see? Do you remember? That was on the day we met at the burial ground."

"I cannot remember. Nor do I know where this will lead us. I am afraid your father was right in believing that you have been in contact with and under the influence of anti-revolutionaries. Ibrahim Siciliano. Mulki, a secretary/typist who when tortured spilled the husks of her protected secrets. Margaritta. What? The Security have broken into her locker and taken out what was there. You've been reading the wrong set of books. You've been under the bad influence of reactionaries. As for Soyaan, God bless him — God bless the souls of the dead — he was a revolutionary and he died serving the Revolution. No amount of misinformation will make the General change his mind. Soyaan is the hero the Revolution has knighted. Schools, squares, streets will be named after him. Yes, my dear Loyaan. Whether some of your friends like it or not, Soyaan is the hero the Revolution has decided to knight."

He got up, cigar in mouth although unlit and as yet unpierced. He walked a little closer to his escritoire, but returned. He bent down. He replaced the cigar in its box.

"And I shall tell you one other thing nobody has. Soyaan was bound for a post abroad. I have it here on record. Soyaan, a fortnight before his death, was appointed the Somali Councillor in Belgrade. Life's irony, of course. But all was set to unfold (he didn't know) and he would've left for Moscow on a special plane. I was re-reading the file before your father arrived. He was on tomorrow evening's list of passengers. Soyaan was scheduled to be on tomorrow's flight to Moscow."

181

"The Somali Councillor in Belgrade?"

"Yes. And better things in store, too."

Loyaan rose to meet the Minister's height. He was taller, but when their stares encountered one another, it was Loyaan's which melted in downcast evasiveness. *Coraggio! What have you to lose?*

"Out of academic interest — but please tell me if you will — what was it that the Russian doctor at the Military Hospital gave to Soyaan?"

The Minister's voice trembled as he spoke in haste to cover the tremor:

"What Russian doctor at the Military Hospital?"

"The one you yourself took him to see."

He turned his back on Loyaan. "I don't know what you are talking about," he said.

"What was his name? Is he still here? Will he be leaving on tomorrow's special plane bound for Moscow? Just out of academic interest. What was his name?"

"I did not take Soyaan to any Russian doctor."

"Whom did you take him to?"

"Nobody."

"You drove him yourself to the Military Hospital. I can name three persons who saw the two of you enter the hospital that day when you returned together from Afgoi. I also know of somebody who saw you consult a doctor yourself. But what was the injection which the Russian doctor gave to my brother, the thing which poisoned my brother's blood and eventually killed him, what was that? Just out of academic interest."

"Have you gone out of your head?"

"What was it, Mr Minister?"

"This is absurd."

"What was it, Mr Minister? And why? Was it because he had written and made statements which proved the culpability of the KGB and our Security Services in harassing the lives of innocent human beings, in torturing them, in depriving them of the right to live a decent life? Was it because Soyaan intended to publish the Memorandum titled Dionysius's Ear? Had he become inconvenient, too intolerably inconvenient?"

"You are out of your mind."

"You could've sent him out of the country. You know you

182

could've made him join the officers in the army whom you deport monthly to Moscow and other places, couldn't you? You could've waited until the day he was supposed to take the plane, the special plane you've just mentioned, to Moscow and finally to Belgrade, no? Too neat a job for our Security men. I smell the KGB."

"But why should we want to kill Soyaan? If so, why then knight him?"

"Heroes are made, Mr Minister. Hero-worship is a phenomenon as necessary as history itself. Every nation needs heroes in which to invest a past, heroes and legendary figures about whom one tells stories to children and future generations."

"But why him?"

"I am asking the same thing. Why him?"

"Yes, why him?"

"Perhaps because he wrote Dionysius's Ear."

"What's that?"

"Dionysius's Ear is the title of one of the Memorandums. Why must you feign ignorance?"

"I've never seen that Memorandum."

"And you've never heard of Mulki?"

"No. Never."

"And you've never heard of a one-armed man who shadows me everywhere I go?"

"A one-armed man?"

"Yes."

"Is he from the Security?"

"You've never heard his name mentioned?"

"That is another service. My ministry has nothing to do with that."

"But you can pick up that phone and ask if the one-armed man is from the Corps if you want, can't you?"

"We don't interfere in the affairs of other ministries or services."

Were those the symptoms of the insane, the brown of Loyaan's eyes which had gone a shade darker than Greek-grown olives? Like ball-bearings in the darkened oil of used grease, his eyes turned and turned.

"I suggest you leave now," said the Minister. "For your own good."

The Minister went behind his escritoire ready, Loyaan told him-

183

self, to press a button of alarm in case something unexpected happened. He pretended he was working. The Minister opened a file and set it in front of himself.

"You won't tell me anything else, Mr Minister?"

"I suggest you leave," said the Minister tremblingly.

"We're going to see you, I hope, Mr Minister?"

"Your father has invited me for tomorrow's seventh-day memorial. I intend to come. I hope, meanwhile, you will have thought about the graveness of your accusation."

"See you tomorrow, Mr Minister."

Chapter Twelve

Like a child not yet two, faced with the difficulty of choosing between a gecko and a scorpion: which to play with, which to disembowel and cut in two. The child's mother, seated not very far from him, is pleased that he has found something which interests him; she is blind and hence does not know what. However, she infers from the gurgling enjoyment in his voice that he is happy, and that he hasn't even wet himself. A gecko. A scorpion. Then the child's eyes, by chance, fall on a grasshopper, hopping thither, hopping hither. Excited by the acrobatics, the child is thrilled. His ga-ga-ga, his da-da-das gather momentum. He crawls towards his choice. His mother, meanwhile, calls to him. Her tone is grave. She waves in front of her colourful rosary, a thing she knows he always loves to put into his mouth and suck and play with. Between the child and herself now: the scorpion. Between him and the grasshopper, his choice, the gecko. And the child moves.

The drums bargained: they would not be silenced. The men who beat them perspired heavily, they sang as they beat, they beat as they sang the praise songs of the General. They were the griots in green.

"Long live the General. . . . There is no General but the General. . . . Long live the Revolution. . . . The Marxist-Leninist Islamic Revolution. . . . Long, long live the General. . . . Paster Noster, the Father of the nation. . . ."

Loyaan lay on his back, awake. No siesta today. The drums wouldn't allow that. Nor would the announcers who heralded their approach by shouting loudly into portable loud-speakers the same things as had been read by the other announcers in cars a couple of hours previously:

"All able men and women of the Village of Howl-wadaag, come. Come to the Rendezvous of the Brooms. Come and sweep. Come and clean. All strong-bodied persons: come and partake in the revolutionary duty of making your district clean as glass freshly wiped and washed, clean and mirror-like. Your district is your mirror. It speaks for you. The General and his honoured foreign delegation have chosen to bless us with their presence, the day after tomorrow.

They are our honoured guests at the Orientation Centre. Come one, come all. Let us clean it as we clean our bodies. All able men and women. . . ."

The drumming was getting closer, the announcer's voice further away; one very urgent and near, the other distant and unhearable. Ladan and Qumman were readying themselves to go to the Rendezvous of the Brooms, each with a broom in hand. They had spoken to Loyaan to lie low, lock the door from inside and sleep, read or do whatever he wanted. Lie low? Sleep? Read? What? Who could do any of these things with that chaos within earshot? The scene of the day presently came up, like vomit, to a throat which wouldn't throw up a drop of soured cud. He sat up. His head beat on the drum of its ache. No siesta today, definitely.

"Come one, come all, Revolutionaries of the Village of Howlwadaag, come to the Rendezvous of the Brooms and let us together paint silver-white our mirrors, our village."

Ladan and Qumman had changed into their work clothes. They would go there, sweep and clean, they would prepare the village's roads just as a mother would a daughter on the day of marriage, skin oil-smooth, every hair in place, the dress the right colour, bride rested, happy, welcoming, receptive. Come: take this bride, our village, as yours in sacred marriage for the brief duration of your stay in Somalia, Mr Visiting President. Come: take this key, the symbol of power, and open the cleaned and shaven legs of our womanhood. Come: take this sceptre, use it as the whip for the sado-masochistic rite to which you've been honourably invited. We host you, we present you with a hand of your choice. We've given one Belet-Weine girl to Idi, we give you another, Mr Visiting Dignitary. Please accept this exchange — not so much of opinion. Our people don't have opinions. We are all after our General. We pray to him.

Ah, at last. They were gone, Mother and Ladan. The drummers had come closer, the announcer's cries had completely faded. Loyaan went and hurriedly put on a pair of trousers. Since he couldn't take an afternoon nap he decided he would go out. They beat the drum, these militiamen in the green uniform of the *Guulwade* — the bringer of victory. "The lumpen in hempen, the green roughness of the uncultivated," Soyaan's definition of the *Guulwade*. Hundreds of jobless youths who would enrol as volunteers first, who would work round the clock doing what job they were asked to. Six months, nine months, perhaps. Then they would undergo a military training of no great worth, would take oaths of loyalty to the General's revolution. "The lumpen in hempen, a creation of the General's notion of the loyal citizen," another definition from Soyaan. They were beating the drum and singing the sycophancies of the revolution's successes. They added: "Come one, come all, Revolutionaries of Howl-wadaag. All able persons. . . ." He couldn't take it any more. The scene with the Minister had returned. The drum beat the rhythm of his periodic migraine. He would go, he decided, and tell them to make noise elsewhere, let people who didn't want to go to the Rendezvous of the Brooms sleep. Yes, he would break the promise he had given to his mother and sister: "We go. You stay. Your sister, your mother will join the men and women and sweep with them." Every family was registered with the Orientation Centre. Certainly somebody of Soyaan's or Loyaan's fame and name would be missed at a gathering such as this. "But we'll go," reasoned Qumman. "Don't you mind. Just go to sleep, lie low, lock the door from inside, read." Lock the door from inside? *Am I a thief? What and who do I fear?* If Ladan and Qumman were there, Loyaan would have to shut his mouth. They would draw the mat from under him, embarrass him in front of the others. "We do this for your own good," they would argue. Husbands went to these rendezvous in order to save wives and children from starving joblessness. Children sang the General's praises at school so that their parents weren't blamed for dissuading them from the right path.

"The Marxist-Leninist Islamic Revolution. . . . Long, long live the General, the Father of this nation."

And Loyaan stood in the doorway. The Green Guards went from door to door just like beggars who chanted alms-songs. They were in front of the house opposite to his family's. Loyaan had the patience to wait until they came to where he was. There were children playfully keeping pace with them, children who sang with them, who marched militarily to the rhythm of the drum. A nation regimented, militarised. A nation disciplined and forced to obey the iron-hand directing the orchestra of groans and moans. In addition to the children, neighbours had come out of their huts to watch this display of revolutionary talent singing their favourites, drumming and marching. This was turning into a circus: an extremely fat woman, no more than four feet, short and ugly, walked out from the crowd and with a

187

raised hand quietened the drums. She would somersault, she said, or dance better than any slim rival, however tall, however handsome, male or female. The crowd clapped. Ladies and gentlemen: let us present a clown. Silence.

"Will you city-criers please let people sleep their afternoon siesta with the necessary quiet?" shouted Loyaan. "You are becoming a nuisance, a noisy disturbance of the peace in the area."

First, there was shocking silence. Then all eyes, a hundred pairs, thought he, zoomed in on him. The children, for their part, were disappointed at the sudden interruption of the circus. So was the fat woman.

There was a stir in the crowd, there were small movements. A Green Guard was making his way towards Loyaan. A neighbour was making her way from another direction. "Please let me pass. Please let me pass." The Green Guard stopped right in front of Loyaan before the woman reached him. He looked Loyaan up and down. He knew he had the power to arrest and detain any offender, anyone who broke peace and order, for at least three months before that person was even brought to court. Was he not a Green Guard, a Keeper of Peace, was he not a militiaman, a revolutionary? "Lie low. Sleep. Read. We'll go." "I have a wife and children and a job to save. I have an aged mother, I have children who go to school. I am the only breadwinner of the family." *No. I am not one of these. I have nothing to lose. Let all present witness.*

"Give me your name," said the Green Guard authoritatively.

"Who are you?"

"I said, give me your name and particulars, *jaalle*."

The neighbour, a large tall woman, had joined them. The neighbour grabbed Loyaan's wrist and held it tightly until it pained him. She covered him with her body as though he were a child being protected from an imminent blow. She addressed the Green Guard in the most appealing of tones, and at the same time pressed Loyaan's wrist tighter to silence him, to make him understand:

"*Jaalle Guulwade*," she interrupted appealingly, "I know this man. I was there when he was born. His name is Loyaan Keynaan. He is a very important man in the government. His brother Soyaan is the man whom the Father of the Nation, the General, has honoured and knighted as the Hero of the Revolution."

"I know Soyaan, the Hero of the Revolution. I know him. Is

there anyone who doesn't? Doesn't every member of the crowd here know who Soyaan is?"

There came a chorus in the affirmative.

"But who is this man?"

"His brother Loyaan."

"Is he really?"

"Yes," said the neighbour.

Heaven's God! What must Loyaan do now? He felt suffocated. He felt he needed air to breathe, fresher air than that which had become heavy with disgust, embarrassment and shame. She let his wrist go now. She stood away from him. The Green Guard to her:

"If it weren't for you, we would take him and teach him a lesson. Thanks for enlightening us on who the man is, the brother of Soyaan, Hero of the Revolution."

Loyaan, loud enough for everyone to hear, said:

"Go to hell, all of you."

The Green Guard, who had heard what was said, asked of the woman: "What did he say?"

"Nothing, nothing. Go, and may the General's blessing be with you."

And she stood right in front of Loyaan, covering him, his wrist in her tight grip, whispering to him, although looking the other way, that she was doing this for his mother's sake, for Ladan and for Keynaan, and for his own good. *There you are. They pull the supporting ground from below you. They pull down the wall you might lean against. They impoverish you. They make you look ridiculous. For your mother's sake, for your sister's, for your father's.* The Green Guard, triumphant, had a point to make before he told his men that the drumming could be resumed. He said to the woman:

"We want you to guarantee before everybody here that this man will behave and not make a nuisance of himself again. And to do that I need your name, and your husband's name."

"But why her husband's name?" challenged Loyaan.

The woman gave her name and her husband's name.

"You guarantee also, I understand, that he will come to the Rendezvous of the Brooms."

"Yes, I do."

The Green Guard gave a GI-salute (something he had learned from American films) and signalled to the drummers to resume their

189

beating. The crowd, terribly disappointed nothing dramatic had come out of it all, dispersed. The woman turned on Loyaan.

"For your mother's sake, for your sister's and your father's, shut up."

At the Rendezvous of the Brooms.

A sprinkling of men, a greater number of women in their cheapest garments gave the dusty road which branched off from the main tarred road a vista of ruggedness and disorder. Women, as a class, formed the majority here, in view of the nature of work to be executed. They descended upon it with a devotion which they never seemed to display when sweeping their own homes. "Fill their eyes with noisy songs which please *him*; provide their eyes with what *he* loves to see. They want all the roads leading off and on to the routes the delegation will take swept, no? Isn't that the only thing which will fill their eyes with pleasure? That is no high task," said the woman who, protecting him, embarrassed him. Women formed the majority of those present here, for they left their husbands and brothers to take a siesta after the day's school, office or whatever. "It is very untraditional to see a man with broom in hand. Most of them don't know how to use the thing, just as much as most don't know how to put water on a fire or are incapable of making themselves cups of tea. The dependence of men on women in this part of the world is of such greatness one is shocked into incomprehension to realise how badly women are treated. Suppose, one day, all women decided they wouldn't go to the kitchens to cook their husband's meals," a woman friend of Loyaan's used to argue when in Baidoa. "Things are more complicated than that," he had said. "There is mutual need: a torturer needs somebody who is willing to be tortured, no?" Qumman and Ladan were there among the women. They had said their say. He should've stayed at home. He shouldn't have opened the door in the first place. And in the second place, he should've lain low as he had promised. "You are going to fall ill," his mother predicted. "You will be sick as usual. Your periodic migraine. See what you've done to yourself. Men of your class and education are asleep. They haven't even sent their mothers and sisters to come and sweep. They are represented by their house-maids. We've come because of this delicate period we're passing through. Don't you understand?"

"Move. Sweep. Don't talk."

190

Qumman and Ladan were full of concern for his safety, just as the other women there were for their husbands' and brothers'. But they didn't have to stick to him, stand by him, remind him of what his duty to them was. They didn't have to hold him down. He was going to go mad if they continued. "Promise is promise. I am not going to say anything. I will sweep like everyone else. But please leave me in peace. Don't strangle me with your concern for my safety. Don't throttle me with your love." Ladan managed to pull Qumman away. "Move. Sweep. Don't talk."

He bent down to sweep. Although his back ached, he didn't mind. He wasn't weaker than the others, he could certainly perform anything they were capable of, women, men, security personnel or Green Guards. "But one thing is definitely clear," he said to himself. "Somalia is a prison. We are the prisoners; the Security, the Green Guards, are the jailers; and the General, the Grand Warder of them all." Would he admit that he wasn't expert at sweeping dusty ground, sifting sand grains from other waste matter? No, he had other things to think about, his interests lay elsewhere. He was ready to speak something which would make this martial government's hair stand on end. "Soviet influence is like polluted oil a huge tanker has leaked. It will spread and pollute every waterway in the Red Sea and surroundings. The fish they haven't already cleaned out of our seas will die of this, just imagine: hundreds of tons a day. But. . . . " Soyaan again. He remembered his talk with the Minister. Keynaan. Ibrahim and Mulki. Ahmed-Wellie. Margaritta. The Memorandums. The Russian doctor at the Military Hospital. The post-mortem which was never performed. He stood upright, he straightened his back. His mother, despite the promise, was only a few feet away. She was keeping a keen eye on his movements. Ladan had gone off as she said she would. But Mother kept a decent distance and was disturbed when she saw that Loyaan was looking askance, behaved as though amused by all this. "Don't say a thing. Just nod or shake your head. Are you all right? How is your back?"

"Sweep. Don't talk. Move."

Women as saviours, women as protectors; women as the backbone of the family's unity and safety. The women who were there gadded about, snatched from the men the brooms they didn't quite know how to use and they teased them. They cracked apolitical jokes, they laughed, they moved about with sufficient ease, yes. However, fear was central to their behaviour. There was something unnatural about it — like grins on the faces of a dictator's entourage, like the contagious laughter of the powerful whose smile makes others giggle with artificial pleasure. These women knew there was a limit beyond which they wouldn't cross; they knew that that was straight politics; that that was men's territory. How wise these women: for this reason they wouldn't overdo the teasing. Would it stretch, would the cord snap? Women had the difficult task of making sure these men wouldn't lose their temper, nor their heads, and speak their minds and in that way endanger their own lives and the lives of the women and the children who were financially dependent on them. Very subtle things happen in coded mannerisms — just as, in the coded stereotypes of cinematography, a murder is likely to be committed in a tunnel; just as only women-adulterers are shown totally in the nude when being unfaithful, but married couples are not to be shown naked when making love unless the act of copulation is of scientific interest. He went back to sweeping. The scene now brought back to Loyaan's mind another he had seen in an extract from a British film about a D-day meet between the forces of the Germans and those of the Allies. "Just like that. Quiet. And safe," Qumman said to him.

"Don't talk. Sweep. Move."

A Green Guard who had assumed the responsibility of a supervisor was shouting at a woman for having taken an instant's break when tired. Loyaan walked over and said:

"Leave the woman alone. She is tired, can't you see?"

"And who are you to tell me what to do and what not to do?"

The woman was pregnant. Loyaan didn't immediately rise to the Green Guard's provocative statement, but crouched by the woman and consoled her with a mere show of sympathy and a touch of hand. He rose to his feet. The sweepers had become a crowd, a forest of eyes focused on Loyaan. There was his mother by him, there was his sister as well. The woman who had previously come to his rescue was there again: this time, she called the Green Guard by name and dragged him away, appealing to his sense of understanding, ". . . the woman is after all pregnant."

"Move. Sweep. Move."

Every time, somebody pricked the balloon of his pride: emotion, women, love, do-this-for-love's sake or that sake. Now they wouldn't leave him, Qumman stayed close by, Ladan at a safer distance. Qumman

192

placed herself within hearing. She kept speaking to him every now and
again. "Why, in heavens, are you doing all this? What will you get out
of that?" Ladan came level with him, making the same soft sandy
strokes of the inexperienced sweeper as he. She said that he should
listen for she had something to tell him in confidence. She said she
didn't believe there was any sense in his being stupid. "Please don't
do anything not worthy of you, of Soyaan's name and what he stood
for, the resistance he represented. You want to rebel? You want to
revolt against all this? You want to do something? Do it. But do it
without parting with your composure; yes, the composure which
defines a person. You pick a dirty fight with a Green Guard. What will
you get? Three months' imprisonment and adverse publicity. No,
what you want, what we all want is change. Do you think the General
has parted (at least externally) with what makes a politician tick? He
smiles at whom he plans to imprison, kill or deport. He tells the
world that he is socialist, that his is a progressive peace-loving govern-
ment. Do you think it is? You know it isn't. Listen to me, listen care-
fully. Don't look. But there are 'strangers' in this crowd, persons whose
provenance is dubious. Don't do anything. Don't look anywhere."
The two moved together, they moved with the row of sweepers, as
though they were part of a group of cotton-pickers. There. He saw
them. Three men in neatly pressed trousers, three men who had each
borrowed a broom from the women. Behind them was the one-armed
man.

>The first pursuer is here. . . .
>The hunters close in: do they feel the danger
>When they wrench his body to pieces, will they hear
>A sigh as his spirit is sucked into the air
>That they must breathe? . . .

Marco, Margaritta and Beydan. Mulki, Keynaan and Ibrahim.
Ahmed-Wellie? Would he turn up unexpectedly? Was he hiding be-
hind the one-armed man? All under Soyaan's star influence. Yes,
including the Minister who trembled, the Minister whose blood boiled
hot with fear of unknown deaths, the mystery of what Loyaan knew or
did not know. *If he were alive, Soyaan would leave for Moscow on a
special plane; the date is tomorrow, if you are interested. No. I want
to know how you killed him. I want you to tell me the name of the
Russian doctor whom you took him to consult for whatever slight
complaint he had on the day you returned from Beydan's place. He*

193

was thirsty. What did you give him to quench his thirst? He swept as he thought, he thought as he swept. He was alone right in the midst of the crowd. He didn't feel Ladan's presence by him. He was lonely. The voice which until recently had helped him with suggestions wouldn't come any more. He was alone. He had not the will-power to look and see whether his mother was still there behind him, checking on him, moving in on him from behind. *Don't lose your composure.* None of that. He was lonely suddenly. The voice was gone. His stomach was cold inside. Cold and lonely.

"Is your name Loyaan?"

He saw it was the taller and stronger of the three. The man indicated that he had a revolver ensconced in his clothing and that he would use it if necessary.

"You've come at last," said Loyaan.

Ladan and Qumman both simultaneously straightened their backs. Their extra senses told them that the time had come, that the Security had finally arrived. But neither was ready to do anything stupid.

"Will you come quietly with us, *jaalle?*"

"At last, you've come."

"Formalities, nothing serious. Just formalities."

"You've taken ages coming."

"Come with us."

Loyaan's neck now ached from looking up at the only small opening in the room's ceiling. It was dark in the room, dusky outside and dusty and windy, too. He could hear the wind blow, he could hear it rage and riot. *A storm of sand, who knows,* thought he, *which would blind them one and all and will free me.* He indulged himself in stupid speculations such as this, but kept staring at the small opening in the ceiling lest he lose touch with the world he was familiar with, the world he was fond of. *I am like the child who holds on to its mother's skirt, the infant that follows the smell of its mother's sweat.* The hole in the ceiling was big enough for a bat to enter through — and it did. The bat came from the evening's darkness, it came from the world outside, free a second previously, a prisoner now, like Loyaan, or like Ibrahim in another cell somewhere else, or Mulki his sister. The bat blindly swooped down and low, it swirled downwards and upwards, expressively nervous and rebellious.

He remembered that they had driven out of the city and turned right, past unfinished buildings, past the cigarette and match factory the Chinese had built and donated to this country. He remembered that they had forked off up and into a subsidiary road and immediately through another returned to the Upper Circular Road. But before he had time to invoke the memory of the Armed-Prophet's name, the car had slowed down and braked. He was transferred to a van and pushed into the back of it, shackled, his mouth filled with a cottony gag, was blindfolded and made to lie down on a mattress, then driven off. They turned round and round, a dirt road, a tarred one, a bumpy drive every now and again, something which reminded him of the story Ahmed-Wellie had told him about being taken to medicate the wounds of a prisoner who had been cruelly tortured to near death. But where were they taking him? Need they dramatise it this way? Or were they going to produce, at the end of this bumpy trip, some evidence as un-challengeable as the fact that Ibrahim was being held prisoner to prove that Mulki had never heard nor known of a Memorandum and never typed one for Soyaan or anybody else for that matter? Were they going to produce, at the end of this, a confession of somebody or other, a statement proving (as much as confessions extracted under duress could) that something contrary to what Loyaan held to be true was untrue? Or should he look for a clue to this mystery elsewhere, put his hand in the hidden pockets "of the politics of mystification" and draw it out, open his palm with the slowness that magicians un-tighten their closed fists just before pigeons white as a saint fly out of them? *Don't part with that sense of composure. They have brought you here. They will come and tell you something, a verdict passed or something. They cannot hold you for ever. You are too precious.* (What a comfort now that the voice had returned, the voice which kept him company when he was lonely, the voice of the angels, of his saint-protector, of his articulated reason.) *Sit and wait. Just sit and do anything you please here, in this darkness, but look the opening in the ceiling, look for it like a spotlight for the main actor, or a ship for the lighthouse when lost at sea.*

"Where is this?" he now asked himself. Definitely, a basement. It smelt of a strange wetness, similar to the smell of a child's one-day-old urine. A basement, yes. Where? There was the smell of burnt oil, the odour of grease. When being brought in, he recalled, his freed hands had touched a washing-line upon which was drying a woman's shawl, or an old man's *cimaama*. On the way here, he had heard a small girl challenging another (rightly or wrongly, he was in no position to confirm) as they played their hopscotch and other childish games. The smell of fire, the cinder perhaps warm from recent use. There were many things which told him he was still in Mogadiscio, perhaps right in its centre, perhaps within a short distance of the former National Assembly . . . ! People talked and said a lot of things. The politics of mystification rendered rumours credible. Nothing was ever confirmed. Nobody knew what had happened to and become of So-and-so. The politics of mystification kept everybody at bay. People were kept in their separate compartments of ignorance about what happened to other people and what became of other things. No information was released until a rumour had been published, and nothing was made official until the General's informants had reported back the mood, the feeling of the general public. If the action was unpopular, one heard an unconfirmed report that so many persons of that tribe, or that class of people, or that pressure group had been imprisoned. The papers didn't carry the news, the radio neither.

Loyaan wondered about himself, for instance. Did anybody know where they were keeping him? Would anybody? No minutes would show how long he had been kept here; he hadn't spoken to anybody who had taken particulars or who had served him with a warrant of arrest. And yet he might be here for six months, a name untraceable, a person unregistered, a man inexistent. As Soyaan argued, it was true that the majority of men and women recruited for the Security were illiterate and hence didn't know how to write reports or read them. But it was also true that when the Service took for interrogation somebody like him or like Ibrahim, the most educated of their ranks were used to talk to them. *But let us suppose I meet the General in person, suppose I tell him all that has happened in the past few days, do you think there is anything by way of documented proof which I can produce?* Of Beria, Stalin said. . . .

Approaching boots. Light in the corridor. Life! Boots! Men! The bat stirred, it pendulated, it swung downwards like an arm of a banana tree. Then flew off. Boots. Footsteps. And the door opened. The light in the room came on. And a man walked in, a man with a cigar in his mouth. The boots which had escorted him returned from whence they came. No writing-pad, no pen. He had not come to take Loyaan's particulars. He closed the door behind him. The blazing light which

196

had been switched on made the room seem longer and not as wide as when Loyaan had measured it, pacing up and down and counting how many steps before he touched the wall at the other end. It appeared emptier, too. Nothing save a straw mat and a pillow, perhaps used by the prisoner last here, perhaps Ibrahim — why not? — used it while waiting to be transferred somewhere else. The man was balding. He was enormous in the upper part and stood on thin stalky legs which dwarfed his hugeness. He was an ugly man, no doubt.

"Loyaan Keynaan?"

"I answer to that name, yes."

"I was a friend of Soyaan's."

"Oh!"

Loyaan wondered if he could ask a favour of the man: "Please let the bat out. Open that door gently, open it so that she won't be frightened." No, nothing identical or similar in Loyaan's and the bat's status. It had come in here in search of the night's darkness of safety. He had entered in search of the light with which to illumine the obscure and mysterious pathways which led to Soyaan's tomb. Granted, he continued thinking, since the man was still silent, there was the opening which it used, but lights flatten holes and confuse colours, in particular strong lights such as this. Let it go back the way it came. Could one breathe life into a corpse out of which the soul had gone? No, he wouldn't ask of him this favour. The man had a long history of cruelties. He was the third man in the Service. The cigar. Of course, it must have come from that box on the glass-topped table of the Minister's today. Possibly, it was the very one the Minister had offered Loyaan, the one he refused to smoke.

"My superiors have been angered by the adverse publicity you've given to Soyaan's name. I've been asked to speak to you."

He took the cigar out of the mouth. He licked his lips. He replaced the cigar in his mouth. Loyaan, meanwhile, followed the bat's movements and was pleased that it had found a hiding place in a corner, apparently darker, apparently safer.

"My superiors are disturbed by what you have said. My men have reported back indiscretions: 'Loyaan this, Loyaan that'. The Minister to the Presidency has asked me to tell you that we've not seen nor heard of the Memorandums, nor of Mulki. As for Ibrahim, the story is different. Ibrahim is with us for a different reason."

"Ibrahim is with you for a different reason?"

"It doesn't concern you. I said Ibrahim Siciliano is helping us with inquiries which have nothing to do with Soyaan's case, nor yours for that matter."

The man put his hand into his pocket and took out a metal piece not unlike a smoker's knife. He inserted it into the cigar which he put into his mouth again.

"Why are you holding Ibrahim?"

"It is none of your concern."

"Yes, it is."

He lit the cigar. Loyaan was tempted to ask for a light for himself. *Insist. Come on. Insist.* The voice was back with him, giving him advice, telling him things, helping him. He wasn't alone. The voice was back with him. *Insist.*

"What? Why?"

"For anti-Soviet activities."

"Anti-Soviet?"

"Anti-Soviet activities."

"But we are not in the Soviet Union. We are in the Somali Democratic Republic, a sovereign African state. Not in the Soviet Union. We are *not*."

Boots outside. Boots which approached and stopped in front of the entrance to the room in which Loyaan and the man were. The door opened. A woman in a veil was pushed in. The door was closed. The man went to the woman and led her closer.

"This is Mulki. Mulki, this is Loyaan."

The man helped her peel off the dark veil with the same care as one would uncover a wound, or royalty a monument. But she kept a safe distance, wouldn't come any nearer. Loyaan had never seen Mulki before and couldn't, for sure, say whether this woman was Mulki; whether she had lost weight; whether she had suffered or anything. The man signalled to her to speak. She said:

"I've been brought here to tell you that I typed no Memorandum for Soyaan or my brother; that I've nothing whatsoever to do with either of them or with politics. I have been brought here to tell you that I haven't been tortured, that nothing has been extracted from me by force."

"What is your crime?"

The man interrupted. "You can go now," he said to her, leading her away himself and knocking on the door which opened and through which she finally disappeared. "There you are. There is Mulki. You have her word."

"All this is like a badly written farce."

"Farce or no, you have certainly been a great nuisance to us. Your father and the Minister to the Presidency agree that you are under the bad influence of some anti-revolutionaries whose company you frequent. I hate to tell you that I once ordered that you be arrested. But for Soyaan's sake and your father's, and because of other considerations, we thought perhaps it would be more convenient for you, for us, for your father and the General if you were offered Soyaan's post."

"Soyaan's post?"

"The General has signed the decree which now appoints you as Somalia's Councillor in Belgrade. There is a plane tomorrow evening. I've had you brought here so that I could tell you myself. This gives you tomorrow, which also happens to be Soyaan's seventh-day memorial, a day of religious rites and prayers, a day for the worship of the spirit of the dead. So prepare."

"I am being deported, am I?"

"No one is ever deported from his own country."

"Bribed with a post, silenced, got rid of?"

"No. Not at all. Saved from ridiculing yourself and embarrassing everybody. You are being given a good chance to serve your country in the capacity of a Councillor abroad. To be frank with you, it is something I wouldn't do. But then I am not the General, nor am I the Minister to the Presidency, two souls generous as the angels which protect them."

The bat re-emerged from her safe corner. The bat flew here, it flew there, undecided, unable to resolve where best to land. Loyaan had a similar problem. What should he do now? How seriously should he take what the man had said? As soon as the religious and other rites were over, a car would come to escort him to the military airport and he would be put in a special plane leaving for Moscow. And after Moscow? Would he get to Belgrade to shake Tito's hand of neutrality? Would the Yugoslavs be interested in hearing the full story of what the Soviets had done? Would they have read, he wondered to himself, that scene in Haykal's *Road to Ramadan,* page 129 (*see how sharp my memory is*) which told about the cable received at a session with Nasser, the telegram concerning a planned coup d'état in Somalia? Podgorney, Brezhnev and Kosygin each read the text of the telegram which would inform the Somali general of the planned coup and initialled it. Did a special plane come from Moscow, a special plane bringing men prepared to encounter a need of such greatness? Suppose he refused to go to Moscow and Belgrade? Would anybody hear of him again? They needn't arrest him, they could keep him here in this dungeon for as long as they wished. Would he emulate that idiot who went on a hunger-strike in a prison outside Mogadiscio? You needed publicity, you needed the world to know of your courageous deed, you needed the external world to write about you and share with anxiety your future release. Suppose he said no, he didn't want to go to Moscow on that special plane, what would they do? Or suppose he said, yes, he would prepare and pack his cases and wait for tomorrow evening, would he believe it? He needed time to think this over. He would love to speak to other friends about this, friends like Ahmed-Wellie — and who else? Well, Ladan. He would love to know what became of Beydan, whether, as she believed, she would survive the childbirth, or the child the womb-push. All this read like a badly written play, with stage-directions almost non-existent, the stage dark and hardly lit, the actresses and the actors unbriefed, and the dialogue unrehearsed. They brought Mulki on a stage only to say that and be taken away? *He allows me to remain silent and think to myself all this time? Something wrong here, somewhere. It is my turn to provoke it; my turn has come.*

"Suppose I say I won't go?"

"No. You won't say that."

"How do you mean?"

"We'll put you on that plane. We'll make sure you go with it."

He reminded himself of what happened to the Eritrean the Ethiopians had drugged and put on a plane bound for Addis. With an Ethiopian passport in his hand, and two Ethiopians supporting him up the stairs of the Ethiopian Airlines plane, the German airport authorities were satisfied with the explanation given. "The man is ill, but says he wants to return home to die there if die he must." In Addis, the *Derg* used another justification: the man had taken the heavy drugs himself. And there lay dead an active Eritrean liberation fighter. Would they do that? Or would they use other methods? What? Ask. Provoke him.

"How did you kill him?"

200

"Who?"

"What was it that the Russian doctor gave to my brother? Curious. Yes, officer, just academic curiosity. But tell me, please."

"Your nuisance again. I tell you we don't tolerate that sort of thing here where I work. Withdraw that immediately."

"Give me a satisfactory reason and I will."

"God takes the breath He lends to one."

"Try another, officer."

"We are Muslims in this country."

"Marxists, officer. Ours is Scientific Socialism, says the General."

"Don't provoke me."

"I have, officer."

"For Soyaan's sake and your father's, don't."

"O.K. Try this. Why was Soyaan knighted when dead and not when alive?"

"He died serving his nation. He died and his last words were: LABOUR IS HONOUR AND THERE IS NO GENERAL BUT OUR GENERAL."

"You read that in the papers."

"I heard them from your father. He told me himself."

"My father is a liar."

No reaction from the officer. Then: "Has he been promoted lieutenant after all these years?"

"Yes, I've signed it and so has the General."

There was a longer pause.

"I was there when Soyaan hiccupped his last. He spent his final breaths calling to me, shouting my name. I was there. My father wasn't."

"Why would your father lie? And why should we believe you, not him?"

Silence.

"Answer me. Why would your father lie?"

"I'd need twenty-nine years to make you understand that."

"That is reactionary nonsense."

And into that gulf of generations went monumental generalisations. Keynaan. Loyaan and Soyaan. What was it that Clemenceau said about the Americans living, in thirty years, the experience of the barbaric as well as the decadent? Could he make someone understand, in a minute, what it meant to be the son of his own father and mother?

201

"May I take it that we can consider the case closed?"

"What case?"

"May I take it, I meant, that you've withdrawn your accusations?"

"No, officer, I haven't. Unless you give me a satisfactory reason. We cannot consider anything closed until you've opened it. And we haven't. There are a hundred questions I haven't had answers for. What Soyaan ate between the time he left my step-mother's place and the time he got to my mother's. I don't know the name of the Russian doctor who treated him for a slight complaint. Nor do I know what the complaint was."

"I am afraid I cannot help you."

"I am sure you can."

"How?"

"For Soyaan's sake and my father's, will you oblige if I ask you a favour?"

"Ask and then I'll tell you whether I can or cannot."

The bat came low, it flew close to their heads like a fighter plane surveying where it would drop the bombs.

"Why does a one-armed man follow me everywhere I go?"

"A one-armed man?"

"Yes."

"Describe him."

Loyaan did so.

"He is not one of my men. No, he is not. There is no one-armed man among those we assigned to shadow you and report on your movements."

"No?"

"No."

"Who is he then?"

"I wouldn't know. Maybe from another service."

"The Minister's?"

"I don't know."

"The Minister to the Presidency knows who he is?"

"I would not be surprised."

"There is a service within the Service, is there?"

"Possibly there is."

"I mean is there a service within the Service, a service especially created to keep a particular eye on Soviet interests in the country, report on anti-Soviet activities, a service financed and paid for by the Soviets?"

If looks could kill! The air was now full of cigar smoke. The man, not speaking, paced up and down and Loyaan's eyes were fixed on him, following every move of his. This probably was as far as anyone had ever gone. Would Loyaan get away with it? There was no reason why not. His name was on that undrawn up list of tomorrow's passengers on the special plane to Moscow. Somebody would have some explaining to do if he was not on it. There was also tomorrow's final seventh-day commemoration of Soyaan's death and he would be missed. In all probability, there would be a government delegation to participate on behalf of the General. They could not afford to keep him here. The man's gaze softened.

"We shall come for you tomorrow evening. Until then."

"Until then."

"Seven in the evening, precisely."

"Seven in the evening, precisely."

Ladan asked: "Seven precisely?"

"Yes, why?"

"Father says eight."

"Has he been here already?"

"He came with that Minister in a long chauffeur-driven car. I rushed to him to tell him what had happened. When he didn't show any surprise, I asked him whether he had seen you. He hadn't, but he knew where you were and who you were with. He said you were being briefed about a trip you are to make abroad."

"And the Minister?"

"Meanwhile, the Minister came out of the car to greet me and Mother. I refused to return his greetings and this annoyed Father. He nearly hit me, but didn't only because the Minister pulled him aside."

"Did Father say where I would go?"

"No. He wouldn't specify, nor answer my question in a friendly manner. 'This is not a thing for women. This is a job for men. A very special job,' he said."

"The Minister didn't add anything to that?"

"Belgrade, he said. You were going to Belgrade, he said to Mother. Not to me. He wouldn't speak to me. He said that to Mother."

"Councillor in Yugoslavia."

"Correction. The Minister didn't say Belgrade. He simply said Yugoslavia. I took that to mean Belgrade."

"But why me, why Yugoslavia?"

"Why Soyaan, why Mulki, why Ibrahim?"

Although tempted, he decided he wouldn't tell her that he had spoken to a woman who said she was Mulki. But was she really? Had Ladan ever seen the girl herself? Would she have known if this was somebody else? How did the Security know he had never met Mulki? Ahmed-Wellie? Or better still, Keynaan? It was Keynaan, wasn't it, who first informed him of the Service's arresting secretary/typist? No, no, he wouldn't tell Ladan. Enough had happened to torment her conscience, to unbalance her mind. Enough.

"I nearly forgot."

"What?"

"Ahmed-Wellie came and went."

"Did he? When?"

"Half an hour before Father and the Minister. He went five minutes before your return."

"And he wouldn't wait? He couldn't."

"He will come tomorrow, he said. He came, in fact, to see if we needed any help, if you wanted to borrow his car or something for tomorrow. Anyway, he is home if you want to get in touch with him."

"No sign of Margaritta?"

"None. Why? Should she have come?"

"You don't like her?"

"On the contrary."

"I thought. . . ."

"Are you talking about that night when she brought you home dead drunk? I was disappointed in you. No. Let me put it this way. We were worried until you turned up. And then — well, it must be said, Loyaan, you were an ugly sight: you had vomited. Thought you would fall ill, just like Soyaan, and inexplicably die, just like Soyaan."

She was silent. Outside, a sick dog began to cough consumptively.

"Listen! "

"What?"

The muezzin called all Muslims to their prayer-mats.

"Listen, Ladan?"

"What?"

Chapter Thirteen

Like a butterfly which fears any figure that grows a shadow, a butterfly which fails to appreciate any fluttering of wings other than its own, a butterfly jittery and jumpy, at the end of its tether. One of its wings has fallen off. One of its feelers as well. It has knocked them against the bars of the window when entering. Below the butterfly, gameful and playful, showily dressed as though for an outing, stands a boy of about four. He has a tennis racquet in his hand. He waves it in the air. The young boy of four waits for the falling, the landing of the butterfly. And. . . .

The goat bleated.

They had dragged it against its will, they had forced it through the outside door, pulled it down and up the entrance. When it glued its feet to the ground, they lifted it up, four of them, four men whose faces were not familiar to Loyaan as he watched them from nearby. The parting streak the pulling had made was still visible on the dusty ground. That was the first, a goat. Many more would be brought, as many as five or seven, depending ultimately on the amount of money Keynaan could spare for this. He had with him the money the family received from neighbours' contributions, relatives and a large unspecified amount from the Minister to the Presidency given straight to Keynaan. This was the seventh day after the burial, this was the end-all of the official rituals. On this day, the family of the deceased would, in effect, stage a massive feast of a get-together and invite those who had in any manner taken part in the previous rituals and feed them of God's generosities what was given, what was contributed, what was shared. The grave-diggers. The sheikhs. The neighbours. Friends of the family. Anyone who had been of help any time during this period. But to the dinner staged by a family of the deceased come uninvited the beggars. To the dinner come uninvited the powerful, Ministers of State, men of unknown provenance and others.

For Loyaan, the night was long, wide-eyed and insomniac. The night unrolled like a cotton thread, unfolding inch by inch; the night wove words of thready thoughts; the night stitched for him a blanket of comfort and warmth; found him a refuge from all which had threatened his tranquillity. A parable of Solomonic derivation, a fable from the Arabian peninsula in which a young man of humble origin follows the hints of a thread up the intricate staircases to the palace of power, lead him and leave him in the open embrace of the princess whom he will love, groom and take care of. The night was long like a serpent, oily smooth and dark, the stars small as unopened sesame. Every movement he heard had a meaning, and if it didn't he gave it one. The Security men were following him and making sure he stayed indoors, in one version. In another, there was Ibrahim who had escaped their grip and had come to bring him the Memorandum which he wouldn't offer them. In a third, there was Margaritta who appeared in her nightgown, a see-through nightgown: she was being chased by the ghosts of guilt, Soyaan's fully untold story. They slept together, he and she, but didn't feel incestuous towards each other, and didn't make love. He lay close to her bottom, which was shapely like a globe, smooth and her hand-filling breasts had lain unaroused, un-sucked, untouched.

"Good morning, Loyaan."

"Good morning, Mother."

"Did you sleep at all?"

"Yes, Mother. I did. Did you?"

"No."

Lies. Lies. But he went back to chewing on the stick with which he brushed his teeth. He watched his mother hammer knuckles against the goat's ribs. He watched her pull the goat by the ear which had a tribal mark, the insignia of the clan that had owned it.

"Not fat enough," she said.

"Not all that bad for what you get these days, what with the drought and the high tax these nomads must pay when they sell a goat," commented the butcher, himself a man from the river people, perhaps from Afgoi. "Not all that bad," he said. "I've seen thinner. I've seen them sell skeletons clothed, as though in haste, with a light coat of flesh."

"He is always cheated."

"Who?"

"Keynaan, my husband. He doesn't know how to buy the best."

The butcher wasn't interested in continuing the conversation once it took this controversial turn. He didn't know how to buy the

206

best either, his wife always said. He would let that pass. He was there to do a job; he was there to kill, slaughter, skin the beasts, charge a fixed amount per head he cut, eat his given share and leave. Now he lifted the goat up as one lifts a dearly loved child. He held the goat up in the air. He flexed his muscles, he showed how strong he was, then dropped the goat so suddenly and cruelly that Loyaan thought it had broken one of its hind legs. He burst into a noisy, hearty laughter, like a beast.

"Not bad," he said.

"Not fat enough," she said. "My husband doesn't know how to buy the best."

Loyaan's thoughts were elsewhere. His mind had gone to graze on a pasture of the shepherded range-land. He saw a man being tortured, he watched the tormentor enjoy himself perversely doing that, heard him burst with the same joy as the butcher's. "Not tough enough. They break," boasted the torturer, "they break when I twist their manhood, they cry with pain." His face was creasy like a river. The weary wrinkles on his forehead branched into the flanks like a tree's branches would, when stirred by the wind of the stream, a stream agitated on the surface like the porridge a child cools with drawn-in breath.

He walked away from the scene; he walked away from where his mother and the butcher were haggling about whether or not the butcher would receive, as gift, the skin of one of the beasts on top of what Keynaan had offered him. Loyaan's bones ached. He had felt the ache previously. Was it due to the humidity of the sea? Was it due to the chill of dawn when he had lain uncovered? His tongue tasted sour like rhubarb. The blood he spat told him that he wasn't taking good care of his teeth, he who was himself a dentist.

"*Nabad*, Loyaan."

"*Nabad*, er, Aunt."

"How are you this morning?"

"I am fine, thank you. And you?"

"Fine, fine. I am glad that you are back among us."

"Yes, yes."

She was The Neighbour, the woman who had intervened with the Green Guards on his behalf. She was glad he hadn't been arrested. His hand scratched his itchy growth of beard nearly a week old. The woman neighbour went in and shouted to Loyaan's mother a greeting

207

announcing that she had arrived, and with her had come So-and-so and So-and-so.

He would have to shave and shower before evening, he would have to prepare for their coming. Unlike Soyaan whom death had surprised, Loyaan would be ready for it. Soyaan had made appointments, he had projects in mind, and his death undid all. Loyaan wouldn't make any appointments, nor did he have any projects in mind. To the question his sister had put to him — "What will you do now?" — he had answered: "Nothing. I see. I wait. But while I see and wait, I also plot, struggle, wriggle, fight. As you've suggested, I shall try not to lose the sense of composure which defines the person I am." Shave and shower, change into his cleanest, plot, plan, wriggle and struggle the best he could, and let nothing surprise him. Would he go back to Baidoa, to his job, to his friends, would he? Come to think of it, the regional authorities could take disciplinary action against him, for he hadn't reported back to duty, he was four days late, hadn't tele-graphed an excuse, nor could he produce a medical certificate if asked to. Unless Ahmed-Wellie forged one for him. Unless he got somebody else to do it. Why, why was he thinking of all this now? Had he resolved the mysteries which kept him in Mogadiscio? Was he resigned to his destiny, the fate of the powerless loser, knees touching the ground, his head bowing and prostrating before the potency of the General and his Minister? Why, why, why? They wouldn't come at dawn as they came for everybody else. They'd appear just before dusk, not to imprison him like Ibrahim, nor torture him like Mulki and a hundred others, but to deport him to Moscow where the cold snow of indifference would freeze the marrow in his bones. The rheumatic chill of dawn, the fear as one got up to answer the knock on the door: these had been spared him. For Loyaan was special. He was the brother of Soyaan, the knighted Hero of the Revolution.

"Good morning."

"Good morning."

Women. One after the other. Women who filed past the butcher in his singlet and his shorts, a pair of trousers cut down unevenly by hand. The butcher, Loyaan watched now, was sharpening *pangas* and a set of small knives on a stone which served as a hone. He then beat a small knife against the panga, he made music and he danced.

The goat bleated.

"If you don't behave yourself and shut up," he said to the goat, "I shall cut your neck before your time."

The goat raised its neck upwards, stamped its feet on the ground. And the butcher felt insulted. He dashed at the set of the small knives and with one of them he poked the goat in the ribs, saying he would give it another chance. "So keep quiet. Or else. . . . "

The goat bleated again.

The butcher ripped off a little of the goat's tribally-marked ear and held what he had cut up in the air, saying: "That should teach you a lesson."

The sun's light was so bright Loyaan had nowhere to conceal himself and his rage. He came to the butcher. He took his arm and shook it the hardest he could.

"What are you doing to that goat?"

The butcher struggled and freed his arm.

"I am training her so that she can grasp the meaning of death before I slaughter it. Your father has, with the money he paid for her head, taught her what it means to be separated from where she was born and her tribal masters. She grasped that being dragged here. Now I've cut the tribal ear. A little later, I shall gladly administer death to her."

Loyaan wasn't certain if he understood any of that. He went away and entered his room, thinking: *What really is happening to me, what is happening here? What sophistication, what articulacy? Or am I hearing things? Or, worse still, am I too tired to catch the significance of all this?* He would shower, shave and. . . .

He had showered. He had shaven. He was talking to Ahmed-Wellie who had just turned up. He was saying:

"You shouldn't have bothered. Really."

"Once in a lifetime. Come off it, Loyaan."

"Really."

"I have only taken the day off. And have come to see if my being here can be of any help to you, your mother or your father. 'You shouldn't have bothered, you shouldn't have bothered'. I've taken a day off for less important things."

"Tell you what, Ahmed-Wellie."

"What, Loyaan?"

"Disciplinary action will probably be taken against me, or I will

209

be fired. I haven't had my leave extended. The regional authorities can fire me. Will you forge a health certificate for me?"

"How you like to tease your friends. Just like Soyaan."

"I am serious. Will you forge a certificate for me?"

"I hear you're leaving, Loyaan. If you are, I suspect, you won't need their extending your leave of absence. Or a certificate. Will you?"

"Leaving? Leaving for where? No, I am not leaving for anywhere."

"Yes. I hear you are. I hear you will leave this evening."

"Where did you hear that?"

"I hear you are going abroad. I hear you've been appointed to a post abroad. Yugoslavia, or Czechoslovakia, I am not quite sure. I hear you are leaving. I hear that you've accepted to leave."

"Where did you hear that?"

"That will be a great betrayal to the struggle."

"I said, where did you hear that?"

"Yugoslavia."

"Who told you this?"

"Ibrahim."

"Ibrahim Siciliano?"

"Yes."

"I'm sorry but I can't help being curious about many of the secrets you find out. I want to know how you do it. There are sufficient mysteries to which we have no clues. You appear to have an easy way of uncovering them."

"What does that mean?"

"How was Ibrahim? Where is he being held?"

"You, too, have begun suspecting me?"

"Have others before me suspected you?"

"Somebody has deliberately misled you. Just as they misled Soyaan."

There was silence. The voice returned: *You should move slowly from here onwards; you should move carefully and unerringly as a sure-footed animal. Don't ever be surprised by anything. Place your feet firmly on the ground on which you walk.* And:

"Somebody misinformed Soyaan about you?"

"Things of the past. God bless his soul."

"The present, Ahmed-Wellie, if we return to the present: how did you learn of my departure this evening?"

Loyaan spat and buried his spittle.

"I said I was taken to see Ibrahim Siciliano."

"And Mulki, too?"

"No, no, not her."

"Koschin — what about Koschin?"

"I plan to ask to visit him shortly."

Loyaan went closer. Ahmed-Wellie was trembling, uneasy.

"Are you unwell?"

"No, I am very well. Why?"

"You look pale and you're trembling. Anything wrong? Is there anything I can do for you?"

"No, no. I am well."

"Will they let you visit Koschin, do you think?"

"It is worth trying."

A pause then: "You look unwell. To me, you look ill."

"I am well, I am well."

"To me you look unwell. Have the Russian doctors given you the wrong injection?"

"I am well, I am well. I said I am well." He was nervous.

There was a long silence. Ahmed-Wellie was the first to break it.

"I've just remembered something. I have a patient I must see."

"You are leaving, are you?"

"I must return to the hospital."

"You needn't blindfold anyone or yourself, need you?"

That was lost on Ahmed-Wellie.

"An urgent case. A very urgent case," he said.

"Well! If you must go."

"A mad case of euthanasia wrongly administered to a woman."

"Will you come back?"

"Yes. I will come back."

"Perhaps the woman will change her mind and want to live, and therefore will make you stay at the hospital longer."

"I won't allow that to happen." He was gone the second following that.

The sun wove itself a fabric of schemata on the boundary between morning and noon; the clouds a tent, gauze-thin and white, pitched on the outlying districts. Then, right before Loyaan's and the world's eyes, all suddenly began to disintegrate like a worn-out piece of cloth a thick set of fingers has pulled asunder.

"Excuse me, *jaalle*. Is your name Loyaan?" said a young boy.
"Yes, it is."

The young boy tugged at the rope which he had tied around the goat's neck, a rope which was his and which he used whenever somebody hired him to lead a goat or a cow home. Boys between ten and twelve hung about the cattle market, ready for hire, to take home before one a silly unruly goat or a rebel cow. Many of them were rebellious runaways from the Young Revolutionary Centre at which any unclaimed babies found in the city's garbage bins or unpatrolled streets were trained to consider the General their father, his revolution their mother, the régime's generosities to them their breast-feed. Free to offer services, free to choose, free to move where they wanted: these young runaways preferred this to the indoctrination and free schooling with which the régime was ready to supply them. Some without father, some without mother, and some without both; some did jobs such as this; some roamed about the streets holding out hungry, begging hands to passers-by; others were cunningly clever, intelligent, quick. The boy said to Loyaan:
"Your father said I'd get paid when I delivered it."
"Did he?"
"Yes."
"He didn't pay you?"
"I swear, he didn't."
"I don't believe you."

The butcher came out to receive his fresh victim. As he did this, he complained that he was waiting unnecessarily long for the coming of these beasts. He should not have accepted to charge them by the number of heads he slaughtered but by the hour. "Why am I such a fool?" he asked as he secured the goat against any possibility of its untying itself, and chose which knives he would use.
"I swear he did not pay me," continued the young boy.
"What guarantee do I have that he didn't?" said Loyaan.
"I say it myself."
"I don't believe you."
"I swear upon the three pronouncements of Allah."

Qumman came by and shook her head, disappointed with the purchase. "Pay him."

"But, Mother—"

"A fool who could buy that goat could not have the sense to pay this young boy in advance. Look at what he has bought. Not fat enough. Not healthy enough. Pay him a shilling, let the young boy go."

"Yes, *jaalle* Loyaan. Please pay."

Loyaan sharply turned round on the young boy. "Don't *jaalle* me, you!"

"I am sorry."

"Don't *jaalle* me, you!" he repeated, inexplicably angrily.

Qumman went to arrange in sets of four the stones on which would rest the over-sized containers. There were other women making other fires. There were other women standing mats against the wall. There was Ladan whose job was, as before, to prepare the room for the important guests who would be admitted to sit with and eat from the same plates as the sheikhs. Pillows were borrowed from neighbouring houses, pillows covered in cases on which were knitted flowery designs, heart-shapes; cases used for weddings, deaths and any other festivity; cases which smelled of moth-killer as they smelled of java perfumes, a whiff of oriental scents, some from Arabia, some from India and others made in and imported from Europe.

"Will you pay me or won't you?" the young boy said.

"What guarantee have I that you haven't been paid?"

Qumman was furious. "Pay him a shilling, Loyaan."

To spare himself his mother's nagging about Keynaan's lack of bargaining tact, to spare himself his mother's this-is-not-the-time-to-argue-about-paying, Loyaan put his hand in his pocket and took out a shilling which he tossed up into the air.

"I don't believe you. I bet you don't have a mother."

"I swear on my mother's life."

"I don't believe you. I bet you don't have a mother."

But he flicked two shillings towards the boy who caught them and kissed the money lovingly and noisily, then tossed both coins upwards and caught them again. He thanked Loyaan while rubbing the coins together. He thanked him again while rubbing them against his rough, unwashed, naked-to-the-waist body.

"I've been paid twice," he said triumphantly.

Loyaan who had prepared himself for this eventuality feinted

213

and made as if to catch him. The boy ran, emitting a Red-Indian howl of victory. The boy ran the fastest he could, his feet barely touching the ground.

Right at that instant, however, a woman in the advanced stages of pregnancy was shambling her way through the entrance. One of her feet had gone up, the other hadn't yet reached the ground when the head-on collision between her and the boy occurred. She fell backwards on her bottom, the boy forward on his forehead. His victory cry gave way to her painful groan.

The young boy rose to his feet. He saw what he had done. In the same dizzying second, he scrambled up but gave himself time to check if he had dropped his two coins. No, he had not. It was then that he ran, leaving behind him a groaning woman, heavy with the advanced stage of her pregnancy.

"Help, please, help."

Beydan moaned and lay on her back on a bed borrowed from the woman who the day before had intervened with the Green Guards on Loyaan's behalf. Her cold, almost lifeless hand was locked in his, with her fingers projecting out, twitching, moving, proving to him that she was still alive. Otherwise, she lay quiet, her eyes closed, her breathing small as a child's. Loyaan held his breath in check, afraid he might cough, sneeze or hiccup, afraid he might disturb her quiet. Beside him, on another low stool, was the Holy Koran the woman had lent him in case he was in need of one. The book remained unopened, untouched. Did he need anything else? She removed the General's framed photograph ("My daughter is married to one of his tribesmen") which would have been right in front of him; she also removed her grandson's clothes which had given a disorderly look to the room. Was there anything he wanted before she returned to Qumman's? No. No. Qumman, understandably, felt uneasy about all this. She said nothing, she did nothing to help or hinder; she stayed out of it, indeed she pretended nothing had happened. Ladan had offered to stay by Beydan's bedside. No. She had more useful hands, she had a job to do, rooms to prepare for the honoured guests. Really, no. It was he who wasn't doing anything. He would sit by her. No inconvenience. Honestly. Although he thought to himself that there perhaps were too many coincidences, too many things which had upset him terribly. Ahmed-Wellie, for instance. Why did he behave so strangely as to suggest the impossible were possible? He could not be a government informant. A plant? No, no. He wouldn't grow in their waters. He surely wasn't the type. But how had he known when Loyaan would be leaving and for where? *How did he know that I was at Beydan's that afternoon at that second and minute? How did he find me here, or find me there? A plant of the Service? No, no. I can't believe it.* Their water would be his poison, he would wither, he would die. But to leave as abruptly as that — certainly that sowed seeds of suspicion in the fertile soil of Loyaan's brain.

Beydan turned to him. "Loyaan?"

"Yes, Aunt?"

"I am sorry."

"Sorry about what?"

"I am sorry."

Her face bespoke the pain which she bore with the divine modesty a woman in her state must call upon in order to survive a situation like this. It required an effort to turn. She seemed willing to surrender herself unto the open palms of the Almighty. Women in this part of the world when pregnant moved about their business slow as turtles in the belief that any sudden jerk, any sports activities would be fatal to the life of the unborn. And if Loyaan suggested calling a doctor, she would say no, "No, I don't need a doctor, I can do without." If he suggested reading the Koran. . . .

"I keep wondering will I survive this?"

"Of course, you will."

She made herself as comfortable as possible in the circumstances. She had locked her fingers into a fist and this fist of knuckles was contained in the warmth of Loyaan's understanding touches and caresses.

"I dreamt last night. I dreamt a dream," she said.

"Yes?"

"I dreamt an interesting dream last night."

"What did you dream?"

"I dreamt I had a boy. I dreamt he was given a name."

"What name was the boy given?"

"I wasn't there. Interesting, isn't it? I wasn't there in this dream myself. I wasn't there in *my* own dream. But I dreamt it all the same. I dreamt I had a boy. But unlike in dreams I usually have, I wasn't its centre-point, I wasn't even there."

215

"But you had a boy?"

"Yes."

"Isn't that what matters? You had a child, a boy."

"Boy or girl. But that is not the point."

"What is the point?"

"I wasn't there in my dream."

"You weren't in your dream. Does that mean anything?"

"That I wasn't there means I must have died."

"No, no."

"What does it mean then?"

"According to Jung, and Freud—"

"Who? According to whom?"

"Jung and Freud...."

"According to whom? Who are these people, Loyaan?"

"No. Never mind."

"I thought, for an instant, that you were talking about *Juuja wa Majuuj*. I thought you would invoke the dormant spirits of the jinns from their sleep. But that doesn't change anything. *I* wasn't there in my dream. I wasn't its centre-point."

"But you were the one who had the boy?"

"Yes."

"And you spoke of a name given to the boy?"

"Yes."

"What?"

"Soyaan. Soyaan was the name bestowed on the child."

Loyaan must hold firm until he again mastered all his faculties. The shock that the giving of the name injected into him! That put the final seal to it all. It wasn't *he* substituting Soyaan, no. There was a boy whom Beydan had delivered in a dream she herself didn't appear in, a boy who was named Soyaan. It wasn't Loyaan substituting Soyaan.

"You don't want him called Soyaan?"

"No, no, no."

"I wasn't the one who gave it," she said.

"Who then?"

"I wasn't there, remember. I wasn't in *my* dream."

Loyaan would admit that Beydan did surprise him with the efficient strokes she administered to this scene of suspense and shock. She looked very much alive in the drama in which she was taking full part. *Juuja wa Majuuj* — should he tell her that these had nothing whatsoever to do with dormant spirits of jinns, that they were a people known also as Gogmagogs in other places, a people of Gog-dwarves and Magog-giants. As children, the twins had these giants and dwarves occur in the tales they told each other. Cross the Himalayas and you will find them: dwarf Chinamen and giant Cossacks, ugly as *buttafuoris*, small as Satan, giant as the demon. Was Beydan ready to be taken by the hand and led across the landscape of the world's literature and lore? Would she be ready to be introduced at this stage to the Lilliputians, the Yahoos and the Houyhnhnms? Could he present her to the Fridays of Robinson Crusoe, the thousand and one nights of a woman's survival, a thousand nights of marathon parables?

"Do you know why I wasn't there in my own dream?"

"I'll believe you if you tell me."

"When you last came to see me, do you recall I told you about the master-witch your mother consulted?"

"Please, please. Let us not go back to that."

"I am bewitched. *I am dead. I am not here.* The voice you are hearing is not mine. That is why I wasn't in my dream. It explains. I am dead. I am not here with you."

"You don't believe that?"

"Of course, I do."

"As a Muslim, you should believe what Allah has told you in this book of His," said he picking up the Holy Koran from the stool near him. "You will die only when your hour comes, not a minute before, not a minute after. The Koran says that."

"It also talks about witches and sorcerers. The Koran does."

"You confuse magic with witchcraft."

"A very minor difference, thinner than the width of a white hair."

"If I were you, I wouldn't worry about any of this."

"I'm telling you that *I am dead.* Or will be before the day is out."

Silence.

"Dead because I've been bewitched."

"Don't believe that nonsense."

"And I must confess one thing to you."

"What?"

217

"I paid the money you bought me to the super-master-witch of Afgoi to undo the knots your mother's master-witch had tied."

"You paid him handsomely, I must say. Three thousand shillings."

"What is money when one's life is in danger?"

"But how come he has been unable to undo the knot my mother's master-witch tied, if you paid him so handsomely?"

"My aunt has an answer for that."

"What does your aunt say?"

"You were the source from which the money came. You love your mother more than you love me. You care about your mother's death more than you care about mine. Therefore, the spirits of your jinn protect with love that of your mother's. Therefore, no master-witch can do any harm to your mother. My aunt said I shouldn't have wasted the money on him."

"All this is nonsense," said Loyaan.

"Death isn't. Death is the ultimate sense in all that we do or think."

All these follies, thought he. But he hadn't the calm to remain seated by her and talk about her death, what would happen to her child if a child survived her, what name they would give it. Twenty years later, for all one knew, a Soyaan who survived Beydan's death in childbirth might walk a street named after a brother Soyaan knighted by a false revolution, made a hero in order to hide in the virtuosity of the generosity of politics. Loyaan got up. Her snoring breath was regular like a sleeper's. He would tiptoe out quietly and not disturb her; he would send Ladan in to substitute for him.

Outside, the sun, like an enormous ceiling, had covered every spot with the potence of its brilliance and heat. Right in the middle of the dirt road, the women had dug a hole into which they emptied the blood and the inedible entrails. This offered a banquet for flies. This invited the stray cats of the district. This announced that a massive feast was being held. A beggar here. Another there. But these stayed quiet. The beggars for the moment remained out of focus, seated in the shade of the tree, patient like their stomachs. They would wait an hour, two, maybe even three. They would lie low, their profile unseen, better unnoticed, for the beggars of Mogadiscio were being put into a van and driven out of the city for the duration of the honoured president's visit. They had experienced it themselves, these beggars, they knew that the General's was a government which welcomed foreign delegations with the pomposity of red carpets while they, the beggars, had to be hidden and driven out of town — ugly sight that they were. Four more goats had been brought and slaughtered. Loyaan could tell that from the number of heads being buried, the intestines, the plain and honeycomb tripe being washed and cleaned. This would be the food given to the women. What the women wouldn't eat went to the beggars. What the beggars couldn't bring themselves to eat was thrown to the stray cats and the masterless dogs of the district. Men didn't eat the insides of animals, the soft entrails, the bilharsia-ridden intestines, the soft rumens. No, men were men. They had for their share those portions of meat which grew on bones, hard as their member when awoken by soft contact with the inside of a woman, a grotto of mysteries.

"Mother says do you want something to eat?"

"No, thanks."

Ladan wiped her face clean. Loyaan turned and asked:

"What is it? Why are you crying?"

"Onion tears," she said. "Liver or kidney? You can have your choice," she said. "Which?"

"This isn't the time. No, thank you."

She sniffed, she blew her nose and wiped her hand on the edge of her dress. She asked: "Is there anyone with Beydan?"

"She is asleep."

"Poor thing."

"Why do you say that?"

Ladan blew her nose. Then: "Father has found another woman."

"Another woman?" He pretended he hadn't heard of this before.

"The fat gratuity the Minister provided has introduced him to a younger girl, this time about twenty, younger than I."

"A third woman?"

"Are you counting Mother, or is there another that I know nothing about, Loyaan? A third woman? What are you talking about? Mother isn't and hasn't been his woman for more than a decade."

"But she is married to him."

"Officially, yes. She is legally bound to him. But they haven't slept together since two years after I was born."

"She's told you so herself?"

219

"Some women's menopause, luckily, she says, comes early. No progeny: no sense in copulation."

"You would think he is an unthinking animal."

More beggars dropped in on them. More cats. More dogs. Some of the neighbouring women who were helping in the preparations received their share of the meat raw. They would cook it themselves. That was for the children who obviously couldn't eat from the same plates as the sheikhs and the invited or uninvited men.

"Here he comes," he heard Ladan say.

"Who?"

"The patriarch in person."

Keynaan, and with him two boys leading two goats, entered.

"Not fat enough," Ladan mimicked Mother.

"That fool of a father." Loyaan, too, mimicked Mother.

"That wicked woman." She now spoke with a man's voice.

"He's been cheated," he imitated Qumman.

"Your mother is evil."

They stopped. They looked each other in the eyes. If only there were not six unrepeatable days; if only there weren't six unrelivable nights of horror. If Soyaan hadn't died! They embraced. She sobbed and sobbed and sobbed. Keynaan halted beside them. The two boys and their goats passed by.

"Has anything happened?" Keynaan asked slightly anxiously.

"Hasn't everything?" said Loyaan.

They fell apart.

"You had me worried for a moment."

"What did you think?"

Ladan went in the direction of the neighbour's where Beydan was staying. But she said nothing.

"Have you heard?"

"How are they?"

Ladan had disappeared into the hut.

"Beydan or the child?"

"Will you tell me something, please?"

Loyaan regarded his father with contempt. Should he pull his leg, tell him that Beydan was dead, a baby boy had survived? Would that delight him? Would that not give him the chance to contract the marriage with the younger woman?

"Your mother's fault. Everything is your mother's fault."

220

"What is my mother's fault, Father?"

"She chased him, the boy said to me. Your mother chased him for no reason the young urchin could tell. That evil woman. She'll be *my* death."

"If it is worth your knowing, Father, it wasn't my mother's fault."

"I know that woman. Evil. She is evil."

Over his father's shoulder, Loyaan saw Margaritta's car parked in the same shade as the one in which the beggars had sat. He said to his father as he moved in Margaritta's direction:

"If you want to see Beydan, she is in that house. May God be with you."

Chapter Fourteen

*Like a crow, raven black, perched on the highest point of the minaret
of a mosque. Down below, on the ground, the attendant to the mosque
and muezzin is throwing stones at the bird in order to chase it away, stones
which keep falling down on him without reaching the crow. . . .*

The sun held court with the clouds which encircled it. Pumpkin-
yellow at the centre but silver-rimmed, she squatted there, her
presence that of a queen, round and thick-bodied, her bodice light
blue, and on her head a coronet of white flowers.

*It is the dead in them which kills, it is the lifeless in them which
pulls the trigger. Power for love,* he continued thinking. *How one
justifies one's love in front of other persons.* Lies. A wreath of lies,
white as the eyes of the dead, fixed like the daily ration of a prisoner.

Meanwhile, the sheikhs had arrived, the sheikhs and their
hangers-on and also their pupils. Before all of these came the un-
invited who stayed hidden in the wings of the day's shade, from which
they plucked, as time went by, the feathers of impatience. Handsome,
good-looking, tall as a tree, the principal sheikh, the one who had led
the prayer at the burial mound, the one who spoke the prayer louder
and more provocatively when the Minister to the Presidency appeared
on the scene, the sheikh who shouted loudest when he took Loyaan
aside to put to him that question about the Memorandums and the
words Soyaan uttered before he hiccupped his last. How inexplicably
strange, now thought Loyaan, that one of Soyaan's last memorable
statements had never once, during the past six days, stirred the
nerves nor the tips of his own tongue. How inexplicable that it had
never occurred to him to repeat it to anybody, that he had never
quoted it: "Dictators, like our General, like Mussolini, love to be
remembered by history, by posterity, but forget that they will be
remembered for the least banal of things and also for their cruelties.
When I was last in Rome, in fact, when going up to Alassio, I talked
to an elderly man and asked him if people still remembered Mussolini
and if so what it was that the mention of his name reminded them of.

222

Do you know what the man's answer was? 'When Mussolini was here,' the man said, 'trains arrived exactly on time.' " Africa. Malaria. Humiliation. Never mind the comments. But why did Loyaan never remember that? Did that not, in one stroke, paint a full picture of Italy under Mussolini? Not that there was justice, nor that there were equal opportunities, which the peasantry as well as the nobility could take cognizance of. No. "When Mussolini was here, trains arrived exactly on time." So did they in Russia when Stalin plaited his moustache and stood for hours in front of the mirror of power. So did they in Hitler's Germany.

But Loyaan was now in his room, alone, his room which would be used not for the sheikhs nor for the elderly men, or relatives but was reserved for a chosen group of young men of Soyaan's and Loyaan's age bracket, more or less, persons like Ahmed-Wellie (if he came), like Ibrahim (if they let him out), like Samater or Medina if any of them turned up. Ladan and Margaritta had prepared the room. They left in here for these men to appreciate the most intricately done illustrations on straw mats, the most suggestive on cushions. They didn't remove the books, either. The sheikhs would feel offended by so many books in foreign languages. They could recognise photographs of Lenin and Marx from posters and placards and wouldn't want to sit next to them in a room where they prayed for the soul of the dead.

"What are you looking for in here?"

That was Ladan who stood in the doorway and wouldn't walk in for she had her shoes on. Her eyes disapproved; she stared at Loyaan. It was impolite, these eyes of hers said, to trample on the clean mats like that.

"I am sorry."

She knew he wasn't. She had known Soyaan to create a great disorder when looking for anything. She had known him inconsiderate enough to rearrange things from the way he found them. Loyaan hadn't touched a thing. Now he was standing by the lowest of the shelves and had a book in hand. The noise from the sheikhs' room reached them here. The women were a great deal quieter, although their number had multiplied since.

"Tell me what you are looking for, please! "

"I want a safe place for these." He held in his hand a shaft of papers.

"What are they?"

"Documents. Soyaan's articles. Bits and pieces of writing found in his pockets. The sky is too high to reach and hide them in, the earth too earthly and too exposed and the boxes are not sufficiently secretive."

"Give them here, then."

"Where will you put them?"

"Where no one will find them."

He moved towards her light as dust; he tiptoed lest he filthied the straw mats on which he had stamped the stains of his walk. He took good care when he had entered: he would do likewise when he was going out. He could trust Ladan to find the best place to hide these papers before the Minister and his men came, or before Ahmed-Wellie returned. There, at last, he could class Ahmed-Wellie and feel no unease. *Ahmed-Wellie: an informant!*

"Give them here then," said she.

"Where will you hide them?"

"I've told you. Where *no one* will find them."

"Where precisely?"

"Don't you want it to be a secret place?"

He held on to them and wouldn't let go. "Yes."

"I'll hide them where *no one* will find them."

"What about me?"

"You won't need to know if you leave at eight this evening."

"Seven, not eight."

"Father says eight."

"The Minister and the Security didn't agree on the time either. Yes, yes, but I want to know where these are wherever I am taken to. Besides, who says I will go with them when they come for me?"

"Will you or won't you give them here? I have a room to sweep and clean before the guests arrive."

He looked at the mess his shoes had made. He gave the papers to her.

"Take care of them, please."

He went out.

Loyaan saw the sun no longer as a queen of great presence but as a squat figure, ugly as an usurper, who, on top of that, made claims to being a grand thinker, a sage whose capsuled wisdom aroused contempt among her populace. A squat figure who aroused fear in the hearts of the masses. Beside him sat Margaritta. They were silent for a very long time, neither able to think of anything with which to fill the gulf the silence had dug. Both had buried Soyaan for good. Soyaan was of the past. He was of the gone past, he had a tomb, he was dated, you could tell when he was born, you could tell when he died. But you couldn't close the tomb. There was that unsolved mystery: of what did Soyaan die? Of complications. What complications? A dead end. A door opened, however, when you pushed the Islamic button. You could time the life of man as you could that of a candle. Burn it and you saw fire feeding on it, the mouth of fire waxy, the candle all the more spent, consumed. How many burning minutes would a bulb clock? If you knew how many, then you knew its life. Man-years. Dog-years. A candle's hours of burning life. A man's life. God times a man's life as man, the maker of candles times a candle's. *But Soyaan, born the same day as I, dead before I am, mysterious!* Push that button. Close that door. Let us go to science, to medicine, let us be the contemporaries of the twentieth century, contemporaries of its technology. A dead end. Post-mortem: an unperformed medical rite. Draw the curtain, please. See that ward — in there lies Beydan whose mouth foams with the labour of her pregnancy. Will she survive the childbirth? Invoke the spirits you please — chemical, temporal or spiritual. In another ward, there is Qumman telling the beads of her sorcery. Whereas Keynaan philosophises: the dead aren't any more of use to us, but we can be of great use to them. *Nonsense. Haven't you used Soyaan to get to where you have?* Ladan is that Solomonic thread which connects all, which stitches the holes its needle has made. Follow the hints of that thread, follow it with patience. You will finally find the princess. And Margaritta:

"There is this wrong notion that Soyaan was unprepared for death when it came. How can I put it, Loyaan, how can I put it to you of all people that Soyaan was prepared for what was coming to him? He used to speak of the 'thunder of life' as opposed to 'death's shower of quiet and restfulness'. He also spoke about death using Tolstoyan metaphors (he was reading *Resurrection*). He wasn't surprised by death. You yourself have seen the poem he copied on the back of Marco's photograph."

"Yes, yes, I have."

The sheikh's prayers came riding the eared wind. Loyaan knew

225

from what he heard that the coffee beans which had been roasted in sesame oil, the first course of the day, had reached their destination, at this minute perhaps placed in front of the principal sheikh, the one who had mumbled a brief blessing. The sheikh, Loyaan knew from experience, would dip his finger in the bowl containing the roasted coffee beans; he would choose and eat some. He would signal that the bowl be passed to his pupils and others in the room. He would rub his hands together and massage his face with the oil that dripped from the beans, and murmur another prayer. A sudden thought, shocking as much as it revealed Loyaan's character: would it have met with Soyaan's approval should sheikhs and others wish to pray for his soul? Wasn't it that very soul which Keynaan had already sold cheaply to the General's régime? It was illegal to sell the same thing twice, wasn't it?

Margaritta drew something on the dusty ground. She drew a throne. Next to it, she traced, with the help of a stick, a big square which she divided into smaller compartments. Into these she put numbers to which only she knew the clue. While doing this:

"I remember once when he arrived home sick-looking and exhausted. He had been to see the General. They had had the worst of confrontations. This was when the sheikhs were sentenced to death, the night before the day on which they were shot. I remember it was quite unlike Soyaan; he was very inconsiderate that night. He rang the bell cruelly, he made noise entering, he woke the whole neighbourhood shouting. He was hot. He had a temperature. He had had a bottle of whisky and asked for more. He was also quite unlike you in this: he contained his drinks, he didn't vomit, and he still spoke sense. I've never known a Somali like him. Anyway. He entered and told me in a long-winded manner what had been said, what the General had said, what he himself had said. He mimicked the General. He mimicked himself. 'I told him that all he had done was unconstitutional,' he said. And the General had looked at him, he told me, looked at Soyaan with disdain. 'Is it unconstitutional to shoot these sheikhs because they oppose my directives, the laws which I've passed, the decrees which I've signed?' had challenged the General. 'Yes, it is unconstitutional to pass laws, sign decrees, run a martial-law government and then sentence these sheikhs to death. It is against the teaching of the Koran on which they base their arguments. It is unconstitutional,' Soyaan concluded. 'Well, in that case, have I ever introduced myself to you, young man? I *am* the constitution. Now you know who I am, and I want you out of here before I set those dogs of mine on you and you are torn to pieces. Out.' I drove Soyaan home that dawn. I couldn't let him drive himself. That was when I drove Soyaan home in his drunken state.''

"Why didn't you let him stay at your place?"

"He never stayed away from home if he was in Mogadiscio. Qumman, y'know, is a worrisome mother. But that wasn't the point. He said he wanted to be found home if *they* came for him. He said he preferred the dogs barking to keep him company.''

"They never barked, did they?"

She didn't respond to this. "It was before this that he copied the poem on the back of Marco's photograph. His preparation for death, as a matter of fact, dates from before that evening.''

Margaritta fitted the figure she had drawn, a figure without a crown, into the square of the throne. She also traced a palace into which she put a woman huge as her bottom was large. An uncrowned, unconstitutional king. A queen, big as the tears of injustice. A palace. But where did she fit in herself? What role had she played? Mistress to power, to Minister? Had she loved Soyaan and left power and Minister? Did the jealousy of power feel betrayed, unadored, unloved? A stone thrown at a culprit hits but the innocent. Was that it? *Ask her*, said the voice to him.

"May I ask a question which, if you wish, you don't have to answer?"

"Yes, Loyaan. Please.''

"I say you don't have to if you don't want to.''

He avoided looking at her. His wandering gaze registered the horror of hunger on the faces of the beggars whose number had increased; the beggars chased away the stray dogs, and the stray dogs chased the wild cats. To each the prescribed share of alms. But how long would they have to wait? The sheikhs were silent now which meant they were busy eating; they would pray later. A congregation of beggars, there was a prominent conglomeration of tatters which the emaciated bones of breastless mothers filled.

"My question is: in this whirlpool of immense and unregisterable movements, in this complicated circle-within-circle of waves, in this plot-within-plot drama, how central do you believe you, Margaritta, are?"

227

"Do you mean how central or how personal are these things, these plots-within-plots, circles-within-circles?"

"Well, let me rephrase it."

"Yes, please."

"A duel, a personal duel between Soyaan and the Minister to the Presidency for the Trojan princess — was there any such thing?"

"There is an element of that, I won't deny it. But I date everything precisely to the night when he returned from the conversation with the General. I believe the General's hand is behind all this. There is also the Soviet hand, a KGB fist punching the face of the Vice-President for whom and with whom Soyaan once worked more closely."

He consulted his watch. The first group of men had eaten their fill of curried rice, chutney and a jugful of lemon *pressé*. The sheikhs were still inside, praying.

"Nothing personal?"

"I don't deny there is an element of that. Only a very insignificant element, to my mind."

"What do you think Soyaan died of?"

"A man can will himself to die, Soyaan used to say."

"Do you think he willed himself to die? At his age? With his things ungathered, with projects, plans, unattended-to appointments? One can will oneself to death when one is past a certain age, say, sixty, seventy, eighty or ninety. Otherwise, it is suicide."

"I don't know, Loyaan."

She got up. Her face was drenched with tears. *"I am not the centre-point of my own dream,"* Beydan had said.

"I am not central to all that has taken place," said Margaritta. She got up. "Are you not coming in?"

"Are you going in?"

She didn't answer. She entered the house. He studied the drawings she had traced on the ground. The uncrowned king. The queen large as the properties she had amassed. The palace cold as the tomb of death.

Then something strange happened, something which occurred slowly, gradually, something at first meaningless. A head moved. An eye opened, then another. A beggar nudged another in the ribs. An arm rose to point at something, at somebody. Somebody yawned. Another broke a knuckle, stretched legs outwards and arms to the sides. A child stirred in the arthritic embrace of a hungry mother, a child looked away from and let go the milkless breasts of malnutrition. Finally, the entire wreckage arose like a corpse resurrected, brought back to life, slowly, shockingly gradually. The beggars no longer resembled the remnants of a plane-crash. No, they were the passengers of a third-class train, stirring forward, jerking, shaking, speaking, a train's *chunk-chunk* of ham-and-butter, butter-and-cheese, a driver's pulling the chain of the starter "soup, soup". (One of Soyaan's favourite train-jokes he had heard in the Orient, precisely in Bangalore.) But. He, too, stirred. Loyaan also awoke to his senses. He saw what they had seen. He saw whom they had seen.

"Look!" shouted one of the beggars.

Power had chosen to visit them. The Minister to the Presidency and his entourage of cars and security men had arrived. A dramatised delay to create effect, give the word time to spread, the rumour sufficient time to reach the corners of the village. Like the day of the burial when he utilised more or less the same technique, when the water-van was held up for an hour and a half and he, a representative of the General, the giver and taker of life, came at the head of a caravan among which was the water-van. *Biyo* the Somali word for water: think of the Greek *bio* meaning life, or being. There wasn't need for a water-van today. The family had sufficient water. Today, Loyaan's life, Loyaan's leaving for Moscow, his imminent deportation, hinged on the balanced rope of the Minister's decision: he could tighten it more, and with it strangle Loyaan; he could chain Loyaan's legs with that very rope, feed him to the lions, or starve him. Did he think he would get away with this? He would be surprised when the hour finally came.

"Look!"

Fear at its embryonic stage can force one person to cry, another to laugh, yet a third to remain silent, and can make a fourth patiently wait, stare fixedly at the emptiness in front of himself.

There was commotion. The beggars had broken into smaller units and reassembled. They were restless; fear made them so. After all their waiting, they knew the Minister's raising a little finger would suffice to have them put into a van and driven off like their colleagues. After all, they were among the ugly sights of poverty, the bad conscience of the Revolution, beggars who reminded one of the grave situation of the national economy despite the statistics published in

229

government bulletins. One of them started to sing the General's praises and choked on them. Another tried to lift the refrain from where the other had left it but couldn't continue, for the full vocal support of the assembly of beggars was not united behind him. It was like a theatre audience not agreed on whether to clap: the solitary applause died at the immature stage of ridiculousness.

"They are talking softly to each other about us," said one beggar.

"Let us go before they take us away," said another.

The delaying effect had produced its concomitant result: Ladan joined Loyaan outside. She stood by him at first without speaking. Then she took his hand and pressed it with sympathy, showing her support, showing this by standing beside him.

"That bastard! " she said.

"Come on, come. Remember where we are. Mind your language."

"I could kill him."

He moved away from her a little, saying: "Where is the *pudore*, Ladan, where is your composure?"

"Look at him. He brings ten uninvited men as well as himself and wants us to feed him, prostrate ourselves before him, kiss the floor that he and the General walk on. Just look at him! "

From the distance, Loyaan couldn't make out the others of whom the Minister's entourage was composed. He could tell by height and size that the security officer with whom he had spoken was also there, the one who had told him that they would come to pick him up at seven in the evening. Could that possibly be Samater, the man with whom the Minister was talking now — Samater, Medina's husband . . . Samater, once a member of the clandestine movement which Soyaan and Ibrahim had started? If it was Samater, could Ahmed-Wellie be far? Give him another five minutes and perhaps he, too, would come.

"That bastard! " from Ladan.

Loyaan turned round and with touching sincerity said:

"Can't you think of other appellatives, for God's sake? 'That bastard, that bastard, that bastard.' Think of a designation pregnant with generic contempt and universal hate. Traitor. Inhumane. Something like that, an adjective fat with ambiguity."

She reacted by moving away from him. Then she stood between him and the small congregation of beggars who had decided to stay on, come what might. Here he had an audience, thought he. Ladan.

230

The beggars. Perhaps, some of the neighbours would join them too. A speech. Give a speech. Here was an audience willing to hear anything. *Tell them what has happened. Tell them who you are. Tell them what the General's régime has done. Tell them that you are being forced to leave the country on a plane bound for Moscow. Tell them about Keynaan. Tell them about the big Security chief. Point your finger at the Minister and at the big Security chief. Tell them about Ibrahim, about Mulki, about Margaritta, about Marco and about the Memorandums.*

But he noticed that Ladan's stare had hardened. He noticed that the beggars, who had settled into position, moved again. Then voices which came from behind him made him turn: the principal sheikh and his pupils had emerged greasy, sweaty, looking well-fed, with their blurchy *Alxamdulillah* in front of them, like the belly of a pregnant woman. From the other side, heading in his direction and the house's, the Minister and his entourage. Keynaan had escorted the sheikhs out. Keynaan said to his daughter Ladan:

"Go back into the house. Don't stand here."

"Just a moment."

"Get in, I said."

"Just a moment."

"I said, get in."

Loyaan motioned to her to obey.

"I shall go to Beydan," Ladan told her brother.

"Do that."

"Would you like to come with me?"

"No. I'll see this through."

"You won't do anything stupid and childish?"

"No, I won't do anything you wouldn't do."

"You won't?"

"No, I won't."

"Promise?"

"Promise."

Ladan went to the neighbour's where Beydan was, Beydan who had dreamed a dream in which she had a child — when she, the centre of the dream, wasn't even there. The sheikhs took their leave of Keynaan, having thanked him for the meal and blessed the soul of Soyaan, the centre of this festivity although, just like Beydan in her dream, he too wasn't there. Both were centres which could hold no

231

pillars, no columns; a family whose centre-point encountered in wave-lengths of Keynaans. The Minister and his entourage were met by Keynaan's crying welcome. Qumman, too, had come out, helping a neighbour carry away two platefuls of curried rice to her husband and children and some neighbours.

"Come on inside, Loyaan," said Qumman.

"Just a moment."

"Come inside and eat. Your friends are waiting for you."

"Just a moment."

"You haven't eaten anything all day. You haven't had a mouthful. Come on in."

"Later."

Friends? There was Samater emerging from round the corner at the same second as the others in the entourage. What explanation would he give? Friends? Friends of friends? Unprincipled friends? What did one make of them? Would his tongue get caught in the knotted intricacy of his thoughts? Would he be in a position to speak a reasonable thought to the Minister when provoked, when challenged? Would his leg hold? Would he stay his ground?

"Good afternoon, Loyaan," greeted the Minister, his arm locked in Keynaan's.

"Good afternoon, everybody."

Margaritta's shadow crept in on him from behind; it was a long, late afternoon shadow, so tall that his eyes tired following it to the tail of its length. He took this as being very significant. Where there wasn't and couldn't be Ladan, there was Margaritta. He would mind what he said.

"Good afternoon, Loyaan," greeted Samater.

"Good afternoon."

Samater did the same as the Minister: he inclined slightly, bowed his head, greeting Margaritta. But nobody moved. They waited for the Minister to decide what to do. Samater, it seemed to Loyaan, wanted to have a quick aside with Loyaan. The Minister said:

"Ibrahim will be at the airport to wish you goodbye. So will Mulki."

"At seven this evening?"

The Minister sought the big man's approval. Correction:

"We'll come and pick you up from here at seven."

"The special plane to Moscow?"

232

"That is right."

"See you at seven, then."

Quick, quick. Allow Samater no chance to appeal to your softest senses. Quick. Do something. Move. Come on. Do something. Improvise. Say anything.

"Can I have my meal brought to the neighbour's where Beydan and Ladan are, Margaritta, please? Thanks."

He quickened his steps. He wouldn't give Samater a chance to chip in, give explanations.

Everything became disorderly again. This was the beggar's feeding-time. The Minister and his entourage had gone without further incident, for Loyaan stayed out of their way and ate with Ladan in the company of Beydan's music of groans and pained labour. Big plates. Containers stacked with residuals, a bone half covered with meat and half with the scratches of the teeth which had bitten off the missing portions. Bowls into which beggars put as much as they could before they shared the rest with the others, bowls which they would save for tonight or tomorrow. The beggars, on their own, couldn't organise themselves into *mayida* of four or five or ten persons. Loyaan and Keynaan threatened not to put the plates down until these did that. A quick rearrangement of tatters, like the October arrangement of colours in Moscow, or Mogadiscio, a rainbow of heads and scarves, falling into designs of farms, factories, chimneys, revolutions, a Lenin bust, a Brezhnev sketch or a Kim Il-Sung song of praise.

"They've taken Ahmed-Wellie for interrogation," said Keynaan to Loyaan rising up from a bending position. "One of the men with the Minister has just told me."

"How farcical! He behaved very strangely. I meant to ask you if he himself was a plant."

"You never can tell."

"Why have they taken him for interrogation?"

"He had a pile of printed papers. He intended to distribute them, they say. A tribesman of his, whom I've worked with in the Security and who was with the Minister, informed me. He says he had no printed matter on his person. It was in his car."

They returned together to bring more plates for the beggars who now began to stream in from all corners of the village. Suddenly, Keynaan stopped. How discriminatory. He pointed at a young man all in white, maybe a Koranic student, who had joined in with the

233

other beggars. He beckoned to the student to follow him in. He would be fed inside with the friends of the family, and all the late-comers. He would read a Sura or two. Beydan could do with a prayer. The house also. A special prayer. Loyaan would be leaving on a special plane this evening. Keynaan would probably contract another matrimony with a younger woman. Qumman would perhaps pay homage and kiss the Prophet's tomb. Keynaan said to Ladan:

"Feed this gentleman well. Give him a separate room and a prayer-rug. Let him pray for the house, for Beydan and for your brother who will be leaving this evening. And for Qumman. But where is she?"

"She is with Beydan."

"Beydan? How is Beydan?"

"She is in labour. An advanced stage of labour."

"*Alxamdulillah!*"

They brought out more platefuls of rice and curry and meat — no quality chutney, nothing very appetising. *But beggars don't dream dreams in which they themselves do not figure. Beggars are the centre of their dreams; they are all the more rich, in their dreams they have better clothes, they have the best of everything, a garden of pleasures, they wash their smooth skins with a perfume of soaps, they scent the odour of the wealth they have, in their dreams. When dreaming they eat the best,* continued Loyaan thinking to himself; *they will probably be content with what they can get when in their waking hours. Beydan dreamed a dream in which she herself was not the centre but a baby boy others named Soyaan to whom she gave birth in her dream. Soyaan similarly is not present at the festivity staged for him. If souls could eat as beggars do in dreams. . . .*

"Suppose I don't go, Father, what do you think will happen?"

Keynaan motioned to a group of beggars to come closer and form a *mayida*. They moved on their bottoms, as they leaned against one another, as they rearranged themselves.

"I would go if I were you."

Loyaan in turn told another group to come together but to hurry up. *Come on, hurry up, I've other things to do.* They read impatience on his face. They obeyed.

"But I will not go."

234

Keynaan and Loyaan each collected an empty plate, but stopped in the shade.

"What do you think you will do?"

"I don't want to go."

"What do you want to do?"

He looked at his watch: he had less than two hours. He hadn't packed. He had thought of nothing, he was too busy. He needed time to think, to sit down and think thoughts.

"All I know is I don't want to go."

"Alternative? What alternative suggestions have you?"

"I haven't thought of any."

"And I can't think of any presently."

That decided it for him.

"What about if you go and take up the lucrative job in Belgrade? If I were you, I would."

A moment's pause made Loyaan wonder to himself: "Who would have thought that Keynaan and I would ever speak to each other with respect, that we would listen to each other and reason together?" *After a storm, the calm; after a fight, a reconciliation!*

"Let us hear your advice. You claim to be the more experienced."

"If you don't wish to go, think of compromisable alternatives."

He couldn't get over the fact: he was getting softer, he was becoming friendlier, and so was Keynaan. Doors untried had begun to open: the hinges of these doors creaked as they opened. *Who knows? Let creaking doors creak. And use them while you may.*

"Do you think they will have thought of alternatives? The Minister, the General — do you? They will deport me to Moscow, won't they?"

"You will be surprised."

"It is not in their interest to shoot me, nor to send me to prison. I am the hair in their soup. I am the water on which they have choked. They, too, are having a hard time studying possibilities. I bet."

"I wouldn't be so sure."

"How do you mean?"

Keynaan half-shouted as he said: "There are other methods at their disposal. They don't have to shoot you and make you a hero more valued than Soyaan, or imprison you here in this country. There are other methods."

"What?"

"I don't want to miss the appointment for seven."

There were rings of left over rice where the beggars had eaten. It transpired that the beggars had stolen a minimum of three plates the family had borrowed from the neighbours. Night had suddenly fallen like a veil of darkness with which a puritan Muslim woman in the Middle East might cover herself immediately she came into the view of males. The news had reached them that Beydan had delivered a baby boy but that she had died in childbirth. Silence. One death gave way to another just like night to day. Not a tear was dropped, nor a hint of anything else. Simple silence.

"Read."

Loyaan held the Koran in front of himself, open and unreadable.

"Read!" ordered Keynaan.

"Which chapter?"

"Any chapter."

Loyaan turned a few pages and stopped.

"Read," Keynaan said again.

Loyaan read a verse and then stopped.

"Read on. Bless us. Bless your mother who has sinned. Bless your brother who died an innocent death. Bless us all. Bless us so that Allah may deliver us from our sins and the sins we harbour inside of ourselves. Bless your mother, the woman who consulted and paid for evil and the death of others. Bless Beydan. Bless the newly-arrived, welcome him."

Loyaan closed the Koran. He would not read.

"Enough is enough."

Darkness had set in.

No one rose to switch the lights on. There was absolute silence. Ladan held the newly-born, wrapped in an all-embracing towel of Soyaan's. She was the only one standing, rocking the newly-born to and fro, without singing a lullaby. Margaritta sat in a corner, quite broken with tears but not crying out-loud. Qumman went back and forth, bringing this, taking away that.

"Has he been given a name?" asked Margaritta.

236

Keynaan looked at her as though she had fouled the clean air. Margaritta wished she could withdraw her question; she wished she had the energy to do so. Keynaan, meanwhile, got up to say his evening prayers. He started bowing and rising. The child cried.

"Soyaan. Keep quiet, Soyaan," Ladan said to the newly-born. Whereupon Keynaan faltered: instead of bowing, he rose.

It was seven in the evening.
There was a knock on the outside door.